The Diary of Happiness

Archimandrite Nicolae Steinhardt
(Jurnalul Fericirii , 1912-1989)

Archimandrite Seraphim ©

Three solutions
– Political testament –

To escape a concentrationist universe – and it doesn't have to be a camp, a prison or another form of incarceration; the theory applies to any form of totalitarian product – there is the (mystical) solution of faith. About this I will not talk in the followings, faith being the consequence of the essentially selective grace.

The three solutions referred below are strictly mundane, they have a practical character and they are accessible to everyone.

First solution: of Solzhenitzin

In the First circle, Alexander Isayevitch mentions it briefly, coming back to it in the second volume of the Gulag Arhipelago.

It consists, for everybody who passes over the threshold of the Security or another analogous investigation organ, to tell to himself with decision: in this very moment I die. You are allowed to console yourself: pity for my youth or my old age, for my children, myself, my talent or my goods or my power, for my sweetheart, for the wines I won't drink, the books I won't read, the walks I won't take, the music I won't listen etc. etc. etc. But something is sure and irreparable: from now on I'm a dead man.

If he thinks so, unfalteringly, the individual is saved. They can't do anything to him. They can't threaten, blackmail, deceive, trick him. Since he considers himself dead nothing scares, attracts, stir him. They cannot turn him on. He doesn't have – because he doesn't hope, because he left the world – what to yearn for, what to keep or to recover, what for to sell his soul, his peace, his honor. There is no currency in which the price of the treason to be paid.

It is required, however, that the decision be firm, final. You declare yourself dead, you are delivered to death, you terminate any hope. You can have regrets, like Lady d'Houdetot, you can regret but this moral suicide, and by anticipation can't go wrong. The risk of yielding, of consenting to turning somebody in, of confessing crazy things vanished completely.

The second solution: of Alexander Zinoviev

It is the solution found by a character of the book The empty heights. The character is a young man, introduced under the allegorical nickname Brawler. The solution resides in the total non-adaptation to the system. Brawler doesn't have a stable domicile, he doesn't have papers, he's not a registered worker; he is a tramp, a parasite, a punk and a homeless. He lives only for the day, from what is given to him, with luck, you'd wonder how. He works now and then, only when he finds the opportunity. He spends most of his time in prisons or working camps, sleeps wherever he can. He's wandering. For nothing in the world he doesn't get with the program, he won't take even the most insignificant, wicked, non-committing job. He won't consent even to watch pigs, not following the example of the hero of the Arthur Schnitzler's short story: that one, obsessed with fear of responsibility, ends up pig watcher. NO, Brawler projected himself (in existentialist style) once and forever a stray dog, a black ship, a Buddhist beggar monk, silly, a lay iurodivii for (into) freedom.

This kind of man, at the periphery of the society, is immune too: they can't exert pressure on him either, they don't have what to take from him or what to offer to him. They can lock him up anytime, harass, despise, humiliate him; but he eludes them. Once and forever he consented to live his life according to the example and the model of a perpetual night asylum. Out of poverty, suspicion, lack of seriousness he made a credo; he looks like a wild animal, a wretched beast, a bandit. He is Ferrante Palla of Stendhal. He is Zacharias Lichter of Matei Călinescu. He is a lay full into Christ, a never bored traveler, (and Wotan descending on earth what name bears? Der Wanderer), a wanderer Jew.

And he speaks up his mind, he won't stop talking, gives voice to the most dangerous anecdotes. he doesn't know of respect, he looks everything down, speaks whatever is in his mind, he utters truths that others can't afford to whisper. He is the child in the story of the naked king, of Andersen. He is the buffoon of king Lear. He is the wolf from the fable – daring too – of La Fontaine; never heard of leash.

He is free, free, free.

The third solution: of Winston Churchill and Vladimir Bukovski

It can be resumed as follows: in the presence of tyranny, persecution, misery, disaster, calamity, bad luck, danger not only that you don't give up but on the contrary, you get from them a crazy urge for life and fight.

In March 1939, Churchill tells to Martha Bibescu: "It will be war. The British empire will be torn apart. Death stalks us all. And I feel I'm getting younger with twenty years".

More the things are bad, more the difficulties are heavy, more you are wounded, surrounded or subjected to attacks, more you don't see a probable and reasonable escape, more the gray, the darkness and the viscous are intensifying and they coil around you, more the danger confronts you directly, more you are willing to fight and you know a (rising) feeling of inexplicable and overwhelming euphoria.

You are assaulted from all parts, with forces infinitely superior to yours: you fight. They defeat you: you defy them. You're lost: you attack. (That's how Churchill was speaking in 1940). You laugh, you sharpen your teeth and your knife, you're getting younger. You feel the itch of the happiness, the untold happiness of hitting in your turn, even if it is infinitely less. Not only that you don't despair, you don't declare yourself defeated and finished, but you fully taste

4

the joy of resisting, of opposing and you experience a sensation of impetuous, demented merriment.

This solution, of course, requires an exceptional strength of character, a military conception of life, a formidable moral determination of the body, a will of alloyed steel an adamantine spiritual health. Probably requires a sportive spirit too; you have to enjoy the battle in itself – the brawling – more than the success.

This solution is salutary and absolute too, because it is based on a paradox: more they hit you and they wrong you and they impose unjust sufferance on you, and they corner you without escape, you are merrier, tougher and younger!

The same as Churchill's solution is the solution of Vladimir Bukovski. Bukovski says that when he received the first convocation to the KGB quarters he couldn't close an eye all night. Naturally, the reader of his book of memoirs will say, it is the most natural thing; the insecurity, the fear, the emotion. But Bukovski follows: I couldn't sleep out of impatience. I couldn't wait the dawn, to be in front of them, to tell them what I think of them, to enter in them as a tank. I couldn't imagine a greater happiness.

Look why he couldn't sleep: not out of fear, of worry, of emotion. But out of the impatience of shouting the truth to their faces and to enter in them as a tank!

More extraordinary words I don't think were ever uttered or written in the world. And I wonder – I don't claim this to be true, no, not at all, but I cannot help wondering – if this universe, with the swarms of galaxies each one containing thousands or millions of galaxies each one with billions of suns and if all the spaces, the distances, these spheres measured in light years, parsecs and zillions of thousands of miles, all this swarm of matter, planets, comets, satellites, pulsars, quasars, black holes, cosmic dust, meteors, and whatever, all the ages, the eons, all the times and spatial-temporal continuums and the Newtonian or relativistic astrophysics were born and exists only so that these words of Bukovski could be uttered.

Conclusion

All three solutions are sure and without fail.

Other than those for escaping an extreme situation, a concentrationary universe, the net of a Kafkian trial, a domino type game, labyrinth or investigation office, fear and panic, a mouse trap, any phenomenal nightmare – I don't know. Only those three. Each of them is good, sufficient and salutary.

Take heed: Solzhenitzin, Zinoviev, Churchill, Bukovsky. Accepted death, assumed, anticipated, provoked; carelessness and impudence; bravery accompanied by a raging merriment. You are free to choose. But you have to realize that – worldly, humanly speaking – another way to confront the circle of iron – which largely is of chalk (see State of siege by Camus: the basis of dictatorship is a phantasm: fear) – it is doubtful you will find.

You will protest, maybe, considering that the solutions assume a sort of life that is equivalent to death, or even worse than death, implying the risk of physical death at any moment. This is true. Are you surprised? That's because you didn't read Igor Safarevitch, because you didn't find out yet that totalitarianism is not the embodiment of an economic, biologic or social theory but rather the manifestation of an attraction toward death. And the secret of those who cannot fit in the totalitarian abyss is simple: they love life, not death.

The death, then, who, Alone, defeated? He who trampled death by death.

Nicolae Niculescu[1]

Pencil and paper there was no way to have them in prison. It would be therefore insincere to pretend that this "diary" was kept chronologically; it is written après coup[2], based on fresh and live memories. Since I couldn't insert it in the duration, I think it is allowed to present it scattered, the way, indeed this time, the images, the remembrances, the thoughts came to me in that avalanche of sensations that we call conscience. The effect, of course, errs toward artificial; this is a risk I have to assume.

I believe, Lord, help my unbelief.
Mark 9, 24

January 1960

–A glass? I didn't break any glass… I don't remember…

This is my answer… and really I don't remember. Or maybe I did break it? In August, on her and my birthday? Or I didn't break it? I don't know. O yes, I know. Of course I broke it. In August, in the evening, at dinner, the doors toward the patio largely open. But still, it is like I don't remember either. I remember and I don't remember. Everything in this unreal and subtle décor, carefully planned, urges me to take refuge in confusion, to lose myself in anxiety: her glances, warm and compassionate, and their glances, skillful and languid. The slide of consent opens gently in front of me; all I have to do is to let myself go.

I could swear I don't remember – fully in good faith; although I realize that's how things happened, the way she repeats them – a glass of crystal, beautiful – with the precision of a computer memory, with the fidelity of the magnetic tape, with the hypocrite shyness of the diligent student who knows only too well the lesson. I look at her – it is she, but as in a dream, she does unexpected things, she's talking differently; and synchronous with her, the world is another, is surrealistic. Look, this is the surrealism; the objects, the same ones, know another

6

order, they have another finality. So this is possible too. Now, yes, the teapot is a woman, the stove is an elephant... Max Ernst, Dali, Duchamp... But also The Shout of Munch, I feel like yelling, to wake up from the nightmare, to return to our good old earth, kind and gentle, where, quiet things are what we know they are and they have the meaning we always attached to them... I wish to get out from this restless city of Delvaux, from this field of Tanguy, with split members, soft and gathered back according to bizarre affinities other than those established in our world... In our world, on earth. Here it can't be earth. This is not she. This décor, Dostoievskian and expressionist cannot exist truly... I am deceiving myself, I act haughty, I put on airs, I imagine of course this delirious scene for the sake of a role I would like to play...

After all I'm not even sure I did or did not break it. Out of crystal, thick. If I acknowledge I broke it, I tell the truth (the objective truth) and, once I tell the truth, I have to go all the way and confess everything including Nego's hostile talking[3]. (This is the purpose of this nocturnal interrogation, where she is defending me with a so highly suspicious care, she's tendering me so friendly a salvation pole; because she, deserving the highest grade at memorization and unable to forget a detail, look that she passes over the lines when is about me and omits my words or quotes them partially and she answers: "Who said it? I can't remember. Someone, one of the people present there, I just know that they alleged..." This "they", impersonal and neutral, as in logic and structuralism, how it makes me an accomplice and abases me.)

Therefore, talking, I enter into clarity and truth and there are no more places to hide, I step into the zone of light, the caches disappear instantaneously. Or if I don't remember, if I make psychically the gesture of détente and relaxation, loose myself in the mist of confusion, wander in the forgetfulness, I give in to the sweet delirium of evanescence and then I confess again, I confess because now everything is equal to me, because everything is gray and similar, because nothing is important and clear cut. I enter the world of the new novel and the literature without characters: the world of THEY, of the OTHERS, where the I and the SELF vanish; they become confuse in the undifferentiated heap. Personality (what's that?) turns to bits, into fine dust, passes entirely through the sieve.

Whatever I do, I'm lost.

You're lost, you're lost, it rocks me the gentle cradle of yielding and fatigue, of disgust, of surprise, of grateful friendship. (She just does everything that can be done. She wants to help me. In the facets of the crystal shine the lights of the festive dinner.)

I'm lost also because this was supposed to be my destiny – this, not another. Am I not a smeared, a looser, tired of concessions and yielding, of shameful hands, of lusts always awake, satisfied but never grandiosely and fully, always mutilated, isn't it my natural place among filth, among the lukewarm, this comforting latrine of renunciation and obedience, of confirmation of the truly truth isn't the logical end of a long suppuration? What for to still delude myself into the far roads of pride and dignity? Inaccessible. The way is barred forever.

What does it matter if I broke it or not? It does. Something tells me insistently that it does.

Insistently but quietly. I do understand – better and better while the long confrontation goes ahead with soothing gloves – that now the decision will be taken, from now on everything will be triggered. And the devilish trick is that wherever I turn I'm still trapped. Either on the path of truth or of the sliding into the mist of nothingness, I'm still lost, I still have to confess. Only to allure me more intoxicatingly and a little more mercifully the path of forgetfulness, the path of confusion, where all are equal and meaningless, unimportant.

I'm lost!

Lost? Oh! no. Look, from the deepness of Pantelimon and Clucereasa – the outskirts and the village – it dawns suddenly another thought, a third solution.

Oh! no, the humility of yielding is from the devil. Around is not mist, in me is not delirium: I'm fully in the middle of reality, what I see is true. Pantelimon and Clucereasa whisper to me – like some reliable schoolmates who help you cheat: why do you let yourself caught by phantasmagoria? Come to your senses. Yes, it is she. Yes, everything is true. Be calm and cynical and skillful. I repeat, skillful. Yes, there is, there still is an unnoticed third solution. Your duty in this moment is to be vulgarly calm, skillful, insensitive. Be a peasant, little Jew. Be a scandalmonger. Nea[4] Matache[5], robed by the maid; nea Pană the quarrelsome, whom the neighbor wants to cheat; oncle Pandele the troublemaker, old Urcan which can't be fooled. I'm not on Venusberg and this is not the Walpurgia night. I'm in an investigation office of the Security[6], on Plevna way (in vain, putting me black glasses, you drove me around in circles in the yard of the Malmaison barrack), and this is T. who passed on their side… Why? How? It's not possible! I don't know why and I don't care. And regarding the impossibility, here she is. Let's not be scholastic, the oil freezes, no matter what Aristotle says.

The glass? Of course I know. Of course I broke it. (A clumsy movement and how ashamed I felt. A, the shards don't bring luck except in German.) But my only duty now is to be calm, smart and stubborn. Tough. Headstrong. Morose. Laconic. Grumpy.

The third solution. Neither I acknowledge breaking it nor let myself yield to the vertigo. No to the stupidity of fear but also no to the magic of bewilderment. Something else: the lie. Nonchalant and skilled lie.

This is what's left to me, this is the third way; to be a smart peasant and a shrewd townsman. Calm and stiff. At their level. Theirs and hers. Not above. I don't remember, dot and done. And I don't know. And I keep silent. And I shut my mouth. I don't acknowledge. I don't yield. I don't know, mister. I don't remember a thing. Sitting on a fence. Neither in the bed nor under the bed. Neither in the cart nor in the chariot. Like the beans on Easter. Nea Lache at fare: he won't leave one penny from the price; nea Simache in court: we won't let himself cornered. Nea Gruia bargaining: no and no and no again.

This is the third solution – unexpected and strange: the lie. Blessed lie, whispered by Christ. (Christ: It is Him, He didn't forget me, all the bells are tolling. I will be His. I am His. I've always been His. In the most infinitesimal fraction of a second I became His forever.) Shameless, crafty lie, as skilled as possible. The son of nea Tache, the tax collector. My father before my leaving: don't be a scaredy Jew, don't shit in your pants. Surrealism is from Paris, the delirium might be good in Zürich, at the café. Here is not there. Here the train stops in the station not the station at the train. Here is the country of Ion[7], of the Fanariots[8] and of Soarbe-Zeamă[9], here Vlad Țepeş[10] impaled the Turkish ambassadors, he didn't say to them "you shoot first, gentlemen of England", here Petrache Carp showed to Voivode[11] Carol that the corn is eaten with the hand, here is life and death, here isn't sophisticated and supreme décor of a lunatic, neither curtains and delights, nor artificial paradise or hell, here is like in the market, at the counter, at the inheritance lawsuit; it's not with jewels, is with stones and rocks (and suddenly I'm thinking of Brâncuşi, a determined peasant who carves his material with the large gestures of a reaper). Here is the pool Bethesda: you jump or you don't. Here, now, now, now. Here declare yourself boy, here, on the spot; you choose.

Now I have to choose myself, to project myself. Should I plunge? Can I? Do I want to? Do I know? What a curious thing: I see that if I want to take the way of Christianity I have to lie. The same as this people did (in the middle of which I was born and toward whom I keep feeling attracted) – and good for him – when he was forced to bow before the fez, the German, the Muscovite. I must lie the way sometimes in mathematics the solution cannot be find unless you first complicate the data, going around the core of the problem. I must lie. This means the things are not so simple. The world is not simple. This means Julien Benda was right when he said he hates those who complicate simple things but he hates no less those who simplify complicated things.

Christianity, boy, is not the same thing as stupidity. The river Târgul (Town) and the river Doamna (Lady) don't flow for the imbecils and the bells of the Capra (Goat) church don't toll for pious hags only. Even them, although deaf, they still make it out.

She is in a chair about two meters to my left; them in front, at the desk. Ah, you would like me, wouldn't you, to let myself caught in the sorcery of the semi-dream, the intoxicating mist of a surrealist scenography… The intellectuals might be weak, but knowing the books is not useless because it can give you an acute feeling of déja vu or at least of déja imaginé… Being literate has its good side. No, I might be Jewish and sensitive but you forgot (and you forgot too, when you planned with them, because what else could be your help if not the means to attract me at your side, to smooth my way, to golden, to sweeten the gall pill which is of shit? – look, I started talking colorful as never before and how tonic is! how wonderful I feel – that's why the surgeons and the militaries are swearing, to keep in touch with reality, to keep themselves from being lead into indifference, (to make a difference), you forgot I was born in the outskirts and I lived in the countryside. Pantelimon and Clucereasa. Tough. Simple. With wise craftiness. There is still time. Christianity is not necessarily doltish.

Therefore:

 – I don't remember anything. I don't recall breaking a glass. I didn't hear our companion saying anything hostile.

 – Yo! Were you at that dinner? And nobody talked hostile?

 – I was at the dinner, it was my birthday and the day before had been her birthday. But nobody talked hostile.

 – You don't remember?

 – No.

 – But do you remember breaking the glass?

 – Neither.

 – Hey, she's your friend. (And he's showing her to me dramatically.) Do you acknowledge she's your friend?

 – I acknowledge.

 – Then? Why would she say you heard what you didn't hear?

 – I don't know. I don't say she's lying. I say I don't remember.

The teapot is a teapot. The stove is not an elephant. The wheat grows from soil. Out of stone they build houses and carve statues. Christ is not the God of disorder and masks. Jupân[12] Codârlă the dullard.

And she? She is with them – simple as apple pie. She's on the other side. Yes, they did something undone before. They brought, to tell the truth, something new in the world: until now if you wanted to lose a man you were contacting his enemies: the wife he divorced, the friend he broke up with, the associate he dragged to court; the contribution of the new, the most remarkable innovation is that in order to destroy an individual they don't go to his adversaries but to his friends, to wife, kids, sweethearts, those he loves and in which he put, humanly, stupidly, his trust and his thirst for affection.

Vertigo. The vertigo is the most tormenting sensation. No pain is so terrible. The vertigo. The world turns around you, breaks apart, you are broken apart too. The objects are twirling, I have seen an expressionist film after Crime and punishment; everything was crooked: the roofs, the fences, the lamp posts. The torment is atrocious. The inversion: the friend accuses you. The blocks are falling down. She is beyond, now she is more and more bored, ("What do you say? Here's your merchandise!") more crouched. The earthquake splits the land and splits your being, on a median line.

Come on, now, Dostoievski didn't preach the vertigo, but Christ the Lord. Come on, understand, realize why you can't believe it: you are not too scared and you are not sophisticated. Something from the foxy brute of the outskirts man, of the peasant stubbornness entered in you. Come on, you know what you have to do, don't deceive yourself, you already chose; you can resist and you are completely aware, understand – no matter how strange and frightening – realize you won, just embrace the NO, it is yours, surrealism is just a theory, life is not the same as the dream, this is not a teahouse of opium and not a salon of sweet aroma, this is a wicked investigation office, statistics proves reality is not a dream: Valéry was right.

You would like to take refuge in fear, in mist, in nightmare… wouldn't you… It would be easy, – how sweet would be to shelter yourself between dream and life, in confusion or incertitude, among delicious corpses or on the operation table between the umbrella and the sewing machine, in Marat's bathtub transformed in a flying balloon, at Samarkand in a palace from the Arabian nights, in delirium: the delirium, the source of all the compromises. But you can't back up now. Who would shelter you? You're through, little Jew, intellectual, city boy: you put on the boots of reality, your feet will get callous. From now on it's over with delights and allaying illusions, with eyelids closed over lascivious, comforting visions of other worlds, more gentle, more ductile. You cannot take refuge in the imaginary; you're good for combat, good for resistance, good for lies, saintly and carefully concocted, good for stubbornness. You're good for fire. The discharge didn't work, nada. Forward, march!

Nae Ionescu[13] says that whoever doesn't have Romanian blood can be a "good Romanian" but no matter what he cannot be "Romanian".

And this is the truth, if we consider only the human possibilities. But what is impossible for men is possible for God. Through human, usual, natural way you cannot pass from the attribute of "good Romanian" to the state of "Romanian". What about through the baptism of fire like my cousin Teodor at Mărăşeşti[14], what about through transfiguration? How come Nae Ionescu didn't remember of Matthew 19, 26, of Mark 10, 27, of Luke 18, 27? How come he didn't understand there is a way sprinkled with jasmine flowers and miracles, of rebirth, which makes everything to become possible, easy? Who believes the wine can be changed into blood, won't have a hard time to acknowledge that the spirit can perform semiotic mutations with the blood.

Biologically, ethnically, yes. Mystically the problems are posed completely different and what is not possible on a plan is totally possible, fast, on another.

Matthew 19, 26: But Jesus look at them and said to them, "With men this is impossible but with God all things are possible."; Mark 10, 27: But Jesus looked at them and said, "With men it is impossible, but not with God; for with God all things are possible."; Luke 18, 27: But He said, "The things which are impossible with men are possible with God". – Pay attention to that looked at them, which

11

shows how much importance Jesus attached to those words full of wisdom, and difficult, maybe not to understand, but to assimilate.)

August 28th 1964

Nobody makes himself Christian, even if he receives the baptism late in his life, like me. I'm thinking that even in the earthquake-like conversions the calling is always anterior – no matter how deep, subtle or crafty would be hidden. Pascal: Tu ne me chercherais point...[15] Always the inverted logic: you look for what you have found, you find what was prepared for you, given to you.

I draw two conclusions:

First, the true basis of the Christian teaching: the absurd and the paradox. Then, the divinity works in detail and skillful both when He rewards and when He punishes. They are sadly wrong those who believe – and they are not always dimwitted – that they can fool God, they can trick him. Not at all. He gives or He strikes with extremely minute refinement. From here it follows that God is not only good, right, omnipotent, etc.: He is also very smart.

August 29th

Thousands of devils are itching me when I see how Christianity is mistaken for stupidity, for a sort of halfwit, coward bigotry, a bondieuserie[16] (the expression belongs to tante Alice), as if the purpose of Christianity would be to leave the world at the discretion of the forces of evil, to smooth the way for crimes because it is by definition, doomed to cecity and paraplegia.

Denis de Rougemont: Let us not judge others, but when the house of the neighbor is burning I don't stay to pray and to improve myself; I call the firemen, I run to the water pump. If not, it means I'm vain and I don't love my neighbor. Macaulay: it is true that we should not rebel against Nero because every power is from Above, but we also shouldn't jump to help Nero if he happens to be attacked. (Eisenhower and Foster Dulles in the autumn of '56.)

It is one thing to rebel and another to approve. When Jacob II fell, some Anglican bishops followed in exile the pro-Catholic king, or maybe even Catholic, only because he was the legitimate sovereign and he couldn't be replaced.

The helpless and impotent Christianity is an heretical conception because ignores Lord's urge (Matthew 10, 16: "be wise as serpents and harmless as doves") and passes over the texts of Saint Paul (Eph. 5, 17: "Therefore do not be unwise...", 2 Tim. 4, 5: "you be watchful in all things...", Titus 1, 8: " must be... sober-minded", and especially 1 Cor. 14, 20: "Brethren do not be children in understanding; however in malice be babes, but in understanding be mature").

Nowhere and never did Christ ask us to be stupid. He urges us to be good, gentle, honest, lowly at heart but not dumb (only about our sins it is said in the Pateric "to dumb them".) How could He glorify the stupidity the One that advises us to be always awake so that we won't be surprised by Satan. Then, again in 1 Cor. (14,33) is written that "God is not the author of confusion". And the order opposes more than anything the wacky confusion, the undecided weakness, the obtuse lack of understanding. The Lord loves the innocence but not the imbecility. I love naiveté, says Léon Daudet, but not at bearded men. The bearded men are supposed to be wise. Let us acknowledge, they and us, that more evil is caused by the stupidity than the malice. No, the servants of the devil, I mean the şmechers[17], would be only too happy if we would be stupid. God, among others, commands us to be intelligent. (Whoever is endowed with the gift of understanding, the stupidity – at least from a certain point further – is sin; the sin of weakness and of sloth, of not using the talent. And when they heard the voice of God our Lord... they hide themselves.)

– You can abstain from sin out of fear. It is an inferior stage, also good. Or out of love: the way the saints and superior people do. But also out of shame. A terrible shame, like doing an unseemly thing in front of a delicate person, shouting an ugly word in face of an old woman, cheating someone who trusted you. After you knew Christ is very difficult to sin, you feel terribly ashamed.

Room 18

Why does Jesus Christ kiss the great inquisitor in the Karamazov brothers?

I answer to doctor Al-G in his own language, i.e. in Indianist style: to advance him from avidya (ignorance) to vidya (knowledge), to dissipate maya, to clear the smoke, to remove the veil, to disperse the magic. After he is kissed, the great inquisitor, finally, sees the reality. The kiss, on the mouth, acts as a shock, shakes him, awakes him.

An artistic masterpiece has a similar effect: it exorcises too. Faith brings us joy because suddenly reestablishes the accord with reality. Therefore the reality – the incorrupt reality – is beautiful and the resonance is a fundamental law. The generalized Moessbauer effect.

After the arrest of Paul Dim., at the beginning of 1955, Yolanda St. – from the family of Eminescu[18], granddaughter of captain Matei Eminovici (until 1954, before remarrying, she was signing Eminovici) – she said to T.: "He deserved it. I hope he and the others will get at least ten years." (She was very angry.) "And your Nicu[19] thinks it suits him to play the Legionnaire[20]?"

We were admonished then and later because we talked too much, because we didn't keep our mouth shut. To that we could answer: "I believed therefore I spoke – we also believe and therefore speak" (2 Cor. 4,13) or "I believed, therefore I spoke" (Ps. 116,10). Or we could quote a more recent author, Brice Parain, according to whom to speak or to be silent is the same as to live or to be dead.

We were condemned also by a young man whose opinion weighs a lot for me. He (Toma Pavel) evoked Wilhelm Tell. In the style of the new generation, Tell knew to be silent, kept his mouth shut for a long time and to avoid any provocation he didn't even pass by the plaza where was Gessler's hen. Yet at the right time he didn't hesitate, he went directly to action, speedily. Kill it! (Gessler, not the symbol: the hat.)

It is true. The argument is valid and, in fact, resumes the history of the Romanians. I confess that the wise words of the young man hurt me. Yet don't we also have the right to defend our past, our deed? Maybe, in absence of something better, speaking up is not that bad. At least it is worth as much as a confession, it's soothing. Poor apologia; what if it is the only one that I have?

Connected to this is the difficult problem of 2+2=4.

The example of Tudor Vianu and others like him, that were teaching serious courses and instructive conferences or were uttering harmonious and solidly founded phrases, was always given to us – given, if not thrown in the face. But aren't they speaking in desert? we were asking. No, we were answered, because the affirmation of the eternal truths is always welcomed, it is always healthy and useful to show that two plus two equals four. (Two plus two equals four is the formula of common sense, of the natural right, of the incorruptible axioms.)

This story of two plus two equals four I knew it for a long time. I knew for instance from Camus that "it always comes a time in history when those who say two plus two equals four are punished by death." And from Dostoievski, in a different way, that two plus two equals four is not life anymore, but the beginning of death. The man, says Dostoievski, was always afraid of this rule; he keeps searching for it, for its sake crosses the oceans, sacrifices his life in this search, but he is terrified at the thought that he would find it. It is a principle of death and good thing is that sometimes two plus two equals five too. Orwell, however, believes differently, that freedom means the freedom to say two plus two equals four and once this is acknowledged everything else follows from it.

How could I reconcile all these, especially because the silhouette of the scholar that, in the middle of the tornado, enunciates calmly the simple and eternal truths is not without grandeur?

I was confused, until I could clear my thoughts; so content I was with the explication I found that I wrote right away a letter to lady Lenuţa, the mother of Alecu, valiant reactionary, tall and beautiful woman, a Moldavian mastering a tongue without euphemisms. Lady Lenuţa, I wrote (and this mania of sending epistles to one another, loco, was criticized too with severity, being considered plainly playing spoilt, with no excuse), the tyrannies don't forbid the utterance of all the truths but only of some, better said of a particular one, the one that touches the sensitive spot of the respective tyranny. A man can put up with a lot but he startles when you run into what the Englishmen call "the skeleton in the cupboard" or the "hometruth" and you begin to reveal what he does not dare to confess to himself, when you risk touching that fragile and vulnerable point about which the esoteric architecture says it exists in every building on the face of the earth and it can lead in a moment to the destruction of the entire edifice. The skeleton in the cupboard and the hometruth[21] are expressions untranslatable in Romanian, but combining them and passing them into the mioritic space[22], I tend to believe there are a sort of equivalent of master Manole, caught in walls[23] and memory and praying for the poor (or the bastard) creator with untold sighs, like the Spirit for the sinner.

The French revolution was readily allowing the proclamation of many truths but was punishing by death whosoever dared to whisper that the simple fact that you were born noble is not a sufficient reason to cut your head without other procedure than simple identification. (The law from Priar, year II). During the time of Cromwell and the puritans were told many well intended things but woe to those that doubted the absolute validity of the moral prescriptions of the Old Testament in their absolutely literal meaning. And in the beautiful cities Geneva, Münster or Florence, in the time of Calvin, of Thomas Münzer, of Johannes von Leyden or Savonarola one could hear speeches full of truth and exactitude and there were expressed ideas worthy to be paid attention, but there was always a certain scandalous truth – blasphemous – utterly forbidden to public use. The pay of the use: death.

The secret, therefore, Lady Lenuţa, is this one: two plus two equals four is an algebraic formula: to us remains the task to arithmetize it. To say two plus two equals four doesn't mean to declare like Tudor Vianu that Goethe wrote Poetry and Truth, that Voltaire died in 1778 or Balzac, gentlemen, is a romanticist realist. Or to hold, as George Călinescu, admirable, novelty conferences about the life and the creation of Eminescu. When nearby people are cut with the saw, if you want to enunciate two plus two equals four you must shout to the bottom of your lungs: it is a blatant injustice that the people are cut in two with the saw. Under the reign of Robespierre were saying two plus two equals four those who were revolting against the fact that some people were sent to guillotine only because they were born noblemen. (Beaumarchais prophesized something, but he was off the mark.) Under Calvin, the same, those who couldn't help revolting when seeing that are sent to death all the thinkers that do not approve without reserves the theologumens of maître Calvin. Healthy arithmetic would do someone who would express to Caligula his doubts about conferring the quality of consul to a horse. And so on, every time. Two plus two equals four would have been arithmetized by misters Vianu, Călinescu and Ralea by talking, for instance about the canal[24], the road without dust[25].

(And at that particular time, not after even the initiators of the grand work gave up, breaking the vow given by workers at the working place: we're not leaving before we finish it! The same as, of course, more originally would have been if someone would have said before the death of Stalin, the greatest coryphaeus of all sciences, that $E=mc2$ is not an idealistic formula.)

Each time the algebraic general formula must be arithmetized, that is incarnated in that certain truth hidden and condemned by the reigning tyrant. It's the story of Andersen, of the naked king. What good is to say sadly that the union of the Orthodox with the Roman church was done forcibly or to denounce vehemently the Turkish oppression in a time when others were the hot, current issues: the hot, current issues were the prisons, the trials with confessions and self- accusation of the defendants, the administrative punishments[26]; to denounce these would have meant to utter two plus two equals four. Father Stăniloaie emphasizing the great abuses committed by the Catholics under Habsburgs or professor Giurescu condemning the Turkish yoke – despite the fact that the two great scholars were well intended – were taking an air similar to the 21st of Caţavencu and the Europe of Farfuridi[27], let me say this without any malice or lack of respect but without conventional detours too.

I needed a long time to relieve my heart in the letter sent to lady Lenuţa; I was confused and impressed by the figures 2 and 4, with their so concrete appearance, so arithmetic, serious and (quote Manole) honorable; until finally, I understood that this formula apparently numerical is actually abstract and algebraic, requesting to be always translated, exemplified, embedded in time; and namely each time according to the truth forbidden at that time. Ah! poor us, still slaves of history we are, and still under times.[28]

December 31st 1959

On the other hand, the quality of Roman senator doesn't seem to be connected to a certain historical epoch, the way Schelling shows that the romanticism is not a literary school belonging to a stage in the evolution of the taste but a permanent inclination of the human soul. The Jew of over eighty-two years, the short pensioner from Bucharest, showed to myself suddenly, in the simplest way, capable of authentic senatorial feelings.

After I told him how things happened, he said:

–Why did you come back home, imbecile? You gave them the impression that you hesitate, that there is a possibility to betray your friends. In business, when you say let me think it means you already accepted. For nothing in the world you should accept to become an accusation witness.

I know him since the time he was returning home from Pantelimon in the running board of the carriage – martially; during the events of 1919 he circulated in the workshops of the factory in military uniform with the sword out of sheath, but I still feel inclined to believe that he's playing a bit. I look at him furtively, being afraid that I will notice he is bluffing. I show to him that now I won't find anyone and staying at the door of the Security with the suitcase at my side until Monday doesn't make sense, here the heroism being very close to ridicule. And I feel exhausted and I was eager to eat dinner. And I also show him what prison really means, that he is old, he will remain alone with a tiny pension; that he should not expect pity from anyone; and no visits either; besides I am afraid; and I am asked only to tell the truth; and we may not see each other again; and anyway

16

I made him only troubles all his life, at least now, at the end I should help him in his last days; and that without further ado, the perspective of the prison, of the sufferance not to mention the thought of his misfortune, terrifies me.

(The imminence of the pain moves us and the repentance, nice doggie, follows it closely.)

In the well known parody, the mother of Stephen the Great feels pity for her wounded son, opens the gate of the castle and treats his wounds. How far is the parody from knowing the human soul and the surprises that a studio apartment in Bucharest can reserve. (More cool than Paris Mysteries.) Listening to my father there is no doubt for me anymore that Lady Oltea truly behaved as in the poem of Bolintineanu. Since the oldie, the Jew is able to talk to me the way he does, what isn't possible? The artificial is as spread as the natural, the theater is of the essence of life. Corneille describes the people the way they are, and at the end of the school year in the recitations of the students from the elementary grades (I in the third grade: You had faith, King, and that's why you won) they say banalities.

–It is true, says father, that you will have very bad days. Your nights, though, will be peaceful – (I have to repeat what he told me, I have to; otherwise God will punish me) –, you will sleep well. But if you accept to be witness for the prosecution you will have, indeed, quite good days but the nights will be horrible. You will never be able to close an eye. You will have to live only with sleeping aids and sedatives, brutified and sleepy all day and during the night painfully awake. You will torture yourself like a madman. Mind your business. My heart is broken too but you don't have any other choice. Besides, even if you will accept today to be the prosecution witness, don't be stupid, after six months they will still take you. That's for sure.

Especially this last argument, perfectly logic, trader like and lawyer like, impresses me. Just that when you are afraid six months is an eternity.

But father, more and more a Roman senator, continues:

–Prepare, therefore, your things for Monday. Take only worn out things. (Here he was sadly mistaken.) And in these three days that are left don't talk to me of any trial, Security, prison. I want us to spend them in a pleasant and peaceful manner.

That's what we're doing. Strange thing, I do sleep well indeed, I even eat with appetite (the convicted man in the Penitentiary Colony by Kafka was eating too on the torture device) and I behave reasonably quiet.

I'm missing from home only in the New Year's day, at lunch, being invited by the lawyer

D.P. whose wife is an old acquaintance of mine – and my first, my only youth love. They are telling me all (they have two kids) that they participated to a New Year's Eve party where one of the guests fell down dead while dancing. Fine start for a year! they comment. If they only knew that on top of that they invited to lunch someone who will be in three days a jailbird… I ask the lawyer, as if it was just idle talk (although this was the reason I wanted to come and I left father alone), what is he thinking about the article 209 penal code. He lifts his shoulders, pensive, sad: the conviction is sure and the sentence is heavy...

January 3-4 1960

I don't think it will be too heavy, says father. They will give you probably eight years. I will take care to leave for you at Gică or another relative the money I will get by selling the tuner, the gas stove, the gas cylinder, the books – so that you will find something when you get out. (Of the total confiscation of the property of the political convicts he has absolutely no idea.)

Monday morning I find myself calm. I wash myself, I shave, I dress up, I check the suitcase (full of rags). I was not allowed to cry not once during the three days. Father, issuer of the interdiction, not a chance.

In the street I meet professor Al. El., former colleague from Spiru Haret high school, and I start telling him – so emotional that I feel his touched surprise – that there are Jews who really love Romania. No doubt about that, he answers politely, not only politely. I talked to him very declamatory. He stares at me.

When I am ready, I take farewell from my parent. I am very gloomy. Father, however – in pajamas, short, plump, joyous – is all smiles and he's giving me the last advice like the coach before the match, like the companion in the train station, in one breath, after being silent until the last moment:

–   They told you not to let me die like a dog? If that's so, then I won't die at all. I will wait for you. And watch out, don't embarrass me. Don't be a scaredy Jew, don't shit in your pants.

He gives me a pressed kiss, he accompanies me to the door, stands erect and salutes me in the military fashion.

–   Go, he tells me.

I descend the stairs at normal pace, without looking back. I exit through the blockhouse door. There is destiny, there is premonition, there is telepathy. On the street first completely empty, although is not early, suddenly appears from beyond the corner just one person: an officer from the Ministry of Internal Affairs. I shudder.

–   The worse moments during the time spent at the Security. Two:

One night, and it is very late, stubbornly denying – a point of secondary importance actually, who came from Paris with the last novel of Mircea Eliade and the plays of Eugen Ionescu, Marietta Sadova? (I notice that for a fearful like me stubbornness is the only solution) – I am threatened: a confrontation with the chief of the batch.

First I don't understand why the confrontation is presented as a threat. (I am still a freshman.) On the contrary, I feel allayed by the occasion to see Dinu. The perspective of meeting in the middle of the night, in the offices of Security a former illustrious representative of the "pro- Legionnaire" intellectuality, already carried me on the playful and stupid wings of juvenile imagination, that candid and disarming imagination that the most experienced old men, wallowed in mediocrity, washed up by compromises still carry in the most hidden caches, where the stupidity makes its nest and fortifies itself definitively, like treponema chased by bismuth in the depths of the big internal organs: it will be something dramatic and heroic. We will compete in defending each other. We will smile to each other. We will shake hands. We will suffer together.

– Bring the chief, mister investigator, bring him.

The investigator rings, gives a whispered order and, after a long silent wait, Dinu Nc. is brought inside.

I was given strict orders to keep my mouth shut, so that many elements of the anticipated heroism were ruined.

I stay put at the desk from the end of the investigation office and I stare; I am focused, alert, all eyes and ears. (All eyes, like Mikhail Strogov watching his mother, Marfa.)

What frightens and depresses me beyond words is the physical appearance and carriage of Dinu. Appearance: skinny, yellowish, unshaved, dressed in shabby clothes that don't stay but hang on him; it's just one year and a few moths since I saw him last time and in what dark side of the moon he already is! And those black glasses that are my nightmare, that – I would come to understand only later – symbolize the darkness as opposed to the light of Christ. (Come and take light... He was life and life was the light of men. And the light shines in darkness...) The black glasses are not just a simple police idiosyncrasy, an intimidation procedure used in the investigation stage. They are not even a refined technique of reaching to the nervous centers that are the most vulnerable because they are the superior ones. They are much more than that – and that's why they are so frightening (Surround me Lord with Thy boundless power and life giving cross and protect me from every evil amen says the short prayer of the investigated individual: on the way from the cell to the office or during the silences of the interrogation or as an obsessive mental background: pray incessantly) –, they are the sign and the seal of the beast, father of lie and prince of fear, king of darkness. The carriage: this skinny and shabby ghost, once introduced in the room and seated by the guard with the face toward the investigating officer and spoken to, right away stood erect. They did not remove his glasses, I am not allowed to speak so he cannot know I am present.

My script is dust and ashes. We are in the same room and still we gravitate in different orbits

– he is virtually in Alpha Centauri –, like the soulless electrons, like the hostile nations from who knows what Assyrian empire based on conquests, like the animal species – ducks, turkeys, cats, roosters, dogs, goats, calves – that carry their life in the farm parallel and indifferently, like all those beasts, caprinae and bovine whose only locus is us, men, so different than them, so reduced to interjections and onomatopoeia in order to communicate with them, so being in circles that never intersect.

The chief speaks in an obedient, prompt, focused tone that evokes a long and painful training. That's how we will all end.

He doesn't deny anything, confirms everything, pronounce my name with indifference, in the queue. (From the file, in the eve of the trial, I was going to find out that my name was the first in the list of friends that he frequents.) The exam is short and the candidate answer quick and well. The candidate even bows a few times. The black glasses give to the candidate an air of obsequious mendicant, of resigned and submissive pauper, the way were the beggars and the paupers – the way it was supposed to be – in the moral novels of the past century, when the society was flourishing strong and stable, when everybody was staying put in his place and was behaving according to his position, when the rich men, calm and not tormented by doubts, were distributing gently the alms, and the needy, knowing their position, were receiving them overwhelmed; when the gentlemen were wearing in the evening only tails (poem dedicated to Anette: sometimes when it rains/ I imagine how nice it was/ in the year one hundred and nine); when those sentenced to whipping in Russia were addressing the executioner, obligatorily, your blessedness.

Most blessed, most generous senior lieutenant seems to say Dinu to Onea (who also took a virtuous air), and I'm not any better than the chief; I am completely silent, according to the orders, I don't shout: Dinu, I'm here, Dinu, don't give up lad, Dinu I decided to behave well. I don't shout because I'm afraid and because I am disgusted and upset like a kid whose toy was taken: pouting, boiling with revolt, huddled in disappointment, burned by deception, I look at D. and the investigator like a babe to mature men who are up only to promise and then not to keep their word, to forget you, to tease you with the cake and then to send you, smiling and cruel, to bed.

The second moment, even more terrible: again confronted with T., this time much more later, when I was brought back from Gherla, first from Jilava, then again at Security, to be witness for a trial. T. has now a sort of statute of professional witness: she was not sent to the penitentiary for punishment execution, they keep her at Malmaison (What was the name, mister, of that Belgian engineer that built the forts, it starts with B? Nah, Bartholdy is the one who sculpted the statue of Liberty in New York...) and they pull her out for all kind of trials as a prosecution witness.

This time – and the investigator tells me from the first moments – I am not anymore what I used to be.

I got wiser, and trickier, now that I am a jailbird, rubbed in inquiries, it's not going that easily anymore with me, I know to defend myself, I learned. I learned their tricks, I saw them laughing. (That's the big difference between us and those from West, the unknowing: we heard them laughing and, unwillingly, with great difficulty, against ourselves, fighting, resisting, we had to wake up, to gain access to the condition – so hard to understand and to realize – of şmecher.)

In the trial of Nego they didn't get anything out of me, just inconsequential declarations (What, you're giving him democracy certificates, you know you're funny? And you're saying there were only trivial conversations?) and they couldn't use me as a witness. I paid dearly for this and later some questioned whether it has been worth doing it. There are some who claim that it is not necessary to resist: you sign everything and at trial, orally, you declare what you want, you tell the truth and appease your conscience.

Wrong reckoning. At trial you can say anything you want, that's true. But did the quick- witted ask why? Why can you say anything you want and state that you withdraw your testimony, that you don't know, that he didn't do it and you didn't hear it and he's a good man and an old progressive and so on, unburden yourself and make peace with yourself and chatter away – as long as they let you. Why? Because everything you say in public (if the sessions are not secret) doesn't have any value and it is not recorded, or if it is recorded is recorded only for the sake of appearances (when there is a public); the statements given in court are not added to the file except if they confirm and maintain what was stated during the investigation. The decision is based only upon documents from the file, where are your signed statements, you clever bunch! What you're saying in the court is like speaking to a radio station without emitter or in the receiver of a defect phone, on the screen of a silent movie.

She gives even now a satisfactory statement for the inquiry. But not only I made progresses, she did too. She files a report so perfect, so standardized, so adequate, she speaks so in accordance with what is expected from her – so tuned –, the officers address her so familiarly and despising- benevolent that I catch again vertigo, this time a vertigo with intestinal spasms and a sort of fiery, hostile lucidity. Maybe now – at forty-eight – it is the moment when I go from childhood to maturity, from dream to knowledge, to awareness[29]. I "get it". This is the world and we are like her. With cabbage in lard and with ham in the attic. The money and the sweets and all the earth fruits. If the hag would have wheels would be tram, if she would have helmet would be minister of war. Now, for the first time, I am really a fanatic. All my old vague attractions toward Legionnarism[30], choked, muffled, unconscious, now startle, come to life. And I am seized contradictorily by pity and a touched, watery horror.

How much stress on details. It's like the keys of the typewriter jump and type[31]. And he said... then I said... and he said again and then I answered... No, the truth cannot be that bad. Maybe I'm deaf, or I have hearing hallucinations. I do not. And why shouldn't be possible? Look, it's possible. Everything is possible. Anything is possible. (If she filed even that Ms Brăiloiu did monarchist propaganda, glorifying Carol[32]. A widow that was strolling the kids of big-shots in the Grădina Icoanei (The Garden of the Icon) park, teaching them French, alone, wretched, only skin and bones and besides despising and hating Carol II no less than myself.) The combinatorial power in the moral range does not have any limits.

You spoilt Bucharester, well-to-do youngster, middle-aged bachelor, Frenchy Jew, Christian freshly tucked in faith maybe just out of fear and out of need for a nest, a den, a shelter, wake up and look where you entered: at the shadow of cross, a torture tool from which the blood flows, where stays One whose lungs, guts, reins are ripped and He's not only tortured and killed slowly but mocked at, especially mocked at – and especially killed like cattle, like the dead hacked with the chopper by a ripper. Slashed guts, sweat, blood, mockery, nails. This is Christianity, boy. Not the bells of the church from Pantelimon on Sundays and holidays, not the Christmas tree in the beautiful house Şeteanu, not the beard of general Zossima, not the candies of the old lady Eliza Boerescu, the widow of Costică, brother of Vasile, minister of Alexandru Ioan Cuza[33], not the juicy jokes of the worldly priest Georgescu-Silvestru, not the baptism in the cell 18 – so humble and therefore so majestic, so hidden and therefore so beaming –, no, not the ecumenicity that you promised so hasty, (and anyway, evoking the luxury of Rome, the splendor of Italy and the refined Latin topology), not the gestures of reconciliation so easy actually and, anyway, source of peace, quiet and subterranean pride, but this: the true cross, enormous, smelly, indifferent; leakage, filth…

Do I really hear it or it just seemed like, but I hear again Look at your merchandise, see who you brought us? It seems like an echo, a reverberation, a ghost pain like from an amputated member. The merchandise, anyhow, is me, that now I am twisting inside, that for the first time I know what pain can be when it means business deadly seriously and with grounds, when it's not damped by the shock of surprise, or sweeten by the strange elevation that inside us abet the first disappointment – and it's counted for what it is and is supposed to be – (Camus: From a certain point of sufferance and injustice further nobody can do anything for anybody and the pain is solitary) –; I, who now knows to speak as little as if the only languages on world would be Algol, Cobol, Fortran, I, who now start to move away with a speed close to that of light: this time I embraced NO and I keep it tight, manly. I lie calmly. I got tricky, didn't I? I heard them laughing, how I wish to be able to tell to my dear Londoners: you didn't hear them laugh[34], to be able to quote Brice Parain: dialectics is the same thing as hell, to show them that not even the two bearded scoundrels aren't better[35] – it's the same everywhere – two scoundrels, two jewels, as lieutenant Onea likes to say.

Would the Londoners hear me? Would they pay attention? Finding the truth makes you lonely. The passing from the pain that cracks your head invincibly to the cold calmness is quasi- instantaneous too, like the light. The light about which Stéphane Lupasco believes that in the moment of final entropy of the universe will reign all over the place because there will not be any kind of particles left except photons[36]. Everything will be light. He was the true light. Light from light. True God from true God…

February 1962

And your joy no one will take from you.
John 16, 22
So shall I keep myself erect! Let I not lose my soul.
Paul Claudel

The cells from Reduit, at Jilava, are especially gloomy and they have the reputation of a regime even more severe than at "sections". At 34 I come from "secret" where I was kept as long as I maintained the hunger strike, in a cell unheated since the building of the fort – at the same time with the inutile belt around the Capital – by the engineer Brialmont. The cold, as terrible as the hunger and the thirst (but the worse is the lack of sleep), entered deeply in me.

I must be looking extremely wretched, because the famous sergeant Ungureanu, who takes over me at the entrance of Reduit, almost smiles to me (the way a gourmand would relent in front of a large piece of well cooked venison steak) and he hands me over to the cell chief recommending him to give me a single bed and to watch me. I am placed in the closest to the door bed, as a suspect and watched carefully by the cell chief, a Bessarabian[37] with a Russian name, a sturdy man, gloomy, with fierce glances; I find out soon that he's dangerous, they say he is a defrocked priest. Cell 34 is a sort of long and dark tunnel, with numerous and strong nightmarish elements. It's a cavern, a canal, a subterranean gut, cold and profoundly hostile, is an empty mine, the crater of an inactive volcano, is a rather accomplished image of a discolored hell.

In this place almost surreally sinister I was going to know the happiest days of my entire life. How absolutely happy I had been in cell 34! (Not even in Braşov[38], with mother, in childhood, in the unending streets of the mysterious London; not even on the proud hills of Muscel[39], not even in the décor of blue illustrate of Lucerne; no, nowhere.)

There are in the cell many young men, subjected to a special treatment by the guards and especially by the cell chief. (The hate of the old men against the new generation; that goes up to allying themselves with the fiercest cops for the building of the common front against the debauched and disrespectful. A sort of generation and age solidarity, very similar to the class solidarity because of which some peasants, workers and small clerks hate the fellow prisoners with degrees, boyars or bourgeois more fiercely than the representatives of the administration.) From the first day I notice in the entire cell a tremendous thirst for poetry. Learning by heart poems is the most pleasant and insatiable fun activity in prison. Blessed are those who know poetry. Who knows by heart many poems is a happy man in prison, his are the long hours that pass quickly and in dignity, his is the hall of the Waldorf-Astoria hotel and his is the café Flore. His are the ice-cream and lemonade served at the tables of the brasserie Florian in the San Marco plaza. The abbot Faria knew what he was doing when preparing for the Monte-Cristo island by learning by heart all the books. And Nikolai Semenovitch Leskov didn't suspect how truthful he was when prompting: "Read and try to gain something useful from it. You will have a lot of fun in the grave." Since prison is like a grave, the advice proves to be excellent: whoever likes to learn poems by heart will never be bored in jail – and he won't be alone.

From this point of view I stay well. I know by heart Morning Star, the Epistles[40], a lot of Coşbuc and Topârceanu (he is especially in high demand), thousands (I think) of verses by Gyr and Crainic (swallowed from the very beginning, together with the Morse alphabet from the Legionnaire veterans); I caught a lot of verses from Verlaine, Lamartine and Baudelaire; the sonnet of Arvers, of course (Ma vie a son secret, mon âme son mystère) Samain – Au jardin de l'Infante – that, whenever I repeat or I teach to someone, directs my thoughts to Ojardindilifant[41] from Medeleni and all the paradisiacal afternoons from the street Pitar-Moşu.

I find quickly a circle of young men that want to learn Morning Star and they were eagerly waiting for someone who knows it to come. In the cell there is a Lutheran parson from Braşov, with aspect of Gösta Berling; his native language is German and he's a poet himself. Ardent admirer of Rilke from which he translated; he knows a lot of poems of the great poet, that he recites superbly, with a vibrant feeling and extraordinarily meaningful; he has a patience of iron and a goodwill that defies fatigue. Everything in him oscillates between demigod and saint. If he would tell us that

Mein Vater Parsifal trägt eine Krone
Sein Rittersohn bin ich, Lohengrin gennant[42]

or if he would tell us that he is Siegfried himself fallen after his Rheinfahrt[43] directly at Reduit, everybody would believe him.

Bruder Harald Sigmund – that's his name, rather Wagnerian – proves to be that miracle that the convict rarely finds but from which, when he reaches it, he finds out what joy is: he's brave, proud, undefeatable, polite as in the salon of the prince de Conti where it is served le thé à l'anglaise[44], always smiling and dignified like the models from the portraits of La Tour, Peronneau or Van Loo, and in high spirits, never sleepy or morose, willing in every moment to learn anything, to discuss, to listen, to tell stories, to communicate everything he knows: a gentleman, a noble, a hero. A man like him arouse in you strongly the nostalgia of the Middle Ages and in his presence you are taken over by a grim enmity toward today's times and against the democracy in the tramcar at peek hours. (What you're at pushing like that? if you don't like it, buy a car! shame on you, are you a lion or something?) Look that he's a lion, look, there are lions too! Look, there are not only vipers and reptiles. Look that life can be something else than the supreme ideal of keeping your place in the line or to evict the neighbor in the adjoining room to extend in his place.

The presence of the youth – incomparably more resistant (morally speaking, otherwise they have all tuberculosis), more gently and more vertebrate than the old men – and the parson made appear in this room an atmosphere of grandeur, of hieratic medieval spirit; invisible purple cloaks flutter in the air, flashing blades of Damascus are shining. Every gesture unveils a hidden Don Quijote-ism. I don't know how, but my arrival, repulsively meager and impressively pale, reeking frost, with even my glances trembling, with an aura of hunger striker, contributes to the accentuation of the atmosphere of noble defiance of reality. There are also two medics, very good people, and some soldiers from the Lord's Army and some sectarians, apiarists and keen after psalms (I know psalms too, mostly learned from the congenial Hariton Rizescu, honorary sacristan in a big church in the center of Bucharest); and they all seem to compete in being gentle with one another and everybody learns verses from dawn to dusk, continuously, and they narrate serious books, and Bruder Harald surpasses himself – he recites, translates, teaches – and relates in detail – with modesty, love and the ecumenical sense of relativity the life and doctrine of doctor Martin Luther. From everywhere – like the clouds in the mountains – it springs and it condenses in cell 34 that ineffable and unmatched atmosphere that only the prison can create: something close to what would have been the court of the dukes of Burgundy or of the king René de l'Arles or of a court d'amour in Provence, something like the paradise, something very Japanese, chivalrous, something that would excite to paroxysm Henry de Montherlant, Ernst Jünger, Stefan George, Malraux, Chesterton, Solzhenitzin, something made out of courage, love of paradox, stubbornness, holy madness and the will to transcend at any price the miserable human condition; something that evokes the aristocratic names considered the most exalting by Barbey d'Aurevilly: Hermangarde de Polastron and Enguerrand de Coucy: something that, I don't quite understand how, it painfully remembers me of the failed attempt to kill Hitler from July 20th '44 of von Stauffenberg and the German aristocracy. Something that awakes in my memory these words of Leon Chestov: "Apparently there are two totally opposite theories regarding the origin of the human species. Some claim that the man descends from the apes, others that they were created by God. They quarrel incessantly. I believe they are both wrong. My theory is the following: those who believe the man descends from the apes they truly descend from the apes and they form a separate race, outside the race of men created by God that they do know they were created by God." Something that sounds like the grand rhythm of Gyr verses: "Where is Voivode Caragea? Iancu[45] wants to see him!" Something that confirms wonderfully the

25

affirmation of Simone Weil: "Because of joy, the beauty of the world enters in our soul. Because of pain, it enters in our body." In cell 34, the joy – rising from aristocracy, poetry and defiance – and the pain (because it reigns a terrible cold, the food is scarce, the water continues to be infested, the room is oppressing like in a horror movie, the abuse is plenty, any inspection of the cops is followed by uppercuts and punches in the head) mix so inextricably that everything, including pain, converts in ecstatic and lofty happiness. When the cow eats grass, the grass is transformed into cow flesh. The same, when the cat eats fish, the fish is transformed into cat flesh. The sufferance we are assimilating is transformed at once into euphoria. The verses of Georg Trakl, learned from father Harald, strengthen too this sensation:

Wanderer tritt still herein
Schmerz versteinerte die Schwelle; Da erglänzt in reiner Helle
Auf dem Tische Brot und Wein.[46]

Yes, in all enters the extraordinary joy after the communion with bread and wine, with the most pure Body and the most precious Blood. Weren't the Hassids getting drunk with plain water invoking the name of Sabaoth? Aren't we able to transform the misery of this gut of stone and abasement in enthusiasm? The lack of enthusiasm, says Dostoievski, is the sure sign of perdition.

The enthusiasm is but plenty in cell 34, and if it's so, nobody and nothing is lost. We are not ashamed of dry exaltations and of a sort of continuous courteous and solemn ecstasy, again in accordance with Dostoievski's recommendation whose words "The man exists only if God and immortality exists" we repeat smiling meaningfully and they seem to us glaringly evident.

Here, in 34, it is shown to me again what occurred to me in 18; that the miracle is part of real life, it is a component of the world. Adhémar Esmein, on the plan of the constitutional right had noticed the same thing when he was saying – against the so-called realists of the juridical science – that fictions are realities too. In cell 34 the miracle is known and accepted as an indisputable fact.

A miracle is also the way we behave toward each other, competing in helping one another, talking delicately, and making the life more pleasant to each other. During a bodily search it is confiscated my only bottle where I was keeping the black liquid that – to my luck – it is served to us in the morning as coffee instead of the more consistent barley. Since I don't eat anything that is given to us, the "coffee" is a precious reserve. The confiscation of the bottle takes proportion of catastrophic loss. The search took place in the morning and for having the bottle I was violently punished and threatened. In the evening, at the taps (nominally, because the bulbs never cease radiating the intense light), when I take off the blanket I find on the bed a bigger bottle. The charity is in accordance with the strictest Christian precepts, because I don't know who put the bottle, I can't ask, I can't find out. This charity (and how did the precious object escape the severe search?) is gratuitous act in full Gidean meaning, it is even more gratuitous than the murder of Lafcadio. The absolute discretion recommended by the Savior is present untainted. This gesture overwhelms me, I feel the thrill of pride, I shake and – could it be otherwise? – I soak my so-called "pillow" with the sweet warm tears of happiness.

January 1960

In the first cell at the Security, Mircea M., former journalist at "Univers", caught in a net of dangerous trouble. He receives me with a lot but somehow forced kindness. You can see how much is tormented by harassment. Being new I had with me a small bread brought from home and I give him the opportunity, after two years, to eat a piece of white loaf.

From inquiry I come back often messed up. Senior lieutenant Onea, from the "methods of simple security", he prefers with me the banging of the head on the wall repeated at long; other times I am trampled (he wears boots). There is also comrade major Jack Simon, mustached and cold, with crystalline voice, who declares to me that he decided, for my quality of Legionnaire Jew[47], to kill me with his own hands. For the time being I am just beaten with the crowbar, a solution disproportionate to the threat but unpleasant too. Mircea M. shows himself very complaisant, soaks both towels – mine and his – and with awkward parental gentleness (he's younger than I am) applies them to the head, ribs, feet, according to the situation.

One late night, when I am brought back, he guesses my trouble although I'm not hurt. In a few words I relate to him – out of base instinct of idle talk confession – what happened. I had been again confronted with her. The officers manifested their malcontent toward the "merchandise", but they didn't insist, and in the end – mirabilis res – lighting at length their cigarettes and starting to chat, they signaled us that we may come close and talk freely. She came toward me, she talked to me. I was not answering. I am awkward, I don't hear well and I have the feeling that it lasts too long. The two continue at their desk their pseudo-conversation of extras while in the middle of the scene evolve and declaim the main characters of the play.

She talked what she talked, then she said to the officers that we're done. Without hurry she kissed me twice, once on every cheek, sweetly.

Mircea M. finds my story sensational and worthy to be put in the annals of the Security. He asks me to repeat it, he tastes it and he won't stop commenting: "Women, mister, women. With them you never know."

It is more complicated. But the outburst of disclosures passed and I forgo more detailed explanations. The news I related, anyway, pleased him, amused him, calmed him: he's not anymore under investigation, he is in the enchanting realm of gossip, on the unending caravan road of the male surprise in front of the feminine Sphinx. Ich bin der Räuber Orbazan.[48]

Every night, my comrade prays shortly. (At Security it is allowed to cross yourself. I was going to find out that in prison is not allowed.) When he stands, I stand too and I stay stone-still near him, troubled that I cannot associate except by a vague and inconclusive gesture of politeness. I don't cross myself.

In the second cell, N.N.P., converted to Catholicism, encourages me. He prays a lot, he recites the rosary of Saint Anthony. I tell him that I want to be baptized. It's more of an old dream, a tendency, now without chances to happen. I come to understand that, plainly speaking, it is a persisting desire, reaching the stage of impatience.

When I come back from the court clerk's office where I was informed of my sentence (and I couldn't stop a nervous twitch: thirteen years and forced labor seemed to me melodramatic terms), I show him that is very unlikely to resist until the end and I should better be baptized. But how? Because of the destiny I won't be able to do it. N.N.P. – an older prisoner than M.M. – assures me that now I won't be kept much longer at Security and without doubt I will find in prison a priest willing to baptize me, clandestinely, of course, but validly. All the cells in prisons are full of clerics of all kinds, just that they are generally fearful, the deed is serious; I receive the advice to use the first opportunity, since I am determined.

The impossibility.

That is what is asked from us.

Otherwise there is neither escape nor beatitude. (And no petty peace either.)

The juridical amendment does not apply in the moral life: on the contrary, c'est à l'impossible qu'on est tenu[49]. The legal precept (à l'impossible nul n'est tenu[50]) has a validity strictly limited to the contractual domain.

Just that there are two kinds of impossibilities: there is the impossible impossibility and the possible impossibility. The impossible impossibility – the physical one – is unimportant and meaningless. The example given by the old jurists – although today is not funny anymore – is as conclusive as it can be: you cannot oblige yourself by contract to go in the moon. Of course this doesn't say too much. But it is not this that is required. You are required something else. You are not required to go in the moon. You are required – and this is something radically different – the moon from the sky. And preferably blue.

As long as we don't surpass the possible, the accounting, we can neither think nor demand the paradise.

What could I have done? asks one who executed the orders given by a tyrannical regime. What could I have done? asks the soldier who received an atrocious mission. Nothing, of course, there was nothing they could have done. And they shouldn't even be blamed for doing nothing, for obeying and executing. That's why the trials of Nüremberg are a mistake and a shame. Something they could have done, however – and at no risk: they could have abstained from committing the sin of stupidity, meaning they could have abstained from being overzealous, quite on the contrary: to execute slowly and unwillingly, to delay a little bit, to make a virtue out of laziness, to take it very easy. This is what they could have done – and unfortunately many haven't done it.

And if one would have wanted (and could have done it) to be a saint or a hero or a Christian, that's what they would have done: the impossibility. He would have not executed the order no matter what! (And to an action that transcends and break the monotony of the automatic life we can assume that God would not answer by indifference.) It is possible that the definition of the heroism and sainthood is just this: to make the impossibility possible. You cannot – man on the street – step on the moon or Mars, but the moon form the sky you can conquer: you just have to do something that is out of the question in the frame of fearful prudence and of the logic affiliated to accounting. The unhurried, crafty, reserved execution of the tyrannical orders, for instance, relates to the possible impossibility and the freedom to refuse. The laws of the world, therefore, are not a total hindrance on the way to paradise: they are just a more difficult hindrance that can be removed by reconsidering the notion (superficially examined) of impossibility.

(The man on the street. As if one could not enter in a church – whose founders knew to say no to the Roman emperors – or they wouldn't have a house, where they spend their night, time of reflection: because if the owl stays near the wise goddess Pallas is because only after the haste of the day follows the thought, nocturne and calm.)

The barren fig tree. This is, I think, the sense of the apparently so unfair parable, where Christ takes exception to the tree, tells to it "leave from my face" rather than curses it. Like Jesus would asks us to act according to terms and regulations, as in a bank. Good reason, indeed: it is not my time! Anytime is the time to do the good. Anytime is the time to oblige Christ. And as the kingdom of God will come when you least expect, furtively, the same the facts that predict it don't care for terms and contracts.

Or as if friendship would consist in answering: I will help you if I can. With such friends… Friend is a man who helps you without the verb being followed by an adverb of time or place or mode. And how much the Lord likes to call us His friends!

–   From the parable of the minas it follows that the man who left very far, who called his servants and gave them his wealth, is God Himself: the one who, returning one mina – as much as he had received – answers: "Lord, I knew you to be a hard man, reaping where you have not sown, and gathering where you have not scattered seed", the master don't contradicts him, on the contrary, he confirms the characterization, repeating it (Matt. 25, 26). And right away follow the strange words: "For to everyone who has, more it will be given, and he will have abundance; but from him who does not have, even what he has will be taken away."

It follows that to God you cannot apply the simplistic ideas that we men are forging about justice and that our relations with God are not based on an accounting do ut des, in which we would be always passive creditors and beneficiaries.

God reaps where He has not sown: it means that we have to give something from ourselves, to endeavor, to loan, to take initiatives. The attitude: what evil have I done! I haven't wronged anybody! I do what I can! if I can't do more! is – according to their saying –the attitude of a slob, it's in contradiction wit the parable of the minas and shows that we have not understood how grave is the sin of sloth and how concretely God means the prompting: the heavens are to be conquered. Nor how seriously, insistently we are required the effort and the aspiration toward impossibility, if not the impossibility itself.

– God is not joking: "Leave your country and your relatives and the house of your father", "Take your cross", "Come after me", "Take heed", "Cleanse and purify yourself!", "Go and shout", "Arise, take up your bed and go".

You cannot stay: there's no place for setting in, for comfort, for complacent dreaming; Oblomov is doomed; in laziness, sickness and madness no one can find a pretext. (And not even in justice: the fig tree.)

But Marta, then, why is she rebuked? Because she is detained by trifles, she toils in vain, she agitates. The Lord calls us for an important job: death is at the door and we, with the cigarette in bed (like Oblomov) or breaking our backs over some dishes as if they are some essences (like Marta)!

– The most useful phrase for getting close to Christianity and to start seeing a faint trace of light consists in these few amazing words of Sir Thomas Moore (Saint Thomas Moore take care – rightful care – to address him the English Catholics), spoken to a friend to whom he wanted to prove the absolute trust he gives him and the serious sincerity of his words: I trust I make myself obscure.[51]

More stunning words were never uttered, except: I believe, Lord, help my unbelief. About which I say to myself that if out of the whole Bible would remain only them, would be enough to prove the divine essence of Christianity. Although Papini says that the Beatitudes are the text that the terrestrial globe and the humanity can invoke to justify their purpose in a cosmic contest, to me "I believe, Lord, help my unbelief" seems even more obscure and apophatic, more final. It's paradoxical, it's the mystery of the faith act itself through which effect even the covalent links of the genetic code – and only mystery doesn't lack to them! – are left behind by far. I don't believe and I still pray. I believe and still I know that I don't truly believe. I believe, since I call Christ "Lord". Yet I don't believe since I ask Him to help my unbelief. (And whom do I ask to heal my unbelief? The One in which I will believe!) The causality is abolished, the law of temporal consecution, as everything that is material or psychological, vanishes. I believe and I don't believe simultaneously. Division. Contradiction. Hence the incertitude, the anxiety. The conscience poisoning everything, poisons the faith too, and in the moment we become aware of it we turn it into unfaith because by thinking the faith we pull it out of ineffable, out of candor.

But the way out, the hope, nothing is lost: because, humbly, I add: help me, keeping in mind that my human condition is indubitably linked to paradox and contradiction. The simultaneity of the text would lead to desperation if not for that short help that – tiny salt grain, infinitesimal catalyst with huge transmutation powers and unsuspected combinatorial consequences – it solves the quadrate of the circle and transforms the shout of confusion into the tears of trust.

– There, in the Security cell where I stayed with N.N.P. – the nephew of the painter Gh. Petraşcu – I was destined to fell the most atrocious unhappiness. The coincidences worked with an inflexible precision. I was caught in the trap, tormented by something that I couldn't be absolutely sure – but it seemed impossible to be otherwise –, in the situation of being unable to open my heart to anyone else, not even the kind man at my side. And locked in about forty square feet. The chasm was nearby: swarming, as in Poe's tale, with snakes, rats, smelly water, darkness and worms. The space, I mean the time – in my case, as opposed to the tale – was closing inexorably. And regarding the troops of general Lassallle – that in Poe's story bring the solution delivering the prisoner from the Inquisition – I was told during the investigation: suppose your Americans left with the wheelbarrow, (maybe that's why in jail slang, the common law prisoners – they, the penguins – were calling us Americans) and still they would have been here by now, as for the troops of general Lassalle not a chance, the miracles of the XIX century are finished. Then I knew the horror face to face, I knew what is the wall of Sartre, the darkness, the scoffing, the corner. Therefore I didn't escape. Crime and punishment. Caught in the furnace, inside. The hole, the chasm there, patient.

Then I plunged in the unknown water, not knowing how to swim, with close eyes; in the heated furnace. Believing only half, or a quarter, or even less, almost naught, but so wretched, that the sorrow itself replacing the faith, I entrusted myself. Unashamed. I was not ashamed to pray. Maybe that's why I was heard.

– But I think the best is, after I let (and I will still let) the images and the thoughts to unfold at will, to tell the story by thread, in detail, how the events occurred, to start with the beginning. Finding out in December 11th that Trixi has been arrested (the "Marchioness" on the phone: she's not home, she checked into hospital), I knew that soon will be my turn. The passing of a few days without anything happening was arousing my wonder. From all the people that drank tea with the Rosenkavalier teacup set, I was the only one still walking free. I talked to my father. Father encouraged me saying it's possible that nothing will happen to me, but we ought to examine all the possibilities. We confer and I reach in my mind the superstitious conclusion that if I'm not arrested till the end of the month, it means I escaped. From the day of December 31st I make a sort of magic milestone, something whispering to me from unknown depths that I'm not wrong. Thirty-one... Actually thirty, who's gonna start making arrests in the New Year's Eve day?

I communicate this precise term to dad. If they don't take me by then we will celebrate the New Year's Eve with pomp. Father agrees. He's over eighty-two. He wants some turkey and without fail carp caviar.

You're asking yourself sometimes how come the cancer sick – visibly loosing weight, warned by the doctor's performing so many analysis and biopsies – how while suffering so violent pains still doesn't realizes what happens to him. But I'm not any different. The days are dripping and although it's not possible not to know perfectly well that it's impossible and unimaginable not to be arrested, I begin to have more and more idiotic hopes. I even have the crazy thought that, who knows, maybe they all really conspired and to me, only to me they didn't reveal anything. I play a role for myself, I forge an non-reality from where the logic has been kicked out with a fillip. I taste, as usually, the deep charm of the Christmas days – since always the most beautiful of the year, even made out of stone and brick and still it's not possible not to be moved – that pass well. In the day of twenty-four I read as always the Christmas carol by Dickens and I can't help again to have my eyes soaked with tears.

Then I start thinking of the New Year's Eve party; I hasten to prepare it. This term that I established myself completely arbitrarily – my mind aches – it's meaningless; I could be arrested as well on first, second or third January. No, my intuition is good: something without name makes me feel sure that if the day of thirty-first passes, I won't be arrested for ages. Until thirty-first I feel the danger intense, imminent, stalking me.

Meanwhile I meet often with Madam Z., lady Lenuţa, mother of Al. Pal. The simple faith, superstitious maybe, of the boyar lady impresses me. From morning until evening she is at the Batiştei church with acatist. She knows, as opposed to her less intelligent (second) husband – un ancien beau[52] – ("Don't worry, they can't be that bad. They will reprimand them, they will scare them and then they will let them go with a warning.") – that the things are irreversible; still she hopes. (She has and she doesn't have cancer.) It's my first contact with the miracle as a daily fact, asked, expected. Lady Lenuţa believe in miracles; the miracles fulfill, otherwise she won't be here at the Batiştei church waiting for father Cazacu, to give her an acatist, she would be at the pharmacy.

Father Cazacu makes its appearance, tall, formidable, with a vladica beard, and with the voice of a town crier, of a God herald. I cross myself, that's not a problem, I've been crossing myself since childhood. (Only in the cell, with Mircea M., I couldn't do it: it was the last, desperate, doltish attempt of the enemy. Once I amazed Madam Băl., so friendly with me, by crossing myself at the gate of the

Legionnaire cemetery at the entrance of Predeal, when you come from Azuga and Buşteni.)

I hope and I don't hope. Twenty-seventh passes, and twenty-eighth, and twenty-ninth. Therefore caviar, turkey, fries, peas, fruits and a cozonac[53]. I have a lot of errands to do; the turkey will be cooked by a neighbor in the adjoining block-house. A sort of agitated pseudo- certitude overcomes me and then turns into a secret assurance: if twenty-ninth passes everything will be alright. The first day of January falls this year Friday; Saturday 2nd is a legal holiday. Sunday is Sunday, Thursday evening is the New Year's Eve party – and the work starts again Monday 4th. Monday 4th is on another planet, in a different eon.

(I was going to find out later that it was the day of the car accident in which Albert Camus
died.)

Father is very busy with the preparations for the New Year's Eve. He keeps asking me when
I'm going to buy the bread. I should buy a lot of bread and as soon as possible. And let me not forget the carp caviar.

Twenty-ninth and thirtieth go by untroubled. Nobody knock at the door, we sleep in peace. My conviction is that nothing can happen anymore. Stupid and animal conviction. I know only very well that I am the only one left not arrested and it's not possible not to be arrested. Afterward, how would I look if I won't be arrested? Won't people say that it's curious, suspect, devilishly fishy[54]? Among the people that were coming to father Mihai only he is still free; and what things are said about him! Do I want the same thing? Why am I the only one not arrested? I thought I read in lady Lenuţa's glances – because in her behavior toward me there is only extreme courteousness – a hue of tormenting, unlikely suspicion. By chance am I not the denunciator, the squealer? (The slang expression is now on the lips of the high society, since their members are the main clients of the prisons.) I know myself clean, so I walk proudly with Madam Z. on the streets around the Batiştei church and I explain to her the two etymologies of the name: from Giambattista Vecelli or Vevelli, the favorite of Voivode Radu Mihnea the Great or from a small river, Batiştea, tributary to the river Colentina – poor show of elementary erudition that allows us to surpass a bit the vileness of the situation. I assure her that I am resigned, that I will not leave Dinu anymore, that... – and I switch to my poor French – I will stand by him dussé-je en avoir pour quinze ans[55]. Maybe, – not maybe, for sure – I exaggerate on purpose – or unconsciously – though I am afraid (a fear deeply rooted in my body) and for quite awhile. I am horribly afraid, I had no idea how coward I am. It's a terrible discovery, and I don't see any remedy. I am afraid, this is the truth, totally, I enter in fear like someone in a scuba diving suit. I am able though – still able – to check it, to hide it. My teeth are not yet clattering, I am not yet yellowish, I am not yet throwing up green gall. But it will come, judging from how afraid I am. For now I am still modifying the list of dishes for the New Year's Eve party with my father, I am shopping, I parade on the streets with lady Lenuṭa and I look for a transcendental refuge in talking French; for ears as those of Madam Z. my French must sound very labored.

Autumn of 1966

In the play of Arthur Miller, After the fall, there is written a phrase whose absolute but also prophetic value, the years confirmed and amplified; the years during which the drugs, the hallucinogens, the compounds of the lysergic acid – especially LSD –, marijuana (the pot[56]), mescaline, peyotl, olilouqui, teonanacatl (I know them from Gigi Tz., who copied a list from an American journal) or the narcotics – opium, hashish, heroine – and all the products deified by Thomas Learey and his numerous faithful, become masse merchandises and goods in high demand: But no pill can make us innocent[57].

Yes, pills can give sleep, or rather the sleepiness or the evasion through disconnected indifference. However, not the innocence. That one can be given (back) only by Christ, through his paradoxical way, as always: giving us the feeling of guilt.

–   Paradoxical are the works of Christ with the sinners, the life and death.

Karl Barth: the grace of justification is our life, the grace of holiness is our death. This means that, in the operation of justification Lord says to the dead (I mean the sinner): live! Then, after pulling him from sin, in other words from death, and called him to life, He tells now to the enliven one: die! The repentant sinner – the former dead called now to life – has now to die for the worldly things. "Under these two determinations and not others must be lived the Christian life."

Look, the whole dialectics of mors et vita[58]: first it enlivens you, then it kills you: so that you can be truly alive. A, if this is life, life it's not easy, it's a kind of death. We keep saying: the life, life is so and so... but maybe we don't even know what is real life (as we don't know what is death), maybe we just stray in the oppressing heat of the shadows of a limbo and among the confusions of a vague language...

–   From the sentence of Arthur Miller it follows also that the happiness and the peace cannot be created by us alone, the material way – but they are given unto us from above.

Another proof of the existence of God.

December 31st 1959

I am not at all surprised when my father wakes me up very early in the morning of thirty- first. I am perfectly calm, I slept, I jumped over the fence, and on the New Year's Eve day I don't risk anything. Why then my father wakes me? He worries about the bread.

I look at the clock: five. I assure father that I have plenty of time.

It's not about the bread, he says. You have a business to attend. At eight you are convoked somewhere.

And he shows me a small note. Yes, it's an invitation in the street Ştefan Furtună, at eight o'clock. As witness. I understood. I understood but not entirely: why as a witness? Why didn't they come to pick me up at night like all the others?

I grin to myself, sour, offended, in the bathroom mirror while I shave myself. I am not scared as much as offended, deceived: in the last moment! Grabbed, you can say, from the running board of the train. How ironically; somebody is playing with me without hurry, like the cat with the mouse. That's why the cat is devilish, because she's the only animal that mocks the pray before eating it.

I am as angry as it can be. The ironic and acidic smile of the pessimist, who knows that everything ends badly, doesn't leave my face not even when I'm ready.

In the last moment. Scorned. Like a mouse. After playing.

Father is a short man, rather fat, with a crooked shoulder – and he limps. He was an engineer and he worked until he was seventy-nine, in 1956, in a factory not an office. (At Scăeni, lately, when I asked about him in the furnace hall, the glass blowers were answering pointing with the chin or the finger above. I thought they like to joke, to make fun of me, what was I doing there. No, father climbed up on a furnace, an inch from the ceiling; you could reach him only after climbing some gangways and many metallic, perpendicular flights of stairs as on a ship. Father: if an engineer cannot replace any of his workers and to make his hob as good as him, he's lost.) He fought in the war as officer and he was decorated. He obtained citizenship by special law voted by the parliament before 1914. But after all what and who is he? An old Jew from Bucharest, a short pensioner, a few memories, some friends, a few decorations hidden in a box, one son. We live together in the same room. An entire life I didn't cause him any trouble; he's not a bad boy, he says, but he is an old child. For sure he sees how afraid I am and how offended by destiny I feel in this morning, and how tormented I am. And what danger threatens even him.

Shorty (that's how I call him, I don't exaggerate) seems however very calm. He urges me to put my things in a small suitcase (it's the suitcase of Lilly's mother, I won't be able to return it) and he encourages me. The calmness of my father is transmitted to me a little. But still I feel very agitated and malcontent. And especially fooled. In the last day! In the last moment! In thirty-first!

The subpoena came in the afternoon of thirtieth, being handed to my father who signed for it. But he didn't show it to me when I came back home, rather late, in order to spare my night sleep. (And I feel for the first time, imperceptibly and vaguely, a harbinger, a premonition, a first appearance of the aristocratic and generous spirit that I will meet often and plenty in the prison; for now is just a sort of sublimated image, a flickering, a gentle tremolo, but the gesture of my parent – for whom it has not been easy to be silent and to behave as if nothing happened – cuts my respiration.)

– In prison I hear – the various versions differ considerably, about the film The General of la Rovere.

It's a production of the Italian neo-realism, and also the recount of a case of transfiguration, with an aroma of a Pirandello play.

A punk from Rome ends up, through a maze of circumstances, in the situation of playing the role of a count-general who's the chief of the Italian resistance in the south of the country during the German occupation. A certain physical resemblance makes easier playing the role that in time he came to fall in love, as well as the environment, so new and surprising for him, of the political convicts, where sacrifice and honor were common things. Although the Germans use him only to discover the identity of the chief of the resistance in north, he cannot betray the man on whose identity he is edified from the beginning.

Like the actor who doesn't want to go down from the throne in the play The emperor, the punk enters in the shoes of the character. In the end, summoned to fulfill his mission and to reveal the identity of the man wanted by the Germans, the former crook, pimp and card sharper, taking his false identity seriously, accepts to pay the imposture with the price of blood. The prison director, a German officer, sends him to the firing squad, not without showing respect. The false count-general ends his life solemnly, tragically and chivalrously. And maybe not even the true general de la Rovere would not have died with more courage and fierce grandeur.

The hero of the film changes, the game becoming for him reality; the character he plays fully substitutes him, or maybe he surpasses the character, according to Jean Genêt's theory that sometimes the imposture is more convincing than the authentic model.

The story of this film conquers me and impresses me tremendously (the magic attraction of nobility and the disturbing possibility of transfiguration): I always listen to it attentively and equally moved. This Christian-Pirandellian transformation of the hero seems to me so wonderful, the pathetic poor thief transformed in a noble hero!

The same thing is the example of the Spanish actress who acts in a play the role of a nun. At the end of the show, she categorically refuses to undress the frock she wears and declares that she truly wants to stay a nun and she went right away to the monastery of the respective order.

The public, kneeled, open the way for her through which she passes.

The Roman actor who, playing the baptized Christian, declares himself Christian indeed; the people boisterously applaud the so natural acting of the interpret touched by grace until, being understood it is not a joke, the neophyte is put to death.

Alphonse de Chateaubriand in La réponse du Seigneur: the becoming is the general rule, anyone and anything can become anyone and anything. The bird can become rose, the man: saint, hero.

After they close the store and they pull the window shutter, the young Japanese clerks don't go home in a hurry; they gather together to listen, full of revering feelings and until late, stories with samurais lead by the Bushido principles.

(Surprising that in The myth of the XX century, Alfred Rosenberg saw only the confirmation power of the blood, the blood as static seal of conservation. When the blood, irresistible elixir, can change and wash everything and everybody.)

I am the general de la Rovere! Anyone can make himself anytime samurai!

The Christianity is transmutation, not of the chemical elements, of the man. Metanoia. This is THE GRAND MIRACLE of God-Christ: not the multiplication of wine, fishes, bread, not the healing of the born blind, the weak, the hunchback and the lepers, no, not even the resurrection of the daughter of Jairus, the son of the widow from Nain and of Lazarus – all good signs for those with little faith or made to fulfill the prophecies or to show the glory of God or manifestations of the mercy of God (I feel pity for the crowds; And seeng it, the Lord felt pity for it), all these divine concessions –, but the transformation of the being.

How far can it go: until the required crucifixion with the head down of Peter, who denied Jesus.

December 31st 1959

I have with me the suitcase, a few pills of vitamin C and aspirin in my pocket and a thick book.

At Security I am received right away with a lot of politeness in a large and beautiful room, I am seated with honor in a chair at a small table. At a long table, on the other side of the room, an entire commission of officers is accommodated. They take me an interrogatory starting with the identification. Everything proceeds with a lot of ceremony and affability. Although neither the anger, nor my being upset with the destiny passed, I hold myself quite calm. I put the thick book on the table in front of me and I read from it during the breaks. From time to time I smoke a cigarette (but of course you may smoke, as long as you wish, you are not accused, only witness) or I suck a vitamin pill.

The interrogatory lasts until three o'clock precisely. Anyhow, after ascertaining that I was not called to be arrested, that I won't be detained, I feel relieved. I wander in vague wordings, but my partners know what they want. Two things I don't like at all: the question "What infraction related connections did you have with C. Noica?" and the smiles and the whispering which meet my talking about the encounter at the lake. (That's how I established with her that I will say where I met at Câmpulung Al. Pal., by then in hiding, with moustaches and under the name Crăifăleanu.) Therefore, my answer was known, expected. The questions take a more rapid rhythm, the tone become colder. But I don't give up. I don't acknowledge the infraction related nature. And to my immense surprise, I persist in my refusal and I give them a statement that is considered fully unsatisfactory and insincere.

It follows an entire comedy: they pull the curtains (of dark velvet) to create an atmosphere of panic. Tense pauses. The commission exits and enters again. There are also fake exits, as in theater: the commission stops at the threshold, ready to exit, then it changes its mind and comes back. They promise me the moon on the sky, sometimes very pleasant things. Afterwards are predicted the grave misfortunes and the dire consequences of my fanaticism. I am told I have an attitude problem. They invoke at length the old age of my father that, naturally, I can't let him die – of course – like a dog. About my father they all seem to have the highest opinion. They make me understand that there will be woe to me. From the factory I can miss anytime, that can be arranged in a minute, And what will I have to do? Nothing, really: once a month, or even more rarely, or maybe more often – we will see, eventually – I will make a short visit, not here, no, a very discreet visit, somewhere, at an address, at more than one, in a very regular blockhouse, in a very regular apartment. (It sounds like the description of the Arnoteanu's, or verses of Muşatescu, Toneghin, Pribeagu.) And what a hell, really, it's not possible not to understand, no matter how reactionary I am (– smiles –), partisan of the Nazies and the Jew killers I can't be. I cannot make myself the accomplice of some assassins with the hands red from the blood of my fellows in religion. So blind, stupid, crazy, I can't be. Hence, all that is asked from me is just an act of justice. And, by the way, what is it asked from me? Just to say that in my presence took place hostile discussions and they conspired against the security of the socialist State system and, out of weakness, I let myself carried in discussions and I did not have the courage to let the authorities know right away, but I realize my mistake, I feel sorry and I concur with all of the above.

The statement that I sign at (one past?) three o'clock in front of a commission obviously impatient (the drapes now let the gray light from outside to enter the room – and outside is a bit humid and the street is puffed with nostalgia – this is the weather that best invites to drink) to prepare for the New Year's Eve is sensationally inconclusive for the purposes of the inquiry and it gives me a feeling (I know it is transient) of elevation: not only that I did not accuse anyone with anything, not only that I did not acknowledge anything, but I signed only after were made – on the paper edges – all the small corrections that, fastidiously, I requested. The marginal notes give the statement the aspect of an exam paper corrected by a meticulous pedant.

I can't believe it is I. I played, I see, my part to the end. I discover myself for the first time stubborn. And I notice that I enjoyed playing. But I am still afraid.

Because this was just the first act – if not the prologue. I am given a grace period of three days to think until Monday, January 4th at eight when I have to come back and then they'll show me. The politeness, however, doesn't stop completely. I am threatened but also advised; the promises are not yet retired. They have the air that they granted me the satisfaction of a first round for "saving the face", being established that Monday will talk business, and will go from airs to submission.

I feel, however, after the greetings, extremely relieved and happy. Shadow: before leaving, alone with me, the officer that returned me the ID bulletin tells me grave and cold: watch it! The tone is – how should I put it? – fatidic.

They talked all the time about my father. They put a lot of faith in his power of persuasion; in the wisdom, the sense and the seriousness of the old man. He will tell me what to do. Without doubt. They even leave me three days to consult him. But this little suitcase, why did you bring it in? Ah! in view of the arrest, this is a provocative gesture. We didn't call you to arrest you. If we would have wanted to arrest you, we would have proceeded differently. (Which is true.) We called you as a free witness to state true things, to help the inquiry, and you come with the suitcase! Provocation! Never mind, go home, talk with your father, you trust him, and come back Monday…

They all are more and more hurried…

– These things of the faith, began, therefore, long ago. Rudolf Otto classifies: mysterium fascinans, mysterium tremendum.

Let me take them one at a first. The fascination started from forever, which is from childhood, in the town bearing the name of a saint or of an outlaw: Pantelimon. By then, completely separated from the city[59]. Once the evening came, not one Bucharester would dare to enter the outskirts. The lads, jealous and proud of their neighborhood, had their private domain. There were also plenty of drunkards, of course, dogs that were barking in the silence of the night or sometimes were striking at the passers by, bad roads, dust, mud. But everything, and not only for the child that I was, it projected itself on a background of patriarchal peace, on the everybody's belief that the world in its most hidden depths is not at all hostile and evil; that, if need be, people will not let you down, a piece of bread and a glass of wine you will still find somewhere; that – until the moment of death, of course – you will not be thrown out of your place and nest; that astounding and terrible things will not happen. (A sort of shelter – of the Mother of God especially – that guarantees to the decent people – and if so we are all decent people – the remote and improbable nature of the tragedies.)

At the church Capra, placed in the side toward the city, on Sundays and holidays almost everybody went; at least nearby. As factory owners and invited by the priest Mărculescu, my parents were coming too. The church, lacking any beauty but spacious, had bells with grave, long tolls, in contrast with the lowliness of the place, tolling often, insidiously and nobly. They, that I was hearing clearly, although they were very far from the factory, made the sonorous and the emotional background of my first years. They defended me, at least for a while, and still they chased the evil spirits, the hail and the wicked crafts; they sweetened, with sound, the growing horrid or deceiving features of the reality: the surrounding reality, the inner reality (where the latent image passing from negative to positive, began to grin at me defiantly). Blessed be St. Paulin of Nola, the initiator of the use of bells in the churches. Blessed be father Gala Galaction because he found – multi-faced as he were – for some of his books titles with such a wonderful echo: The bells of the Neamțu monastery, By the Vodislava water, The corner stone, The little church in the flower beds. (From Pantelimon to Fundeni were spread gardens, groves, lakes, pastures good for rest and behaved weeds, small vineyards – and you were encountering flocks rather than crops, mioritical detail lost beyond fences and clearings. They were strengthening the opinion of Eminescu: the gentleness of the Romanian people has its roots in its pastoral prosperity, always superior to the agrarian peoples.)

There were also – I remember well – the Easter bells, different: they were not prompting tenderness, as on Christmas, but they were stirring, persisting, denying your peace.

(On Christmas all were good: the pine-tree and the cozonacs and the carols and the little baby Jesus. On Easter all were strange and oppressing: the fast and the funeral liturgy and the bad cross and the fearful nailed Christ.)

Every man has its own childhood alley. (Bucket that balances at the beginning of the ancestral sin.) Mine was there, in the so common Pantelimon, between Capra and Fundeni – and in the endless courtyard of a timber factory, maybe the cleanest industry, deeply penetrated by the smell of cut wood and sawdust. (After rain, out of soaked planks and logs a stinging perfume emanates.)

The fascination of the Romanian outskirts from the good times. The fascination of the soul for the place he stumbled into? For me a strong capture – although with such modest means. What can be more inconsequential, more vanishing than the acacia of poor courtyards and the pubs of shrewd townsfolk?

From the beginning, from the eternity of my childhood. Tremendum came later, much later, on not delicate ways.

1961

At Jilava, section 1, in the cell number 9, a long time with a Macedonian[60], Anatolie Hagi- Beca. He, Macedonian and Legionnaire; I, baptized Jew and Romanian nationalist: we become friends right away. (I am accompanied by my fame of Jew that refused to be accusation witness in the trial of the mystical-Legionnaire intellectuals.) We soon arrive at conclusions that make us both happy. The thing that we realize is that both he and I are equally in love with what we find suitable to call the "Romanian phenomenon", in other words the Romanian people, the landscape, the sky, the customs, the interiors, the fields, the mountains, the onion, the țuică[61], the hospitality, the equilibrium in our space. We consider ourselves especially justified to love in full knowledge, because we are, each in his own way, half inside the Romanian space and half outside, in a especially favorable position to catch, to understand and to suffer. Romanian by blood, Hagi-Beca came, however, in the country twenty years old, from abroad; in my turn, born and grown here, I am a foreigner by blood. Together, we make up, who knows, a whole person, like that character from Napoleon of Notting Hill of Chesterton, real only by the merging of the minds of the two heroes of the book. One arrived from outside, the other built inside but from another leaven, we discover ourselves equally charmed and infatuated with everything that is Romanian.

January 4th 1960

Monday at eight o'clock, after three days of celebration, I find the door of Security locked. Of the ridicule of waiting in the front of the jail (or, anyway, its antechamber) I still didn't escape. With the worn suitcase, as in the train station: on an empty platform, in a halt, to get on third class wagon, in a train that won't come. Or on foot, na Sibir. The sadness of a recruit with its box, in a station forgotten in a field, where he changes the train. Toader Mânzu, without the dog, after the train left.

After a while, a hurried soldier appears and opens some locks, some chains; I am allowed inside and invited in the witness room.

The same commission. The luggage provokes again – this time from the beginning – explosions of indignation. Therefore, you still didn't learn your lesson. You still came in a provocative manner? You were contaminated by the Legionnaire fanaticism? Take it easy, we won't give you the pleasure to arrest you. In vain you want to become a hero. Didn't you talk to the old man? What did he tell you?

The first thing I do, pushed (I was going to be told later by Alecu) by a demon of pride and the need to show off (and to gather courage) was to repeat the words of my father precisely, melange of Regulus and Cambronne. Then I take a C vitamin from the pocket, I put it in my mouth and I feel proud and, yes, very calm.

All those that compose the group are addressing me in turns. The game from the preceding meeting is repeated identically, except this time the hurry disappeared completely and everything is more stressed and professional. I am threatened then I'm taken easily. Everything is repeated. The threats are repeated in avalanche, now the accent falls on them. The phrase with the father that is going to die like a dog comes back very often, although his prompting – transmitted uncensored – cooled a lot their feelings of compassion and respect toward the "old man", and also the trust they put in his elderly wisdom. The curtains are drawn again back and forth to create again, alternately, an atmosphere of horror and an atmosphere of relief. Although is only the second representation, the impression of repetition is strong enough so that instead of fear I feel a sort of amusement.

The hard tone intensifies but not enough to think they lied when they declared that no matter what they won't give me the satisfaction of being arrested.

I keep myself firmly, and more and more stiff, caught in this subtle and absurd game of the interrogated that wants to be arrested and the interrogators that do whatever they can not to arrest him. Actually, the dialectics accuser-accused does not disappears except the signs of the equation are now reversed. I advanced too much in the adverse territory – now I am self inflicting fear to myself in order to not tempt the odds – not to understand (or to have the feeling) that I have to be arrested.

At few minutes past four the arrest still seems improbable. Then, suddenly – is this the moment established beforehand? – the things take a completely different turn. The questions go quickly, the voices are working only on high tones, the words become exclusively crude.

At five o'clock I finally hear you bastard, jackass, punk. I am ordered to get up on my feet, to empty my pockets. The vitamins, the notebook, the watch, the handkerchief, the belt from my pants. You'll see, you, fanatic, you, jewel. I am put under arrest.

1969

Even now, after the baptism, I am dirty. The thorn is still in the eye, the sting in the body, the messenger of Satan still buffets me (and walks psychosomatically everywhere, as the king in his palace). That I will escape temptations proved to be a doltish, proud self deceiving. I ignored 2 Cor. 12,7. But that Christ is the Truth, the Way and the Life I believe absolutely festively.

Aiud 1961

Plotinism.

There is degradation.

At the beginning is the Word, the Logos. The people are destined to word.

The word turns into speak.

The speak turns into automatic stereotypes. This is the decayed phase (quick, Kali yuga[62]) of the slogan. Heidegger established too the difference between Wort[63] and Gerede[64].

The character of Saltikov-Scedrin (Misters Golovliev), that floods everything under the avalanche of words. The abyss of pettiness of Duhamel in Chronique des Pasquier: without bottom; the chilling secret of stupidity and meanness. Ferdinand and Claire: the whispered perpetual commentary of trifles. The inexhaustible generator power of idiocy; the thicket of the exegesis of triviality. The egg and the hen. Soma and the cell.

Through words people communicate ideas, sentiments, information. And that ecstasy in front of good, beauty and truth that don't allow you to be silent. (The counterpart of the eyes closed by the orgasm.) In front of the Beauty, he explained, the solitude becomes unbearable. And it is such a beautiful night, sir...

The verbosity is just a background noise. And the slogan – frozen lava – transmits the lie in stable, congealed form.

1971

I didn't know.

I didn't know – the answer of those that are told about torture, gulags, prisons, complete confessions of the accused, political internment in madhouses – "it doesn't hold", is not a valid excuse. Nobody is supposed to invent the gunpowder or to discover the quantum theory. But otherwise, the elementary awareness is a duty. Especially for a Christian, that has to watch always for temptations. And stupidity is a temptation. But not only for the Christian –and this because of a simple experimental observation: nobody knows anything, but everybody knows everything.

The ignorance, the animalization, the blind passing through life and things or the careless passing, are from the devil. The Samaritan was not only kind but also watchful: he knew to see.

Otherwise, why would God tell to the people: this is your time; or why would urge them to see with the eyes, to listen with the ears and to understand with the heart; or how would they know that the Lord is hungry, thirsty, stranger, sick or in prison so that they could feed Him, offer Him to drink, to receive Him, to dress Him or to be able to come to Him?

Jean Cau tells it to Roger Garaudy (who also says that he didn't know) the best way: then how come I, that I wasn't university professor and member of the central committee, I knew? Millions of people on the street how come they knew?

The truth is that there is no need of who knows what secret information, there are things that anyone can find out, just to be a little willing. (The spies oftentimes transmit uselessly, two times uselessly: because it was known, because they are not believed.) There are things that you feel if you don't shut your ears and don't cover your eyes on purpose. He who has ears let him hear. But what if the man is stupid? Stupidity is no excuse because no one is so stupid – (I'm not talking of oligophrens and psychopaths, these poor people are excluded) – that he can't figure out that two plus two makes four and not nine.

It is not convenient to acknowledge, we take shelter under the objectivity of science, but they are elementary gifts, we have them from nature and they lie in the soul, the heart, the reins, the mind, the lungs, the guts, the cells and the synapses of everybody. Everybody knew that Herod was a scoundrel, Robespierre a canaille, Stalin a villain.

Lit matches thrown into gas.

Did I ever know anything? Did I know a thing about the wonderful world in the middle of which I found myself? about the hidden sufferance? about the unknown heroes? about those that twenty-four hours out of twenty-four were keeping their dignity in cells conceived to lead not only to denunciation and filth but to fall and dementia?

–   In most of the cells, one of the favorite puzzles are the words said by the Savior on the cross: Eli, Eli, lama sabachthani?

Since Christ could say God, why have you forsaken me means he was man too and not God.

Panait Cerna: "you moaned too when the iron pierced you."

This argument I consider totally unfounded and from the words on the cross I deduce, on the contrary, the absolute proof of the validity of the crucifixion.

I have on my part Dostoievski, Simone Weil, Kierkegaard – and the entire synod of Chalcedon. I also have two paintings, one of Holbein (at Basel) and one of Velasquez (at the Prado museum). In both oîf them the light rays from the sky are missing, the tragedy is irreversible, without remedy; he departed this life: not only the torment and the prophecies but the entire hubbub, finished, death is not clinical, the resurrection is chased among deceive and empty noble hopes, never will live again this body now contorted, bleeding, pierced, dirty, slashed. The resurrection is utterly impossible. That's how Dostoievski says – openly – that Christ appears to him in Holbein's painting and the same precise, black, cold impression I had looking at the Resurrection of Velasquez, that was exposed at Louvre and where the foreground is dominated by the intense yellow – forget it if you can! – of a cloak; in the background are the pitiful crosses, the lead sky. The crosses seem thrown into distance, already forgotten – the way you would forget in the haste (and the executioners truly worked under the stress of the haste) an inconsequential or embarrassing thing –, Christ is completely alone and abandoned, a crucified near another two individuals, somewhere at the dirty outskirts of a city, on a pile of thrash, stones and slag, in a torrid afternoon and – because of the low clouds – sultry heat. You don't see as in The dictator of Jules Romains the powerful and the melancholic structures of the suburbs of a great modern city, but the massive bulwarks of an ancient town, cold and evil rather than melancholic. A closed system, as the physicists say, when they predict the inexorability of the entropy. From the dust that looks like lye, the low clouds, the faint glances of the crucified, the grumpy outbursts of the executioners leaks like a brown wax, the wax of the seal that closes. From the surface that covers everything like a bell there is no exit. The transcendence is a theory, the resurrection seems, no, it doesn't seem, you can see clearly that is a puerility. They got what they were looking for. Poor people. Let's be serious.

I show to those that put the problem of Eli, Eli: so much the better that it is so, only so could have been.

The crucifixion is not farce and deceive only if you first see that any miracle is impossible, any resurrection is a fairy tale. If the Monophysites, the Dochetists(?) and the Phantasiasts(?) would be right, then I wouldn't have converted to Christianity. It would mean that the resurrection was, at best, a representation. Let it not be! Only the human despair on the cross proves the integrity and the seriousness of the sacrifice, prevent it from being a game, a trick.

The Lord had come determined to drink the cup to the bottom and to baptize Himself with the baptism of the cross, but in the garden of olives, when the moment was getting closer, He still prayed that He be spared from emptying the cup. Of course He adds: Your will be done. The hesitation was real. And on the cross, despite the communication of the idioms, despite the fact that He had full knowledge of the resurrection, the human nature seemed to have overpowered for a while – the way, the counterpoint, on the mount Tabor the divine nature predominated –, because otherwise He wouldn't have said the natural I thirst and the allzumenschlich[65]: My God, why have You forsaken Me?

The act of the crucifixion was so serious, authentic and total that even the apostles and the disciples were convinced that the hanged man on the middle cross will not rise. If they wouldn't have been so shaken in their faith, Luke and Cleopas would not have walked so gloomy, dragging their feet on the way to Emmaus, and they would have recognized right away their Teacher, and they wouldn't have been so amazed when they realized who He was. (They were feeling so lonesome, so deceived in their expectations, that they prayed the first passer-by, un stranger, not to let them alone, to stay with them.) Even Thomas, would not have put so drastic conditions (and, truly speaking, offensive) if he wouldn't have been sure that the resurrection, the way things happened, was not possible.

Nobody could believe. The resurrection was definitive for them too, as for the scribes. And it was necessary, for the certification of the sacrifice, that the crucifixion would give an impression of end, of solved, of case closed, of triumphant common sense. It was not enough – for the resurrection to be what it was – it was not enough the horror of the torture, the nails, the spear, the thorns – in the painting of Mathis Grünewald from Unterlinden the thorns pierce the entire body entered in putrefaction – it was absolutely necessary – for completion, for strengthening – to also seem catastrophe, confusion, failure.

Only the shout Eli, Eli proves us that the crucified did not play with us, he did not try to comfort us with hypocritical mitigation. (As always, He treated the people as free and adult beings, capable of dealing with unpleasant truths.) As opposed to Buddha and Lao-Tze, He doesn't give aphorisms and allegories but flesh and blood, torment and despair. Pain without despair is like the food without salt, like the wedding without music.

(And if the good thief is the first man that comes into the heaven – before the prophets, the patriarchs and the righteous of the Old Testament – maybe he owns this not only to his earthquake- like conversion but also to the fact that was colleague of sufferance with the Lord. Because one thing is to stay at the feet of the cross and to suffer, no matter how sincere and excruciating, and another thing is to be on the cross. The pain of another is not your pain, you appropriate it only through a theoretical process, not through feelings. Only the good thief feels like the Lord.)

The incarnation was total, as the synod of Chalcedon teaches us. Okay, total, but Christ on the cross did not cease to be also God.

I: it cannot be contested the permanence of the communication of the idioms, but after a few hours on the cross the human side must have been predominant; otherwise the tragedy was not authentic.

I insist: what do they want the Dochetists, the Phantasiasts and Monophysites – and the atheists? Should Christ have winked from the cross to His people to let them know: this is only for the sake of appearances, don't worry, we know what we know, see you Sunday morning?

What horrible "spectacle" implies, without knowing, the Monophysitism!

Scripture arguments: in Romans (8,32) Paul writes: "He who did not spare His own Son". This "did not spare" proves also that what happened on the cross was not a symbol, but a real sufferance. Only through the combination of the physical pain and of the moral torture one can obtain the final concoction: the supreme sorrow.

Again at Paul in 1 Cor 1, 23: "But we proclaim Christ nailed to the cross", and in 2, 2: "I resolved that while I was with you I would not claim to know anything but Jesus Christ – Christ nailed to the cross."

Why the addition "Christ nailed to the cross" if not to put the accent on the most crazy and scandalous aspect? The wise reason would agree finally with a God crucified symbolically and conceding to suffer apparently (otherwise people don't understand), but the paradox and the craziness (i.e. the Christianity) shows the divinity not only seated on the cross – solemniter – but truly nailed; where He suffers with the nerves (the legends and the sagas of the Middle Ages, who knew what pain is, keep referring to the nerves), the fibers and the soul of the poor man, up to the last consequences (and Christ has, despite the heresy of Apollinarius, full human soul). If He would have kept – at least partially – the impassiveness on the cross, if He wouldn't have fully tasted the hopelessness of the man, the event consumed on Golgotha would not have been – for philosophers, priests and the masses – a stumbling and fooling block but "script" or "ritual", therefore admissible, comestible.

In 1 Cor 6, 20 and 7, 23 Paul insists: "You were bought at a price."

At a fair price. In full. God did not swindle anybody: not the devil, not us; not Himself. He did not pay with the appearance of sufferance, with a mythical cross, or with fake money. The price was not paid by a phantasm; flesh from our flesh, blood form our blood.

And in Hebrews (2, 17; 2, 18; 4, 15): Therefore He had to be made like His brothers (us) in every way (only without sinning); Because Himself has been tested in every way as we were.

As we were in every way and tested in every way as we were: therefore with the human despair too.

March 1966

As always I find at Dostoievski, told without detours, what I suspected; in the confusion, light – suddenly. Regarding the vision of Holbein I find the exact text: "The painting is not beautiful… it is the cadaver of a man who just endured endless tortures… if such a cadaver (and this is precisely how it must have been) was seen by His disciples… how could they believe, looking at it, that that corpse will rise?"

THEY DIDN'T EVEN BELIEVE IT!

"If death is so terrible and the laws of nature so merciless, how can you master them? And those people that stayed with the dead, they felt for sure in that evening a terrible sorrow, a deep distress that suddenly blew all their hopes and almost everything they believed."

HE DIDN'T WINK TO THEM!

Socrates and Jesus Christ

Logically, the death of Socrates, the man, should have had the seal of disorder, blood, treason and rage: but on the contrary, it was as serene and dignified at it can be. Of Christ, on the contrary, bears – entirely – the seal of tragedy, disgust and horror. Socrates dies calmly, surrounded by faithful and respectful disciples that hang to his words while he – imperturbable and radiant – sips the painless poison offered with a lot of deference by the executioner. Abandoned and betrayed by His own, Christ writhes on the cross, tormented by thirst and covered with insults. Socrates dies like a nobleman, Christ like a villain, between two bandits, on a waste ground. Socrates thanks to the gods that he escaped the vicissitudes of the material world, Christ exclaims: Why have You forsaken Me?"

The difference is total between the two deaths, and precisely the divine one seems inferior, dubious. The truth is that it is much more human; that of Socrates, in all its greatness, seems – by contrast – literary, abstract, directed, and especially not realist. Socrates – in good will and partly successful – raises himself from the statute of man to that of god, Christ descends not bothered by filth to the basest strata of the human condition.

Dostoievski was planning to write until 1882 an epilogue of The Karamazov Brothers and then a life of Christ.

Probably God did not want a fifth gospel.

March 5th 1960

The van brought us slowly and with jolts and jerks from Malmaison to Jilava before noon. We descend: Fort 13. The reception is given by lieutenant Ștefan, walk of primate, face of anthropoid, gestures and glances of a penitentiary colony sergeant in a noir film. He is enjoying himself, plays his role in slow motion, as a gambler who takes his time spinning his cards.

We spent the rest of the day in a quarantine cell, small, incredibly dirty, with the barrels full. In the evening we are transferred to the snake pit, a vast cave, sinister, stinky, that, although electrically illuminated, keeps some dark corners.

Everything – as so many times in so many places in prisons, but now is the first contact – it shows so lugubrious and oppressing that it doesn't seem real. Charming is the presence of doctor Voiculescu, very old, only bones, gentle, mannered, peaceful, noble, sharp minded but broken by fatigue.

Strange sensation of immense happiness. Reasons:

Because finally I am rid of the inquiry. Prison, after Security, is a haven, an oasis, a heaven. Then, the first meeting with the Legionnaires (in quarantine is not only our batch); from them I hurry to learn the Morse alphabet and verses of Crainic and Gyr – my hasty enthusiasm amuses them. Of course, and the very allaying presence of doctor Voiculescu. But also the remembrance – exalting – of what happened in the van.

Where I was placed, in a partition, a hole, a lock-up with Sandu L., former Legionnaire. Just squeezed together and he starts talking to me. He tells me that he sincerely regrets having been Legionnaire and he asks my forgiveness, maybe it is very unpleasant for me to stay with him and so tightly. Am I not horrified? He barely finished talking and the ceiling of the van opened; the blue of the sky opened too. I answer him that I don't see why is he talking of forgiveness, and if it is so then I ask forgiveness too because I am Jewish and he has to stay glued to me, that regarding the guilt we are all guilty, all alike, all together. I propose to him that since now we asked to each other forgiveness, to make up, to hug each other, to address each other by the first name. Under the light of the bulb in the lock-up on wheels we kiss and – considering the ridicule an empty word and a vanishing feeling – we know suddenly and plentifully – under the blue sky – that state of unspeakable happiness compared to which any drink, any trip, any passed exam, any notability are nothing, dust and cinders, deceive, emptiness, desert, resounding bronze and noisy cymbal, state that follows the fulfilling of an action according to the divine prescriptions. Waves of joy overflow upon us, they spill, they flood us, they overwhelm us. I ask Sandu – and if I copy Saint Seraphim of Sarov from the scene in the forest with Motovilov, I am doing it unintentionally

– if he sees on my lips the smile that I make out on his: of the hesychasm originated in the uncreated energies. Because in the tight corner fitted with us also Grigore Pallama, not to mention Saint Seraphim of Sarov with Motovilov after him.

The behavior of the guards is so bad, the atmosphere so dramatic, the remembrance of the scene with Sandu L. so acute, the perspectives of long sufferance so clear, that I cannot help circulating from one end of the cave to the other in a state of extraordinary exalted agitation. I start to feel that Christ is present in the prison. I can't believe that everything can be so complete, that I have part of so much blessed luck.

Doctor Voiculescu and bishop Leu (very wretched, walks in clutches, dressed in fleecy clothes like a shepherd in a high mountain sheepfold) are interrogated at length by the guards who, probably, are bored. Both of them are humiliated and insulted, swore at, made a pigsty. The others are getting away more easily.

–   Therefore Christianity is possible, therefore one can behave Christian, make Christian gestures. Christianity can be arithmetized. I am ready to believe that not in vain the bells of the Capra church tolled for me.

February 25th 1960
Paul Dim., witness:

He's calm, he speaks stressed and sparsely, with the offhandedness of the old jailbird, with the cold politeness of the fallen angel or the ruined but proud boyar. As opposed to us in the box, he did already a few years of jail, and this time he was already arrested for some time. He knows very well what he is not supposed to know and what the tribunal cannot inform him: that Petru Dumitriu, revered writer, big shot of the literature and big profiteer of the regime, remained on the other side.

It is played a delicious scene à la Donizetti or Rossini. Did they make accusations hostile to the regime in your presence? Yes. (Obviously content countenances of the judges. The prosecutor inflates visibly, like a pumped tire.) In what way? They systematically calumniated progressive writers. (More and more enchanted countenances of the same judges, together with the president, Colonel Adrian Dumitriu.) Can you give examples? I can. – Pause of grand effect, the witness works with methods of professional actor, he doesn't hurry. – Come on, give them! – I heard them calumniating with violence the progressive writer Petru Dumitriu in whose works the accomplishments of the regime are reflected, criticizing him, claiming he is just a hypocrite, that he is not a true democrat, that he writes only for personal gain and actually his novels are the work of Madam Henriette-Yvonne Stahl…

The homonym president cannot interrupt him because he is not allowed to inform him that the other bearer of the name of the unction streamer saint, Petru, is in connivance with the imperialists now. Thus the witness, the third Dumitriu (actually Dimitriu), keeps going with the progressive novelist, with the calumnies, having fun, we having fun, until he is invited to retire, which he does after bowing with glacial politeness.

Perfect, not less than Sam Weller, posing as witness in the lawsuit Bardell versus Pickwick.

– The definition of life, according to André Breton.

Life, says André Breton, is the way an individual seems to deal with the unacceptable human condition.

– Paul Dim. tells to Al. Pal. and me not to hurry to stay by the door to be allocated to cells; to stay at the end, together. We might end up in the same place.

We do as we planned, prolonging our stay in the sinister hall which for sure seems like taken from Rocambole, from Les mystères de Paris or Les misérables.

Voiculescu, Leu, Sandu, Streinu, the Legionnaires from Aiud, the Saxons: from Codlea they left; Paul and Alecu turn to French and the conversation takes a strictly bawdy and gossipy turn. Joky (or Szoky) Cristea, Nicodames, Puşa Măciucescu, Tea-Room, The Mystery, The school of gossip, Dangerous liaisons, five to seven. Done with the eloquence and the sublime. Toward one or two o'clock, probably, the cop in charge rejects me when we advance all three. Paul and Alecu leave casting at me desolated glances. After half an hour I am taken out myself, alone.

– Many are wondering in the prisons and in the literary critic: where is God in the work of Proust? In the novels of Mauriac?

Where is it? Let me tell you where is it. It is not on a certain page, because the authors are not theologians. It is nowhere. It is everywhere as in the world.

– Some clarifying thoughts about freedom: Alfred Jarry: There are people for which to be free is a bore, a hassle.

Thomas Mann: Liberty is a pedant and bourgeois notion.

Both put under question the survival chances of liberty in the world that Ortega y Gasset called it, more pertinently than anybody, of the masses.

Alexandru Herzen: the masses don't care about the individual freedom, the freedom of speech; they like authority… by equality they understand the equality of oppression… only the civilized individuals want liberty.

Let us, the intellectuals and the political convicts, be less convinced that everybody is dying after liberty.

Denis de Rougemont: Liberty is not a right, is the assuming of a risk.

Let us be, then, less sure that people are willing to risk. Rights, yes, as many as possible, but the risks they consider just obstacles, intrigues, insults.

John 20, 29: "Jesus said to him, 'Because you have seen me you have found faith. Happy are they who find faith without seeing me.'"

Let us understand that liberty is above any act (risked and irrational) of faith, therefore a bet. II Cor. 3, 17: "The Lord is the Spirit; and where the Spirit of the Lord is, there is liberty."

50

If we are not free we are not worthy to be called – as Christ like to consider us – His friends.

Revelation 3, 20: "Here I stand knocking at the door."

Let our hearts melt at the thought of that popular pictures where God with bag and stick waits for us to open the door, if we want, according to our free will.

Nicolae Bălcescu in The History of Romanians under Michael Voivode the Brave: Whoever fights for freedom fights for God.

Phrase little quoted by the today's admirers of Bălcescu.

– The great writers truly forge a world and beings, similar to God.

There are in Balzac two moments that seem to me supreme and that they show how real were for him the characters built by his pen. Which show that from a certain level (artistic, moral, soul-wise, carriage-wise) upward, the noblesse goes without saying. I am not a racist, would suit me well to be! but I can't swallow the scarecrow of absolute equality and tolerate it (which end up being what it is: all the animals are equal but some are more equal than the others) and I am thundered by moments of life when I don't feel like laughing thinking of Gobineau, or Houston Stewart Chamberlain.

In Ursule Mirouët, the letters of François Minoret – a dishonest and hateful character – Balzac reproduces them each time with all their spelling errors, because the man is stupid and uneducated. (And you can tell that the author enjoys the exercise, and he likes to imitate the speaking of French with Teutonic accent.) However, when toward the end of the book, Minoret is unhappy, discovers the repentance and he confesses, the letter that he now sends is transcribed with a correct spelling. And Balzac explains why: I corrected his spelling, he says, because, it is not right to laugh on behalf of a man stricken by misfortune.

These extraordinary words prove:

a)   That Balzac was a creator in the precise meaning of the term, since he can feel pity of his characters as for real people – and to respect them;

b)   That he had the cosmic feeling of unity of the noosphere and of the community of the of the tribute (supererogatory) of miseries among people;

c)   That he was a nice person and a Christian because he abstained (even if only in imagination) from despising his fellow man – which is what it was imposing to him as a human being – when this one was going through sufferance and was proving that he was sorry for what he did;

d)   That he was noble and he did not sinned by adding by himself the particle de at his name;

e)   That for him, as for Dostoievski, the show of human sufferance is holy. (Sufferance is not always useful to the sufferer – see the bad thief – but for the one who watches it does not have moral contingencies. As a show, is always holy. The one who suffers I am obligated to pity him, to help him. The Samaritan doesn't ask who he is, what is he doing, where is he coming from and what is the occupation of the wounded – maybe he was a thief! One that deserved what

51

happened to him?) The faithful does not refuse – because he doesn't know, sancta simplicitas, look, an eloquent example – to give alms to the drunk. The merciful does not care if the beggar sold the coat that he received, even if he went directly to the pub with them. The coat is worn by Christ.

The nature is not capable of this type of delicacy as that from Ursule Mirouët. Nor the history. Nor the intelligence. It comes from grace.

Another incomparable moment in the work of Balzac. That one when, in Colonel Chabert, the hero renounce to all his rights and claims in favor of his wife and stops fighting the lawsuit when he realizes how incorrect and of bad faith she is. He feels so much disgust and despise toward the remarried "countess Ferraud" that he stops opposing, stops fighting and gives up everything. Out of disgust, of nausea. Precisely because he knows. He does not cross his sword with someone who proved to be not his equal.

Corollary I: when the injustice is done to you, you have the right – if you realize how big the baseness of your adversary is – to give up, the renouncement being in this case the most dishonoring slap in the face. You don't fight a duel with a man that doesn't deserve to spill his blood. The Chinese that take their life on the threshold of their oppressor to deliver them to eternal blame. And the gesture of colonel Chaber that – God forgive me if I am blasphemous – evokes the silence of Christ before the şmechers decide to liquidate him, according to the recommendation of the grand priest Caiaphas, and they pretend, ladies and gentlemen, to judge Him.

Corollary II: when the injustice is done not to you but to another, (although, even then, it is still done to you) it must denounced, taken down, corrected. That's how the errant knights were behaving. Don Quijote.

Iorga[66]: "You have the right to forgive only what was done to you." The man, if he reasons like a Christian and wants to behave in accordance with the Christian doctrine, he may – and he must – not to take into account the injustice committed against him, the insults thrown at him, as an individual. But if he occupies a position of responsibility or he manages the public affairs he does not have the right to invoke the principle of forgiveness in order to remain distant and cold in face of the evil and to let the scoundrels pray on the innocents.

The tragic error of Lord Halifax was this, to have confused two distinct situations. And not only that of him, of all the airheads who believe that "thou shall not judge" and "who am I to judge?" refer also to the interests of the community, of the humanity. It is the opposite way around: vigilance, defense of the good, the shepherd is loved by the flock because he guards it and is willing to die for it.

(When you cannot correct the injustice you still have the solution of resignation if not entering in a monastery or suicide. Cato in Utica and Ian Pallach; the Buddhists from Indochina; blind and simpleton these ones, but honest and logical with themselves.)

Again the problem of Eli, Eli.

"I prefer to believe in God rather than see Him in all His glory"
Paul Valéry (The letter to Mme Emilie Teste)

God, who abandoned Christ on the cross, isn't He completely absent for us too?

One thing that we don't want to understand, that not even the contemporary of the Lord did not understand. Those that were waiting the coming of Messiah in glory. What they couldn't understand, what we can't understand: that God, as Kierkegaard says, is not a huge red parrot.

If suddenly in the market, out of the blue, an immense violently colored bird would appear, of course that the mob would jump to see and would understand it is not common thing.

The faith, the repentance would be too easy this way. Breakfast in bed. Take the money, give me the honey.

We are required however to believe in complete freedom and you would say that – worse that that – the scenario unfolds als ob[67] we would be not only completely abandoned but also – which puts the cherry on the cake – the providence on purpose does everything possible so as we won't believe; it likes – one would say – to accumulate the difficulties, to multiply the risks, to count the arguments in order to make the well intended desire for devotion in impossibility.

The roads that lead toward faith bear the same name, all: bet, adventure, incertitude, mind of a madman.

Dostoievski: if God did not descend from the cross, the reason is that he wanted to convert the man not through the coercion of an evident exterior miracle but through the liberty of belief and giving to him the occasion to manifest its courage.

When the Lord was told on the Golgotha: save yourself and then we will believe, the mistake was linguistic, the rationale was based on a confusion of terms. If He would have descended from the cross there would have been no need to believe anymore, it would have been just the acknowledgment of a fact (as in the case of the red parrot: the descent from the cross would have constituted an irresistible red parrot).

We are required – invitation to temerity and exciting adventure – something more mysterious and stranger: to contest the evidence and to give credit to a non-fact.

He works on hidden ways. Incomprehensive ways, say the Frenchmen. And the Englishmen even more precisely: He moves in a mysterious manner.

–   Léon Bloy: "O, Christ, who pray for those who crucify You and crucify those who love You!"

February 24th-26th 1960

First we are brought in a sort of waiting hall, an antechamber, and judging after the faience that covers all the walls up to half, it must have been the vast kitchen of a boyar house in the old times, or of a boarding school. They sit us on long, parallel, benches, one at a bench and at extremity, you would say that it follows to be communicated the subjects of an examination and they are afraid we will cheat. We are forbidden not only to talk but even to look at one another. It is cold and we are hungry. We remain for an interval of time that seems depressingly long, then the guardians – it was their lunchtime – they pull from their briefcases packs with food. They all swallow vigorously, smacking and munching, I am taken by an atrocious hunger and I suspect the same humiliating sensation at the others because, without exception, we stare with envy at the silent consumers. We can look at them. Sensation of skinny cur, in a cage. (Just that we cannot walk from one end of the cage to the other, nor near the grates like the beast can.)

Sometime later, Păstorel addresses the officer who enters congenially and jokingly to ask for a pen and a piece of paper. He wants to write some verses that he composed at Security and it would be a shame for the Romanian literature to be lost." What kind of verses? Ah, not hostile, lyric, patriotic. How did he compose them? Ah, in his mind. But now he would like to write them down; because of the age, he might forget them.

Making verses mentally is, anyway, a performance, maybe not like scoring a goal or improving a record, but still is a performance. It can be felt a wave of admiration. And Păstorel smiles, distantly but friendly. (What wouldn't do a man for a cigarette? What wouldn't do a writer for a pen?) Although the officer and his subordinates keep themselves hard, they watch each other and they fight the magic, in the cold atmosphere (literally and figuratively) of the former kitchen suddenly enters a spring breeze, a patriarchal fragrance of Cotnari[68] and a breath of Humulești[69] mirth. The childhood alley doesn't seem to have moved in the lost territories of the far away galaxies. The foreheads lighten up a little. You would say that the Medeleni of brother Ionel[70] are somewhere around, maybe also the Ancuța's inn of comrade president Sadoveanu[71] is hidden somewhere under some huge cabinets at the end of the hall. I heartily rejoice, spake Mihai Voivode Sturdza, that I see cheerfulness and mirth in the country of Moldavia. To the congenial tone that asks the unthinkable, the officer cannot answer harshly. The officer is rather young, and I come to think that maybe he feels like a high school student who has the touching opportunity to talk to one of the authors reproduced in the school textbooks. Păstorel doesn't get silent, he got wings and he slaps the vigilant sergeant that intervenes in the discussion with:

"You should know that I am not only a writer but also an artillery captain." With these last words you would say that the walls vanish and from forests where the light and shadow chase each other playfully come in procession, among us, majestic shadows and gracious shadows – Stephen of Moldavia, Neculce the country boyar, the sly Creangă, mister Ibrăileanu[72], Knez Moruzzi, the traveler Hogaş[73]; not only persons but even buildings and objects are coming: the hut of Creangă, the linden tree from the Copou garden, the restaurant Le paradis general, the Academy library in a spring morning when the readers are scarce and the leather binds of books shine gently, Bucharest from the old times with its entire cortege of gardens and grills, and the other Moldavia, from the Icoana street, where at a table resounded the poor epigrams based on which Al. O. Teodoreanu is now here.

But our projection outside time and space – and how yoga-like, and Honigbergian would it seem to the author from Paris, whose Night of the Sânziene[74] had an important contribution in shaping the scene we all play, the absurd scenario, the appearances deeply rooted in misery and fright – doesn't last too much. The aura of mirth and the mist of Cotnari, of the color of grapes polished in the light of the hot sun of ancient summers, surrounds only Păstorel. When, breaking the magic of the calm that fell from all places, from upward, Dinu Nc. open his mouth asking for a cigarette, the officer shakes, exits from the power of the Romanian literature and of the merriment tradition, steps bitter and resolute in the domain of the hostile contemporary philosophy and suddenly breaks the veil: "You shall not think we are so stupid, mister Noica." Dinu, of a strained ascetic weakness, bows monk-like, submissive – with pensive, burdened, meditative eyes. Defiance, thinks the officer, and he reprimands us all, in group, coldly and solemnly, not without a last nuance of consideration (as I didn't hear during the inquiry and I won't hear again in the prisons): "We know very well what you represent and you are not misleading us with gestures good for pilferers."

In the huge courtroom that gives an impression of emptiness, we are seated in the box, still on benches – as in school, many of us are former students from the Spiru Haret high school –, now packed and crowded. They place us in order as we came in: I find myself between Noica and, at right, Vladimir Streinu. Pillat, Sandu L. and a few strangers for me occupy the first row: the co- authors of the conspiracy brought before justice which now I see for the first time. The four women (Anca dr. Ionescu, Marietta Sadova, Trixi and Simina Caracaş) are in the back of the box.

In the huge empty courtroom there will be during the trial four compact groups of human beings, separated by spaces of void that remembers the dizzying distances between the swarms of galaxies. (The binder that the public, the relatives and the press would make doesn't exist.)

The first group is ours, of the prisoners in the box, counting twenty five, crowded on the benches, looking straight ahead (again, we are forbidden to look anywhere else, and especially at one another), surrounded – similarly to the electronic orbits from the periphery of the atomic nucleus – by a circle of conscripted soldiers, all equipped as for battle, with automatic rifles pointed toward us, striving to stare fiercely at us. The courtroom is morose, the hues are dark, but the presence of the soldiers – posted in firing position, as if they would guard the gang of Terente, Coroiu, Brandabura or Zdrelea the Turnip, caught in the power of the night and the heart of the forest or in the reed thicket, and not a bunch of pale, skinny intellectuals, dressed in clothes circumstantially ironed in the Security laundry, tired, lacking sleep, ringed, many passed beyond the noon of their life, almost all with a sedentary illness, of inhabitant of the large cities: colitis, rhinitis, constipation, tuberculosis, bile calculus – seems a direction mistake, an exaggeration with a hue of ridicule.

The second group is constituted, far at the end of the courtroom, and barely visible, by the Security officers, the investigators, the inspectors (some in uniforms, others in civilian clothes), came to watch the unfolding of the trial, to take notes, to verify, as in a strange theatrical representation where the director's rehearsal, the general rehearsal and the premiere would be muddled in one single Kafkian show.

There is a third swarm, at our left: the defense lawyers, superior as number to the accused, because there are even two-three for one client, and some of them are accompanied by a secretary. They are, in all the room, the most lonely, unhappy and – I suspect, then I find out with certitude – the most fearful. Impeccable dressed, looking like a million bucks, as for wedding, they look very cool and they miss only the flower in the buttonhole or the top hat and the gloves of the executioner for the capital punishments; otherwise they are dressed up to the nines: coats of dark color from a silky material with metallic sparks, corners of white handkerchiefs emerging from the upper pocket of the coat, freshly and carefully shaved cheeks, haircuts licked by the tongues of tens of cats. In their festive carriage they are, compared to the securists that do their dreadful job (you know the craftsman from his work; the craft needs time, you don't learn it by eye; the craftsman brakes it and fix it out of fear), to us which had no choice (we did not eat mushrooms) and to the members of court, militaries detached from work (the cooked birds can't be find in the fence poles[75]) the most ridiculous: because they have to play a double role (and they are distributed in the most embarrassing role: of the good kid, mummy's boy) and they came, if it's so, on their own will.

On the judges chairs are five bored, impassible militaries: in the middle Adrian Dimitriu (this one not bored, but worried, because he is in charge: his honor used to be a lawyer too, now in role and uniform of colonel).

As soon as I see myself seated on the bench I accomplish the only deed that I consider worthy in my whole life: to Noica, on whose face you can read the despair and in whose eyes, (those eyes that look in vain after Mihai Rădulescu) shines an atrocious unrest, I whisper pulling his sleeve as long as the hubbub of our installation didn't stop and I can still talk to him shortly: Dinu, you should know that none of us are upset with you, we love you, we respect you, everything is fine.[76]

God is favorable to me: the face of Dinu brightens up, he squeezes in hurry my wrist, sighs deeply, unburdened. I did something good in this world.

With Vladimir Streinu I just furtively change glances and at times a timid smile; we will often touch each other elbows during the trial and we will have a good laugh when the prosecutor, unleashing himself, will make against the reactionary intellectuals in the box, the eulogy of Eminescu, Tolstoi, Gyotee.

For the poor lawyers is very hard. They know they are the most supervised, they don't even have the certitude of the condemnation as those from the box; they sweat, they wipe discreetly their foreheads, some with the white handkerchiefs from the upper pocket of the coat, others with bigger, household, colored handkerchiefs, pulled form the pockets of the pants, like practical old men. In the pause, every defendant is given the right to speak five minutes with his counselor; the meeting takes place on one of the benches in the end of the courtyard and in the presence of the respective investigator. Out of pity for the lawyer – the man tremble afraid not to be told who knows what hostile imprecations – I limit myself to the most ordinary words and I indicate imbecile arguments and motivations. I am answered by a grateful glance.

Mister Bondi, that represents Vladimir Streinu, characterizes his client as being from always, from youth, uninterruptedly, with tireless perseverance, a brave, convinced, fierce enemy of the Communism... I mean of the Legionnarism. A sort of canned laugh breaks the stiff solemnity of the séance. Streinu, near me, startles, then he smiles too.

Another counselor that gets in trouble pretty bad is Mădârjac, of Păstorel. (At the last words the author of the Chronicle will succeed again in creating a breeze of humanity saying that he makes epigrams as the hen makes eggs.) Mădârjac, interrupted by the president to be asked severely if he shares the opinions of those in the box, answers hastily: God forbid... The president takes notice of this act of confession of mystical faith, of this manner of speaking showing purposely a certain mentality and he invites him gravely to weigh his words. It doesn't pass more than a few minutes and willing to show that Teodoreanu by his jokes did not pursue at the restaurant Moldavia the fall of the regime, Mădârjac, again pushed by the friendship elan, he stresses his words with the ecclesiastical equivalent of parole moncher[77] – at which maybe he was thinking, but carried by a subconscious respect, absolutely naturally in what, after all, was still the praetorium of a judicial instance, he replaces it – and namely with "God forbid". This time Adrian Dimitiriu is angered and he threatens the lawyer from heights generators of ice and full of implications.

Poldi Filderman, in order to defend doctor Răileanu, reasons coram populo[78]: If I would think he is Legionnaire, I, who was tortured by the Legionnaires, for nothing in the world would have accepted to become his lawyer. Since he cannot say that the whole accusation is baseless, he considers fit to call the others in the box philosophers of the blood and death, inveterate Iron Guardists[79] and direct spiritual descendents of the Captain[80]. Then, to prove his first assertion, takes off his coat, makes the gesture of opening his shirt, and because he affirms that he was beaten at feet, "where he bears the signs of the Legionnaire bestiality", he mimic the gesture of taking off his shoes. A discreet sign – of the bored president or maybe the hurry (because to each lawyer were conceded only four minutes) or maybe starting the gesture was considered eloquent enough, determines him to stop and to renounce the live exemplification.

Among the approximately twenty witnesses of the accusation (the prosecutor and the defense agreed to gave up the others) is remarked the journalist Radu Popescu, by a declaration of unexpected virulence and length; he is also dressed fancy, like the lawyers; he moves, while he's speaking, as a professor at cathedra, with ample and studied gestures as they say were those of Maiorescu[81], he scolds Noica as the fiercest drill sergeant would do with the most worthless recruit. He recites without stop his entire tirade. At the end he wipes himself too with a handkerchief pulled out from the back pocket of his pants: on the forehead, the face, the hands.

At a certain point a small old woman in black, with a cloak – she looks like Barbara Ulbrich or rather the director of the girls school from The crime of Sylvestre Bonnard, the one who transfigured herself when she found out that her modest visitor is a member of the Institute of France. The old lady answers to the name Popescu-Voiteşti, she is the widow of the geographer, she is retired and she does typewriting. She typed Waiting for the judgement day, the novel with Legionnaire subject of Pillat. Summoned to explain for what reason, seeing what is it about, she didn't notify the authorities, she mentions with a calm and low voice the following: first, when she types, she focuses on the words not on the phrases, and even less on the overall meaning; second, she understood it is about Legionnaires but she felt that the novel is plainly anti-Legionnaire, because the youngsters that were belonging to the movement were shown by the author in an unfavorable light. Unfavorable? Yes, of course, since they were missing classes, they were not giving their exams regularly, they were coming home late, they were upsetting their poor parents that were working hard to pay the tuition and to buy them books.

Charming is a friend of Păstorel; swarthy, short and stout. He is also one of the guests from the restaurant in Icoana. Retracting his statement from the inquiry, he doesn't want to acknowledge the hostile aspect of the sayings of the accused. The president insists a lot, in the courtroom a vague rumor is produced (in the back), followed by perplexing amazement. It seems that in the unfolding of the scenario it occurred a breakdown; of course it is inconsequential, but it spoils the impression. The witness is, I think, Macedonian his name is Arsenie Taşcu-Dumba, and he must belong to those Aromanian families that through Ragusa, Vienna and Transylvania came in the kingdom[82]. (Others, like Şaguna, Starcea, Capri, Hurmuzachi, Grigorcea, Flondor remained in the Habsburg state on Romanian land.) There is a branch Dumba that was ennobled by the emperor, living at Court, remaining loyal to the dinasty and the city of the imperial waltz. (Iosif Roth described in Radetzky Marsch the –strange – case of these exponents of the "co-inhabiting nations" that remained until the end devoted servants of the empire. To them was referring Rebreanu with his David Popp from The catastrophe. And isn't Avram Iancu[83] one of them?)

Later, in prison, I was going to find out how sure are the friendships established by Macedonians, how faithful, and steadfast they are – although they give themselves with great reluctance. The threats of the president, more and more annoyed, fail. The president proposes to the prosecution organ to demand the arrest of the evidently lying witness. (The scene risks taking a fully Ionescian[84] character: if Păstorel, asked by the president, maintains his guilty plea from the inquiry – and how could he not maintain it? – it means that the witness, claiming Păstorel's innocence, lies and he is supposed to be sent in the box as perjurer based on the very words of the person who wanted to defend.) The prosecutor reflects but he doesn't ask the arrest. The witness is granted two minutes of reflection. The witness is troubled, frowns, a diffuse redness covers the darkness of the cheeks, he strains his little body. After the passing of the two minutes the witness states that the accused did not speak in a hostile manner. The president, the prosecutor and the judges sign with the shoulders, the heads and the hands that the witness is an idiot – and they send him back with feeble threats. He won!

From the summation of the prosecutor I am especially interested in the long part where he makes the analysis of the summations of the defense. He declares them generally healthy. He distributes grades, qualifications, references and critical remarks. The student-lawyers stay put with the hands on the desk. At the end – Mădârjac was mentioned negatively only in passing – you can see they are relieved.

When we were told that we will have the right to say a final word of defense, we were cautioned that we can only acknowledge out guilt and ask the indulgence of the tribunal. Can the diseases be invoked? They can. For Păstorel is given a certificate of pulmonary neoplasm.

Many confine themselves to acknowledge and to wait for the verdict. Pillat, first, started: "Although I have never been a communist, because I always considered inadmissible a materialist doctrine of violence, I couldn't help not to…" The president entered in frenzy; Dinu is interrupted brutally, the automatic rifles seem dramatically pointed toward him. Alecu, emotional, makes a general mea culpa, shows that he sees in Marxism the only solution and I think he sheds tears; the generous boyar from '48[85], that lives at the bottom of his soul, took the lead of the conscience. Otherwise than Alecu, Dr. A. Vl. apologizes with prepared words and cliches and wipes his eyes emphatically. Simina talks spontaneously and quick, as from a motorcycle, you can tell that in her veins throbs the blood of a former member of the Foreign Legion of Africa, an adventurer boyar, a musketeer, a paladin that – for who knows what reason or to come in the help of the weak and small or to defy the strong – doesn't spare neither the words nor the fists or the sword. Noica, dignified and pale, does not acknowledge himself guilty to the code of the tribunal but he considers himself deeply guilty toward the friends he dragged here after him and he asks them to forgive him. Marietta Sadova is pathetic, she cries, she coughs, chokes, evokes the sixty soviet plays she staged, invokes the fact that she never had estates or ranks.

What about me? I prepared carefully from the cell, the eventual final word and I recite it without interruption: "The facts being what they are, I have to show two things: first, that I never had the intention of plotting, second that if I should have known that the volume of Emil Cioran[86], The temptation to live[87] could be interpreted as an attack against the Romanian people (which is not) I wouldn't have read it and I wouldn't have associated to its spread, because I had, have and I will always have toward the Romanian people only feelings of deep respect and boundless love."

Skillful words that – God knows why, because they weren't any better than those of others – are listened by all four groups of the courtroom in silence. Dr. Al. G. told me later, in room 18, that I moved him.

When the court retires, we remain under guard in the box. The détente is general. The lawyers smile like the students after exam. The officers and the investigators are relieved as after an inspection. The soldiers stretch their legs. The chief of the guard, a gypsy sergeant that is also the Security barber, uses the opportunity to climb the platform and to sit on the chair of the court clerk.

From there he looks at us overwhelmed with happiness, like the traveler that would rest on the royal throne during the visiting of a palace, or as if he would mount, in a parliament building, an illustrious tribune. The excursionist thinks, from the painstakingly reached peak, that the sight that unfolds in the valley is only for himself. How happy is the temporary court clerk! He shows all his teeth. Maybe he is, at least now, the only one truly happy out of all who are here, all slaves, all actors with various parts in a strenuous and tiring play.

I wonder, doesn't have this whole masquerade the congruence point in this utmost passing and doltish happiness of the large-lipped among whose ancestors is not possible not to be an executioner?[88]

The tribunal reenters: the sentence will be pronounced after three days.

60

We are taken out hurriedly. Between the exit door and the van we make out a lead sky, an evening of sleet, pokes of fresh air.

Interlaken, summer of 1938

It happens to be a cold day and the hotels are full. They explain me the reason: it takes place the congress of an international religious association, The Oxford Group. I had heard about them. It is lead by a very energetic orator and propagandist, Frank Buchman. The title of a book written by one of his disciples: For sinners only. The rather mundane reputation of the movement does not attract me; I'm wrong, maybe, as in the case of the wisdom school from Darmstadt[89].

In the hotel where I was finally received there are living only members of the Group; I have no choice but to stay with them for dinners and they mistake me for one of them. Most of them are Englishmen. It seems that in another hotel, more luxurious, there is a lady from Romania.

The mountains are hazy, the moist makes people to drink an increased number – astronomical – of tea cups. The contact with these Englishmen – sincere, always in good mood (for them the world restarts anew every day like the first – better said the sixth), preoccupied with establishing and observing the most precise and busy schedules, ready at every hour to discuss the most delicate and private problems with complete detachment; with simple manners, polite, absorbed without any trace of hypocrisy in everything that is linked to the spirit and soul – is pleasant, amusing and even delightful. Everybody talks, confess, ask indiscrete questions followed by long silences, handle tea cups and biscuits dishes, pulling out from the pockets notebooks in which they write hundreds of addresses, titles of books, names of religious associations. I feel charmed.

At the beginning a sensation of not being in my place. Then I go to all the conferences of Buchman (a bit declamatory and the stress on schedules and organization), I participate at the meetings and the councils of the association. I am so caught that I give up a trip on Jungfrau for the sake of participating at a meeting of the Group. I am especially taken care for by a young office clerk from Bedford, whose name is Manning and he's a great guy; and an Irishman, older, tall and bald; they are my pillars, persevering and never awkward.

I'm not interested in what is the purpose of the Group, what is separating them from numerous other Protestant sects and unions. But is my first daily and sustained contact with people whose main preoccupation is the faith in God and the care for salvation, that made pecuniary sacrifices to come here at Interlaken, that take very seriously everything they do and discuss. No matter how frivolous one would be and still would feel attracted by these pure people. A lot of ingenuousness, summary theology, reduced general culture at most of them, conceptions often candid. Yet also freshness, charm, an impression of well aired rooms, not a trace of artfulness, guile, surfeit, fermentation.

The name of the Irishman left my mind, or is somewhere hidden in caches of gray matter that are inaccessible to me. I am therefore forced to mention him as the Irishman when I pray for him every day, and for the Oxford Group. In the morning before their departure he comes to me hurriedly; I was looking for you, he tells me, I wanted you to know my last night dream: the Lord appeared to me and entrusted me that He will call upon you. He notices that I look at him puzzled, because he repeats, explanatory: you will be one of those who believe in Him.

Montreux, 1938

The train that goes from Berna to Montreux bares the name Edelweiss, it's electric, sumptuous and cosmopolite, as in a Paul Morand's novel. Gallant Europe, Closed during the night, Open during the night, Gingerly stocks.

In Montreux, from the windows of the hotel, the sight has a solemn and perfect beauty that oppresses me. The live postcard in front of me shines of blue and green purity. The Oxford people I saw them as one coming from a France exclusively preoccupied of vacations, beefsteaks and strikes. Et un Pernod pour Arthur. France sick of intelligence and practical spirit, on one side, and these childish Anglo-Saxons, yearning for faith, enthusiasts on the other side. Alkohoolfreies Restaurant: the first advertising board I see in Switzerland, puerile but certain proof of an idealistic concept of life. From here to Schelling and Fichte is just a step.

I can't believe what the Irishman told me. Not in this life, maybe in a future reincarnation. I even have the feeling of being deceived. No, I cannot convert to Christianity. A world obsessed with Pernod. The doltish grin of mustached Arthur in the commercials. (There is another one, a neighbor, but alive and he drinks only water). How far is Christ. From them, from me. From all. I swear to myself, however, that I will never say a bad word, I will not grin when someone will be talking of the Oxford Group in my presence.

–   There is no need to spend a lot of time in jail. What is man, what is the real human condition, how is our situation – and that Christ is there under your nose, that He sees you, that He saw you, he saw you since always – it can be understood in a few minutes. Like the military service, it is an incomparable exercise of self-control.

London, May 1939

The family of pastor Lound lives in the very center, and in a very elegant neighborhood, close to Regent's Park. I was recommended and received as paying guest[90], deliciously hypocritical formula to say they rent me a room. I arrive in the evening after a terrible trip with the

plane: the storm haunted without ceasing above the Channel, we all vomited, (including the crew) all we had inside, in some bags at first than wherever happened. Barely arrived on the land of the Albion I encounter the British kindness, sweet compensation for the ironic French coldness: at the airport, some strangers hurry toward us with little bottles of cognac and they prompt us to drink: the remedy, they say, is obligatory after the stirring of the guts. The driver of the taxi manifests too his solicitude, and the maid of the hosts smiles to me with deference and lets me know that for this evening I am excused for wearing the smoking. The welcoming words of the master of the house are charming too (let someone tell me, after I went through Security, I made five years of jail and three years and half of unqualified work along the gypsies – that politeness is an old fashioned vanity, let him say that and I'll spit him in the face – let my mamma die, let I be crazy, let my eyes jump if not): in our house please feel as in a hotel, but allow us to consider you a friend.

Madam Lound and one of the girls (assistant at a dental clinic) are a little bit more reserved; the pastor and the other daughter (she is teacher in a town at a certain distance from London and she stays home from Friday until Sunday) are the gentleness and the simplicity in person. I see well that as cold as the Englishmen are abroad, as friendly are in their country. Hospitable, open, understanding: they acknowledge to everyone the right to be crazy, to go to heck if we wants it – and on the way he chooses; the need of faith they consider to be the most natural thing.

In the afternoon, sometimes, mister Lound invites me in his working room and makes me coffee in an electrical coffee pot. In the morning, before the consistent breakfast, he always takes me with him to a short walk, at military pace, through the endless Regent's Park. He shows me all sorts of elegant villas (some in very bad taste, imitations of the most various styles): they belong or they belonged to famous personalities. There are ponds in the park, I rush to some very lovable ducks. To see them more closely I squat, I call them, I tell them utzi-utzi. The ducks quack very mannerly, as long as they should. Returned home, the pastor recounts during the co-called breakfast that I, when he showed me the architectural beauties in the park, I abandoned them and I went to worship some ducks[91].

From London I write at Bedford to Manning, the young functionary that I met at Interlaken. He answers me soon and he invites me to participate to a reunion of the Group at Eastham, which is a suburb of the capital.

Suburb, it's a joke, because I travel with the underground and then with the train more than an hour and a half. I find again in the town hall of Eastham the same atmosphere of sincerity and naïve purity from Interlaken. The speakers talk enthusiastically and seriously, the public listens attentively and seriously, everybody takes notes, write down the number of the biblical verses that were quoted: it reigns a diligence that is not surprising to people convinced that the Lord will come as a thief, that He can come any minute, unexpectedly, why not right now!

During the break, the conversations are as animated as at Interlaken, they give again addresses to one another, they recommend to one another journals and books, expositions and courses, again they make to each other, unashamed, the most intimate spiritual confidences. Tea is served on little platters. I don't know how they manage to do all at once: they walk, drink, crunch biscuits, talk, write, preach, inform each other, salute each other, smile, meditate... I meet again the Irishman, who comes slowly toward me and reminds me the dream he had. I listen more carefully than at Interlaken, but with increased unbelief; and with an inner smile, not malicious, but anyway, condescending. It seems to me very moving – you will be counted among His worshippers –, and still childish. And a bit o pity for this man, of course well intended, but I don't like that he trusts dreams; and he lacks the shyness for his fantasies.

At London, however, I go often to churches, cathedrals and chapels, to visit them and to wait. To wait for something that doesn't come. I go to the church of my host where I don't take communion, although I am invited to. As an argument I invoke the fact that I didn't go to confession. The pastor, who has good knowledge of Catholicism and Orthodoxy (he was for a few years the appointed priest of the English church in Paris), is impressed by my motivation and he doesn't insist. Mister Lound is middle church[92], almost high[93], the faithful that does not come close to the altar out of lack of confession seems to him worthy of respect.

I go to a lot of associations and religious centers. On the London streets their names appear often, as the commercial firms. Here religion is everywhere, you meet Christ at every corner. They say the Lord. On the continent religious discretion is strict. In England no, they speak of the soul and faith in the most natural way. How many times, passing a building bearing a board with a name of religious organization, I entered! Inside there are séance rooms, libraries, files, batches of journals and booklets, photos, testimonies, telephones and secretaries. Offices. (But is it any different in Babylon? Quote Pierre Benoit: le Pape, c'est des bureaux[94].) I am received affably by peoples a little hurried, that listens to me, they summarize their respective belief. This part I find quite stereotype. But I am always moved when I am proposed with unforced ingenuity "a couple of moments of meditative silence in two" or a prayer. Let us pray[95]: and they kneel in the middle of the office, of the parlor – waiting room, archives room, as if they would pull a white handkerchief from the pocket to wipe the glasses. They load me with papers and booklets, pamphlets, as they like to call them.

And in Hyde Park, where I like to stop for long near the preachers. A group of sectarians sing: I come close to them with the hat on my head and the umbrella in my hand. (It is a bright day with no trace of clouds; if it would be raining, I would have taken, naturally, the raincoat, not the umbrella.) They ask me to take off my hat because their song is a psalm. I answer them politely but, out of a sudden stubbornness, I refuse to uncover myself at their command. Why did I do that? They insist, persevering too, not upset, because they are used to the various tricks of the devil. To the end, they leave me to God's judgement and I leave – full of sorrow.

March 6th 1960

Therefore, finally I am taken out, brought to an office sheltered in the small niche of the vaulted corridor; interrogated, identified, undressed. I am left only with a towel, o toothbrush, a toothpaste, two pairs of socks, a shirt, a pair of underpants, out of which I make a small parcel. I look at the clock above the vault of the niche and I see that it is much more earlier than I thought. A very tall and sturdy guardian makes me a sign to follow him. (In the interrogation room they were chatty, now they are mute.) But he doesn't lead me toward the row of metallic doors loaded with locks and bolts, behind which I suspect the cells. He go outside, in the yard. This night at the beginning of March is a blizzard night. It remembers me of The clubs jack of Edgar Wallace: "He was taken from a gutter in Lambeth young Gregory said the Cocaine-man , and he was dead before the agent in charge from Waterloo bridge, who heard the shootings, could arrive at the place. He was killed in the street, at night, on snow and wind, and nobody saw the killer. After they took him to the morgue and his clothes were searched they found nothing but a small metallic box full of a white dust that was cocaine and a playing card, the clubs jack!"

I'm in undershirt and underpants. The guardian shows me a huge pile of suitcases, bags, rucksacks, packages, sacs and he orders me to move them from the yard to a small room close to the entrance of the corridor along which are the cells. Some suitcases are very heavy. I'm working, trembling and clattering, because it is not only cold, it's also a horrible current, about two hours. The guardian, wrapped up in a huge Siberian fur coat and shoed with hip boots over his boots, raised his fur collar, pulled the flaps of his bonnet over the ears and he crouched – he looks like the invisible man from the film after H.G. Wells – on a pitiful chair thrown in a corner from where he probably watches me. He is of course cold and – I don't know why – I have the feeling he doesn't like seeing me fumbling around in the snow, undressed, skinny and wretched.

I finish happy that I didn't show any sign of weakness, starting to warm up. The guardian makes me a sign again to follow him, shaking a ring with a lot of huge keys. He stops in front of cell 18, opens the door with difficulty, yawns and pushes me inside.

–   After all it is possible that God doesn't even need to punish us. He turns His face away from us: which means He withdraws His protective grace and leaves us at the discretion of the events and interconnections of the material world. We enter in the zodiac of the hazard and of the mechanics: woe to us!

March 7th 1960

They pushed me inside. Now I stay stone-still near the door. I'm looking. I am in a huge hole, an incredible stench hits me. The room is strongly illuminated. A sort of night asylum geometrically amplified. I am taken by a double and contradictory feeling of emptiness and overcrowdedness. On both sides four rows of iron beds that mount up close to the high vaulted ceiling. The window, in front of me, is nailed with planks, and beyond are the bars. In the space between the innumerable beds, a narrow table, two wretched and also narrow benches. In the right corner, in the back, a tub and a covered barrel. That's all. Down, along the beds, rows – that seem to me without end – of boots.

Some sturdy snores do not break the deep silence, like the isolated clouds that do not change the unity of a violent blue sky. A couple of breath rattles. The metallic noise of the bolts and the keys didn't wake up anybody; and this amazes me.

I start trembling of cold, frozen in my summary clothing, with the pack in my right hand, blinded by the aggressive light. The breaths are various and dissonant. I stay like this a long while and wait but I don't see any movement. I look for a place for shelter where I could sleep. I see none. And nobody is seeing me.

After I scrutinized a long time the walls with exterior sarcophaguses I turn my eyes down and I see a melange of dust, concrete, gravel and mud. The room seems to me extremely hostile, evil, I feel ridicule and lost. I feel vanquished by fatigue, but especially frightened. As at an examination for which I don't know the subject. A completely different kind of horror than at the Security.

(The premonitions are not always valid. I didn't know at the threshold of that stinking hole, intensely illuminated and caught in a whirl of snores and silence, that in it I will find access to happiness.)

For the time being I look up and down, right and left, everywhere, insistently, scared. Light and emptiness.

(Everything can be defiled; here even the light is cold and evil. How you felt from sky, bright star, son of morning. Winston Smith in "1984": in the place there is no darkness[96] – and what turns out to be that place: the inquiry offices and the prison! However he wasn't deceived: there is always light, but what kind of light? The kind that probably was sparking the fall of the angel Lucifer, when God saw him falling, lightning, in the deepness.)

Suddenly, up above, from the left, on the highest row, a hand stretched a finger and signals me to mount.

To mount – but how? The hand – which obviously is gifted with the sense of seeing and understands that I am turning around searching for means of ascension – is joined by the second, her sister of course. They sketch a climbing. With my pack, wretched, with scared gestures, clattering, I found myself monkey enough to climb up using the iron beds. A muffled up apparition, short and awfully skinny, of a pallor which might belong to another chromatic prism than that of our universe, move closer to another mummy and urges me to stretch myself near him; he covers me with half of a shabby blanket. And he is whispering to me: sleep a bit because it won't be long now.

–   Maybe the most terrifying words spoken by the Savior are in Luke 22, 67: "If I will tell you, you won't believe."

This is the human condition. We don't believe Him. We don't believe each other. We don't want, we don't know, we don't dare, we don't strive to believe the others. Experiences are not transmissible. We eventually understand some things – what good for? we are not believed. We can speak but we cannot establish the communication, make the connection. What's left to do than, following His example, to shut up (not frowned)?

–   Not even ten minutes elapsed and it starts a noise more than deafening; the noise of pulverized stars which in Le Napus of Léon Daudet causes the instantaneous disappearing of people? A long hubbub, a demented uproar; explosion that I would never forget, that, even afterwards, for years, would awake me at five, even a couple of minutes earlier, out of anticipating fright. This sonorous rush – of alarms? bells? trumpets? fire arms? – penetrates the most Freudian layers, more Jungian, more Adlerian of the ego and settles its den in unknown places of the being.

The miracles exist. God always works. The foretelling of N.N.P. comes true at once. Hardly the trumpet gust ended that my benevolent neighbor recommends himself: he is an orthodox hieromonk. Near him, another two ghosts wake up, one stout and heavy, the other slim and young: they are two Greek-catholic priests.

I know, in the middle of the tumult that arouses in the cell after the end of the reveille, when a sea of bald heads fills the space and in front of the barrel already formed a line as a comet queue, I know that I fell in the hands of the living God.

–   I trust I make myself obscure.[97]

–   My monk is Bessarabian. He is a young man, sentenced for having visions and for sending to the Cults Department a letter in which he was protesting against the closing of the skete where he lived. I barely have the time – I mold the iron while is red – to tell him that I am a Jew and I want to be christened, and he already agrees. He is gentle, with slow gestures and silent. The two Greek-catholic priests are very different than each other. Father Nicolae, from Alba, young, is skimpy and agitated, a jokester and enjoying idle talk. Father Iuliu is big, strong, kind and very retired. You can read on his face the pain caused by the fact that his daughter, a nun, is imprisoned; she was part of a batch of mystical nuns. Speaking of strange pairing of words and situations, I say to him, I was part of a batch of mystical Legionnaires. But father Iuliu is upset for other reasons too: being a catholic priest, he signed, unconvinced, in 1948, for the conversion to Orthodoxy: he cannot forgive himself this. Now he's here for stubbornness in Catholicism and activity in the service of Vatican. The obsession of his first act doesn't leave him and I find myself in the paradoxical situation to console him myself, telling him that only in Judaism, Brahmanism and Buddhism the facts remain recorded forever and they can't be erased, while in Christianity the faith and the repentance cleanse them completely (Christianity, therefore, discovered the antigravity) and, actually, even in Judaism, Brahmanism and Buddhism there is a law of compensation and hence his present sufferings balance the past mistakes. Father Iuliu listens to me, sighs and approves with his head – but it's obvious that he is still aching.

Father Mina, the Orthodox monk, imposed me only a few lessons of catechism and we are doing them sitting on the edge of an iron bed, with the back toward the door, close to each other, speaking in whispers. We are, of course, both in convict uniforms: boots without straps, striped cloth, a little bonnet (this time with horizontal stripes) on the head. The jacket doesn't have buttons, the pants, too short, are ready to fall. Actually everything here, in Jilava, has the most violent aspect of jail, of brig, not of grave prison. The building is creepy but the interior looks like a fare, a painting by Breugel, Chagall, a bedlam, Mărcuţa[98]. It's an unconceivable agglomeration, you can barely move, the noise is formidable, although they speak only in whispers (at least theoretically), the line for the barrel is uninterrupted, the most funny questions are circulating (how do you say chaffinch in French? what peace treaty ended the Seven Years War? how do you say brass in German? what's the name of the three parces, the nine muses, the three graces, the seven wise men of the antique world? the seven kings of Rome? the three masters of Babylon, what about in Syriac?

–   what were the first names of the Buzeşti brothers[99]? who composed Tzar and carpenter? what's the capital of Swabia? which are the rivers of Eden? what about chervil, in French? quince in English?)

Buggy mambo rag.

We eat in two series, at ten minutes interval. The food is incandescent, mostly barley. Spoons are only for the fifth or the sixth part of the prisoners. The first series is forced to finish quickly so that they can wash the kettles and have them prepared for the next round. But how can you eat without spoon and in five minutes a hot dough like the hypothetical magma or soup out of which the mono-cellular life sprung on earth? Almost all the food remains in the kettles: it is thrown in the barrel, which gets filled to the top. Washing the pot in which there was the gluey barley is an utmost laborious work. (What were the twelve works of Hercules? Who composed White cross of birch? Where is buried Alexander The Great? Turnip in French is navet. God forbid, it is poireau. I'm sorry, poireau is leek. Be serious mister, it can't be leek. He was a military attaché at London. That's why he knew English. At Răcăciuni, they signed it there. It believe they say Messing. You know, I think you're right. Ah, dill is easy, is fenouil. On the contrary, is aneth.) Al. Pal. and I happened to be on duty in the room the very second or the third day. A certain benevolent advises us to use the ashes from the stove; the water – bad water, smelly, with worms – is very little. We have to wash sixty or seventy kettles, in a few moments. The ashes combine with the barley juice and make a very resilient glue. The little bit of water we had is gone. What should we do? We feel spite: two intellectuals that made fools of themselves out of clumsiness. We exchange glances without any sense of humor. What should we do? God relented on us and made a miracle.

(Miracles will be plenty during the years of prison. One who served time in prison not only that he doesn't doubt miracles, but he wonders how come they are not acknowledged by everybody as the most normal thing.)

–   I didn't know. I lived like a beast, like cattle, like a blind. In prison, toward sunset, I found out what is kindness, politeness, heroism, dignity. Big words! Empty words! Big and empty words for şmechers and squealers; big and useful words when you feel their cool breeze in the lake of fire and you can taste their experimental charm. Let everybody believe what he wants, on absolute value I can't talk, one thing I know: that these big words and the qualities they show were better priced than a strap, a string, a nail (the nail that Geo Bogza learned to respect in the criminal prison), a paper or any other forbidden objects, which could make happy his possessor.

H.G. Wells in The Research Magnificent: two big forces: fear and aristocracy. Now I understand. Fear must be defeated. There is only one thing in the world, just one: the courage. And the secret is to behave aristocratically. Only gentleness, kindness, calmness, beautiful gestures are fun.

I begin to understand that only the character matters. The political convictions, philosophical opinions, religious faith are but accidents: only the character stays after the purges caused by the prison years – or life years –, after wear and tiredness, skeleton, code, electric blueprint.

The miracle consists in the supplementary bringing, completely exceptional, of another bucket with water by the guards form the corridor. We are put with the face toward the wall and the hands at the back of the neck when they open the door: after its closing, we turn around and we find the bucket. Moreover, the food for the second series is late as never, so that Al. Pal. and I can present when they ask us from the peephole some kettles that are so to speak clean.

Manole repeats the prayer of La Hire, one of the captains that fought together with Joanne d'Arc: do unto me, Lord, what I would do unto Thee if I would be in Thy place and Thou in mine.

March 10th-15th 1960

The catechization lessons go very quickly: father Mina is lenient and unpretentious, and it is true that I prove to know quite a lot. The three priests confer among them and then they come to ask me: what do I want to be, catholic or orthodox? I answer them without hesitation orthodox. Very well. The monk will baptize me. But the two Greek-catholic priests will attend the baptism and as an homage for their faith and as a proof that we all understand to bring to life the ecumenicity in a time when John the XXIII is on the pontifical throne, I will say the credo in front of the catholic priests. All three ask me to consider myself baptized in the name of the ecumenicity and to promise to fight always – if I will get out of prison – for the cause of ecumenicity. I promise from the bottom of my hearth.

It can't be known when we will be taken out of cell 18 (it is for transit) and spread who knows where. It is therefore necessary not to postpone. The baptism will take place in the fifteenth day of the month. There will be less than ten days since my arrival in the cell and the effectuation of the baptism. N.N.P. was right.

– Noise, mess, increasing agglomeration (new prisoners keep coming through the door), almost all the time there is not a drop of water, longer and longer lines for the barrel (we are more numerous each day and most of us have bellyache), jumble, cold, yells of the guards, unexpected visits from lieutenant Ştefan: he is swearing terribly, staring fiercely and he is threatening to "jump on our heads"; inspections are made and those found with boot straps are sent to "blackie". There are no kettles, no spoons, no beds... The batch Noica-Pillat, those who are present, don't mind the hubbub and they organize some culture circles: Sanskrit lessons taught by dr. Al-G., history of art (Remus Niculescu), Spanish (Theodor Enescu), general biology (dr. C. Răileanu), history of culture (Al. Pal.), agricultural technique (Iacov Noica), philosophy of the law (Dinu Ranetti); I "open" myself an English course. Prompted by Dr Al-G. (who proves himself to be an exceptional personality: all strength, courage, good humor, deepness in everything he says, obligingness, conduct) some collective seances are held on general themes, which are mandatory for all the "students". The first theme is the theory of act. In parallel are told the great books of the XX century: Doktor Faustus by Thomas Mann (Remus Niculescu), Zauberberg by the same author (I), The grand initiates by Schuré (Em. V.), The revolt of the masses by Ortega y Gasset (T. En.)... There are some more earthly subjects: a gentleman named Radu Ant. – Oltenian[100] and Legionnaire – tells us in detail about the preparation of dishes in griddle.

Prompted by our example, the other intellectuals in the cell – up to then in a munched reserve – start working: a group of superior officers teach: the history of World War II, the campaign in Russia of Napoleon, general principles of strategy. There is also a bunch of young boys – of social-democrat nuance with a touch of nationalism – full of enthusiasm and good manners. One of them is the nephew of Sofia Nădejde[101]. Life's little ironies[102]. (This book of Thomas Hardy should be told too, it is fit, at least the title.) Gentle and kind, the young social-democrats brighten and sweeten our days. Some frontierist students arrive too, boys of good family. (Jean Bart is represented by a descendent.) They are very brave, confident, but although they behave impeccably they don't show too much interest for our intense cultural activity. Remus Niculescu beats us all talking enticed and enticingly about the impressionist painters and their friend, the Romanian baron Belliou (Bellu).

Some time later, in the increasingly overcrowded cell, two skinny silhouettes of a weakness that I never saw before appear: a civil servant from Ploieşti and a Legionnaire engineer, who tells us that he was the commander of the cross brotherhoods[103].

March 15th 1960

The catechization came to an end. The baptism, decided for the day of fifteenth, takes place as established. Father Mina chooses the moment that he considers the most favorable: the return from "air", when the cops are busier, when the agitation is maxim. We have to work fast and to act clandestinely in everyone's sight. The conspiracy in the middle of the day of Wells. Something like the invisible maneuvers of Antonov-Ovseienko. My task is to not go for the walk. (Easy to do since I have a purulent sore on the right foot from the boot. I was not allowed to go to infirmary although I went every morning for report. Doctors Răileanu and Al-G. treat me with a rag soaked in the infested water. One day before a sergeant told me that he won't let me go to the official doctor "even dead". Lord's works, manifold.)

Therefore I remain alone for a quarter of an hour, the duration of the "air" – almost alone, because there are a few others for which the walk was waived for various reasons. Void of noise and activity the cell takes an even stranger aspect, like an empty scene where the piles of scenery are distributed randomly. But especially the difference of noise level compared to the full cell is so striking, that I have the feeling of an absolute silence – the silence becomes, quote Cervantes, a show – and I can quiet down, recollect a little.

When the flood of people comes back with clamor bringing in pairs the tub, the barrel and a "reservoir" of water, father Mina, without taking off the cloak, hurries toward the only pitcher in the room – it's a small red pitcher with the enamel cracked, dirty and disgusting – and he fills it with infested water, fresh from the "reservoir" brought by him and another prisoner. The two Greek-catholic priests and my godfather come to my bed. A few days before I had chosen as godfather Em. V., former lawyer and professor, with extensive knowledge of Latin and Greek, sent to trial for writing the daily order "I order you, cross the Prut!"[104] V. was the chief of staff of Ică[105] and he carried in the car the famous order which for nothing on earth the proud and otherwise very cultivated general Antonescu would have allowed anyone else to write in his name. Why did I choose V. that I didn't know before (as well as most of the people alongside I conspired) and not Al. Pal. – an old friend, well, friend from '54, former student of the Spiru Haret high school too, and besides we decided to consider ourselves childhood friends – or dr. Al-G. whose personality strongly impressed me, and who remained for me the most multilateral being I ever met in prison and the most gifted man with the virtue of courage – Marinică P. was the kindest, in him the kindness turning, through intensity, also in intelligence, tact, politeness, refinement and power of thought, but at a level of less grandeur – or one of the generals present in the room (they would not have refused me) or the gentle Toto Enescu, I can't tell.

Two prisoners, in complicity, step in front of the peephole to block the view. The guard can come any moment to take a look, but now, when the cells are taken out for the walk in turns, is unlikely. Hurriedly – but with that priestly skill where the speed doesn't impeach clear diction – father Mina says the necessary words, signs me with the sign of the cross, spill on my head and shoulders the entire content of the pitcher and baptize me in the name of the Father and the Son and the Holy Spirit. I made a summary confession: the baptism erases all the sins. I am born again, from infested water and quick spirit.

After that we go somehow quiet, somehow relieved – the uncaught thief is an honest man – to the bed of one of the Greek-catholic priests: it is close to the barrel and the tub (we came down from upstairs) and there I recite the (orthodox) creed, as we established. I renew the promise to not forget that I was baptized under the emblem of the ecumenicity. Done. The baptism, in these circumstances, is perfectly valid, even without diving and anointing. (If I will ever escape from prison unscathed, it follows for the sacrament of anointing to go to a priest whose name is given to me by father Mina: this name I would forget and then remember it again.)

The intense rhythm of cell 18 grabs us right away. The Greek-Catholic fathers are on duty in the cell. Father Mina has to wash a shirt. Doctor Al-G. convenes us: some of us stay on the brink of his bed., others in the front bed. We are still talking about the theory of act and I have to speak about the act of creation at Proust. We stay packed and we talk fervently in whispers. Many prisoners attracted by everything that the "Noica batch" is doing gather around us. The abstraction and the documentation spread their magic and they pull out momentarily the people into joy and illusion.

–   Who was baptized as a child can't know or suspect what the baptism means. More and more frequent happiness assaults rush on me. You would say that each time the besiegers go higher and they strike with more power, with more precision. Therefore is true: it is true that the baptism is a holy mystery, that there are holy mysteries. Otherwise this happiness that surrounds me, embrace me, dress me, vanquish me couldn't be so unimaginably marvelous and whole. Silence. And an absolute lack of care. For everything. And a sweetness. In mouth, in veins, in muscles. Also a resignation, the feeling that I can do everything, the impulse to forgive everyone, a lenient smile that spread everywhere, not localized on the lips. And a sort of gentle air layer around, an atmosphere resembling that of some childhood books. A feeling of absolute safety. A mescalinical union in everything and a complete detachment in serenity. A hand that is tended to me and an abode with guessed wisdom.

And the novelty: I'm new, I'm a new man: where from so much freshness and renewal? It comes true Revelation (21,5): I am making all things new; also Paul: if someone is in Christ, is a new being: the old things have passed, look, all things are new. New but unspeakable. I find only trite, stale words, those that I use all the time. I'm caught in the chalk circle of the known words and of the ideals subtracted from the daily décor. Madam Cottard of Proust if asked what is her desire would indicate the situation of a richer neighbor from the corner of the street: she wouldn't even think of becoming the duchess of Mortemart. Our ideal goes up to the very next circle or heaven. But there are others above, unsuspected, unspeakable, unthinkable. And thalassa of Xenophone and the earth of Columbus. The baptism is a discovery.

Cluj[106], August 3rd 1964

I arrive at Cluj at half past five. From Gherla until here I watched over the window of the wagon with the intensity that must have had in his eyes the man who first saw the world freshly created by God, or the convicted to death from the ballad of the prison of Reading. As behind the bars, I felt Christ close to me, when, in front of my eyes still bewildered by the always lighted electric bulbs, were parading orchards, houses, fences, domestic animals; in every thing, in every strip of land throbs the light of the pictures of Van Gogh – explosive –and the relaxing hues of the day toward the end and the thundering joy of the first six days; demented feeling that the ancestral sin still didn't happened.

It is a cold afternoon and the sky is cloudy. At the buffet of the train station asked by colonel Ion T. – ten years in Siberia, ten years of prison, translator of If in Romanian, presently possessor of a few tens of lei[107] – what I desire, I answer greedily: a coffee. After I drank it, with plenty of sugar brought by an understanding waiter that puts it on purpose on our table, we go to the center. The colonel wants to meet a friend he is looking for so we wander around in the city with an aroma of Kaiserstadt in miniature and full of buildings in baroque style (the most evoking of silence and opulence). At each step I have the feeling that I live in the year 1900, that Europe is a vast saloon, that the people don't know what is fear and anxiety. It looks, really, like we were in Stadtpark, the statues of Mozart and Johann Strauss emerge out of trees and flowers, on the terrace of the restaurant a capella is singing, pairs are performing the most beautiful waltz, the imperial waltz.

The train for Bucharest, that he have to take, leaves at ten o'clock in the evening. After a while the colonel find his friend right in the train station, and I remain alone. Money for the bus fare I don't have, there is not too much time until the departure of the train, the euphoria that overcame me since I left Gherla is egalitarian and indifferent, a small rain started, so I decide to walk around the station. First I enter in a bakery staring at the merchandises and the prices. Then, the rain stops altogether and I wander in a small street. It's completely dark and the air is humid; it looks like it still pours a little and there is a breadth of perfumed wind. I think the street is very little circulated; now is empty; through most of the windows you can see the lights turned on. It is not less calm and less blue than in Verlaine's poem that George Mavrocordat was asking me always, insatiable, to recite for him. Actually blue is not a color is a silence too. All the houses are clean, cared for, with many flowers, in that pseudo-cubist style of 1925. But they have something of beings attentive to the exterior form, something of little bonnet and apron, of coffee with milk and croissant with butter; and how silent, comfortable and harmonious all the interiors seem to me seen through the windows!

It is given to me, in a few moments of intense emotion, a better than ever understanding of some of the major secrets of life.

I do understand first that in this world we are completely abandoned by God, as Simone Weil noticed and that this abandonment is also the supreme sign of the "existence" and love of God. God, she says, "retires" absolutely, to allows us to live (otherwise His presence would be equivalent to out annihilation) to leaves us complete freedom so that our daring act of faith should have merit (or better said meaning).

Abandoned completely, destined to live in full dialectic passion, I understand that rational help I cannot receive from anywhere; drugs, alcohol, eroticism, caresses given by illusions or mania are not valid because they make me dependent on the goodwill of others and they are temporary, moreover, subject to the whims of the time that degrades them; categorical and absolute proofs do not exist; the theories are aging worse than the people, the clothes, we are dealing only with signs, and the signs – of course, there wasn't even need for Sartre to tell it so loudly – can be interpreted in two ways; the dialectics awaits us at every step. Therefore, I understand that I cannot put basis except in some vague intuitions – not a trace of evidence, rules, objective guaranty etc. –, in some mysterious prompting coming from a world that I feel and I guess only, from hidden depths, from the domain that Ortega considers that belongs to the faiths, not to ideas.

Without further ado, I am a slavophile too, I subscribe to the new mystique program of Homiakov: the preeminence of the unwritten laws on any formulated dogma, preeminence of the religious and moral law on any logic or rationale. Without further ado, the Jesuit Auguste Valensin enunciate the essential when he admits that, if one would show him, by impossible, on the death bed, with the most perfect evidence, that he's wrong, there is not afterlife, there is not even God, he still wouldn't be sorry for believing; moreover, he would consider himself honored that he believed such, because if the universe is something imbecile and worthy of despise, then so much the worse for the universe, whoever thought there is a God was not mistaken, mistaken is God because He doesn't exist; without further ado I cannot find anything beyond or above the credo formulated by Dostoievski and that he presents very simply: I believe there is nothing more beautiful, more deep, more enticing, more reasonably, more manly and more perfect than Christ, more than that, if one would prove me that Christ is outside the truth and the truth is outside Christ, I prefer to remain with Christ rather than with the truth.

This is all I have, few quotes (from decent people) and a feeling – so delicate, so unsystematic, so fragile. Yet this vague, mince and humble capital – my only gain after years of prison, a small bundle – it is enough to give me a solid foundation and the unfaltering conviction that I know what I must and what I must not do.

The incertitude is the basic law of the occidental civilization – and its zodiacal sign; it is also the basic condition of Christianity. But besides it there are – "unproven" on human plane, scientifically – those convictions stronger than theorems, like the rock. (We have them from higher authorities.) Prompted by them, I will always know what to do, by them I can always reestablish the broken connection with God and joy; over the abyss, the emitter and the receptor may instantaneously communicate.

In the light drizzle, along the street, I understand that we're not supposed to do any evil to anyone, that every disorder, rudeness, brutality, quarrel, anger, despise, insult is from the devil; that doing the good is the most selfish goal because it is the only one that gives peace and reconciliation with oneself; that good behavior and collecting good deeds are our only property that we can always make use of (it can't be confiscated during a bodily search); that since it can happen to anyone to end up alone, in a prison cell or at least in a hospital bed or to wake up sleepless at two o'clock in the night (the terrible hour of lucidity), nothing is more dreadful and closer to hell – I use a strictly selfish vocabulary – than the remembrance of the ugly, evil, mean deeds; than the void of the unused minas and the wasted gifts; that we are supposed to do the good now when there is still time, before coming to the state in which all that remains is to be (manners of to be: after death, in prison, on the hospital bed, in hopeless – or irremediable – loneliness, at lonesome old age, waiting at the red light, abused by an office clerk); that, gathering beautiful memories (but not the regret of some fleeting moments of pleasure, because that's a torment too) we build indeed our paradise, which is nothing else than a sum of good deeds, of noble or heroic actions, of generous behavior whose remembrance is eternally sweet and warm stove, an occasion of righteous and calm beneficial content for being safe from contortions and baseness; that we don't have absolute surety and logic but we know what we are supposed to do, modestly; we know! In other words, God is completely absent from the world but he is completely present inside us, as Kierkegaard said, as St.

Bonaventura roared; God is preeminently present to the soul, even immediately knowledgeable.

I leave Cluj quiet, with my soul rich in peace; I begin to see a quiet wisdom, a modest temperance that could mean the nearness of hesychasm.

Let the carnation blood the hill And Transylvania is a hymn

Ioan Alexandru

– In the train, of course, we cannot sleep. We all are too agitated (Scurtu tells us about his two escapes, from the ferry in the Danube delta) and everybody understands where we're coming from – from the shaved heads, the worn out clothes, the total pallor, the smell (especially) –, they make place for us, they give us food, they put money in the pockets of our clothes hanged on the pegs of the compartments.

From early dawn the fertile and imposing landscape of Transylvania unfolds before our eyes, almost processionally the solid buildings, the spires, the carefully cultivated fields, the reinforced gates, the clearly marked gardens, the windows hidden by flowers, the smooth roads, nicely paved with stones, the fortress-churches... Transylvania, Transylvania![108] We are experiencing an immense proud joy; we are allowed to renew the contact with the country and the state of freedom – (as much as it is; father: don't be sad, you're just going from a large prison into a smaller one, and when you get out don't be too glad, you're going from a small prison into a larger one) – throughout this noble and worthy landscape among all, nothing is sordid, sandy or ugly, there were pains and sorrow and sad birds sang, but no smells of Turkish mud was left, an honorable and honest landscape, and a bit emphatic, mister father, I pray you, servus esteemed friend, the seven burgs, reciprocal, tea with milk, the landscape that tamed even Caragiale[109]. And how clean are the streets, the driveways, the yards, the fields, at least at this early hour...

The patriotism, says Duiliu Zamfirescu, is not a prejudice and also it is not a judgement; patriotism is a feeling. Feelings can have anyone. And which among the psyche's powers are more close to the tears than the feeling? I weep easily, too easily. From prison I gathered a lesson: the expression gift of tears is of utmost accuracy.

3-4 August

In the train I the formula "the devil is the master of this world" retains my attention. I believe the accent should be put on this. The world is the creation of God, but the world contaminated by sin and entered in complicity with the devil, this world – which is not the original - the world that Satan offers and yields at the feet of Christ as being his and having the right to give it to whoever he wishes (and The Lord –Luke 4,6 – does not contradict Him), because it is just a secondary image, deformed, deviated – and which is illusion, that the peasants and the townsmen see it, believe it to be a tavern, but don Quijote knows it is a castle – it's his world.

The cleaning operation doesn't require therefore a recreation, but only an exorcism, an un- bewitching. The proof is the contact with all the masterpieces of art that succeed too to counter- spell, to establish a direct connection with the godhead. The magic veil then disappears and the world – being still the same, but transformed, with the charms shaken off – becomes again the first creation and gives the sensation of happiness. After all, the Lord in His conversation with Nicodemus from John 3 (because of the sectarians I began to refer to the biblical text always citing the chapter and the verse, pedant habit) does not ask from the man a new bodily birth, thus another Genesis, but just to perform an instantaneous spiritual metanoia, which is absolute. Somewhere around are the lightning words of von Jawlenski: the art is the nostalgia of God.

Everybody saw, in bad printed books colored images in non-overlapping positions relative to the black-and-white ones. Well, the devil's world is the same as this slight deviation between background and color, slight but enough to lead more and more accentuated and quickly to other realms.

It is a deviation that must be corrected.

Accordingly, the world controlled by the devil is real, but only according to the above. Because, otherwise, the devil did not create a second world, but still on the one created by God he operates as a parasite; it is the same world but "bewitched" and over this imaginary one (because it exists only through our eyes, concepts, convictions and passions) is he king. That's why my beloved Simone could state very exactly: the things we are chained to are unreal, but the chains that binds us are very real. The structures don't differ, "structurally speaking the devil doesn't work on a different domain than the Good, the Word.

Therefore, the devil can offer us only what he possesses: which is the illusion, Maya (this is the influence of dr. Al-G.), the image displaced during printing. As long as our relation with this illusion or spell is founded on our act of consent, he delivers: he gives what he promised. In the moment of death however (or the shuddering repent or anytime we settle the accounts), when we are recalled to reality (the moment of drawing the balance-sheet at the end of the year has its greatness its little suspected allegory – and doesn't Soll und Haben, the humble book of Gustav Freytag, prefigure in a certain way Sein und Zeit?[110]), of course the established agreement is "liquidated" (see Faust) and the devilish contribution appears to be illusory, simple reflection in the mirror.

Father of lie: because he has power only over the deviated image, only over the error, only over the corrupted essence; prince of fear: because it is frightening to realize that you are locked – engaged (engaged means also hired, employed as a servant) – in a huge, shaky, wrong construction, that cannot but fall like a playing cards castle.

Therefore, the faith in God seems to me in the full meaning of the word the most realist act that can be: it is the accept of truth and the abjuration of illusions. That's why it is required humility, that's why the church puts so much stress on humility: nothing is more difficult than to renounce the make-believe.

When don Quijote tells to the peasants in the tavern that they are truly in a castle, he is crazy because the peasants are in the tavern as long as they think they are there: and the human word being itself "creator", as the word of the Father (Genesis 2, 19), for the tavern castle would be its name. You called it tavern, it is tavern. By the virtue of the divine power conceded to man to define things. Don Quijote, therefore, denies a reality of the plan, of the level where he is too and hence he is crazy. But he is also realist, in the fullness of his mind, because the castle is still castle in the essential world, archetypal, true, (true, not real), among models, just being covered with the veil of spell and able at any moment to be restored, reestablished, repossessed, reintegrated in its initial state through an act of coming back to truth and of repudiation of this world, the world of the color displaced during printing.

The situation of the Christian is as paradoxical as of Don Quijote. He is man and he is required to be God. He was created clean and he is dirty, he just has to come back to what he was fated to be. In other words he must fight to become what he is.

BUGGY MAMBO RAG

Maniu didn't want to listen to me, and I prayed him so hard, ah, if he would have listened to me, he listened to Penescu... Semolina pudding? let me tell you how is done semolina pudding, because I see you have no idea... Ah, you who say you have lived in the countryside, let's see: the hen cackles, the duck quacks, the goose gaggles, but the turkey what is he doing? Well? He gobbles, mister, he gobbles... Natalia Negru, that was her name... No way! This was the woman for whose sake Şt. O. Iosif[111] killed himself, Odobescu's[112] woman was named differently, I don't remember now, I think it is a name with German resonance... Look, first the milk must be without fail well boiled, the semolina is added only after... Cornes grecques, this is how pods are called... Yes, you are right, Tămădău was an operation so carelessly performed that you can't even... You see, the badger, to be honest, I don't know how he is, but the polecat... It's in Dante, mister...

Bucharest, August 4th

I find father in the street, close to home. He is helped by the cousin who came to take him to a walk and to the barbershop. He is short, incredibly short, a lot stooping and he makes small steps, but he walks without fear and his eyes are lively. I take his right arm without being noticed by him and when he turns the head I ask him not to cry.

— To cry? he says. What, am I stupid? Tell me, have you eaten something today?

Upstairs in the room I feel horrified: the couch and an armchair are broken, the springs are hanging, the dust makes everywhere a thick layer, the walls and the ceiling are black, the dirt, the misery and the stale air stink, I see bedbugs crawling all over. A sort of warehouse corner with all kind of old stuff, abandoned. Down, in the room, some old newspapers, all dust. A dirty dish, two sticky forks. I feel like hitting my head against the walls. (By myself, without the intervention of the investigator.) But I don't come from jail for nothing; I remain calm: I will clean.

Gherla 1963

> Français, encore un effort, si vous voulez être républicains[113].
>
> Marquis de Sade

I happen to come together, during a time of moving rage, which often seizes Tudoran, the political officer, with former militaries, gendarmes and Legionnaires just brought from Aiud.

I find out authentic details about Ţurcanu[114] and reeducation.

If the devils, the fallen angels, could invent terrible tortures, only the şmecher order of the people could imagine such crazy and contorted tortures.

Swallowing the hot barley in no time and right away after that a big pitcher of cold water. To climb the wall with bare hands.

Prostrations, continuously until fainting.

To eat feaces. (The one asked to eat his own should consider himself privileged.)

Enormously eating followed by forty-eight hours spent in an overcrowded cell, without barrel and with the door, of course, locked.

Priests forced to masturbate.

Sleeping hours reduced to four, from 12 p.m. to 4 a.m. and even those interrupted at each quarter of an hour.

The obligation to stand up from 4 a.m. to 12 p.m. for two months.

Three alarms in a night. When the alarm is given the inmates must go under the bed face down. The guards enter in the cell with extinguishers and cover the floor and the walls with a white liquid that solidifies turning into a hard crust. The inmates go out from under the bed and they have to remove the crust in less than an hour, when the inspection comes to check if everything shines "bulb".

Arriving to Gherla in the cell where I am, admiral Horia Măcelaru exclaims: heaven on earth! He comes from Râmnicu Sărat where he lived six years alone in a cell; subject to a starvation regime, he ate the straws from the (worn out) mattress on which he was sleeping, all of them; to the end only the cover cloth remained. The leather of chagrin, pictured otherwise. In the adjacent cell Ion Mihalache[115] died, after blinding.

Maybe this is the hell, the madhouse.

On a more temperate level, I come too to the conviction that the political prison was conceived on the basis of the cybernetic concepts of retroaction and spontaneous morphogenesis. Let the prisoners torture each other. Economy of means: the guards will intervene only too little. The convicts will create their own inferno. That's how it happened. Because of the people subjected to the conditions of a "punishment execution room" I suffered much more than because of the cops on the corridors.

The cell chiefs, conscientious, reglementar and fearful, the maniacal comrades of hygiene (What are you doing, mister! you took the kettle after you scratched your butt. Don't you see you have thrown your snot in my bed?) fulfilled the plan based on the true idea that heavy jail is nothing, a trifle, apple pie, compared to the madhouse.

Telling everywhere Huis clos by Sartre I was hoping to reveal this secret and thus to annihilate its effects. I was listened to with attention (the hotel room, which in the play represents the hell, evoked well enough the prison life conditions to capture the interest), but the results proved to be null, according to the advice given by lord Chesterfield to his son: you will hear many beautiful speeches in the House of Commons, some will change your opinions, take care that none will change your vote. Amazing thing, the boyars, the great landlords, the university professors, the bishops and the high rank dignitaries proved to be less exigent about the hygiene than the shepherds, the workers and the peasants, that most of them were – according to their own saying – disgusting and gingerly to food and they kept imposing prophylactic rules more severe than at the Pasteur institute, or rules for using the barrel and hands washing more strict than the tribal rituals or the defecation ceremony of a brahman.

Gherla, May 1963

Twice operated, horribly meager, barely walking, most of the day in bed and covered with the blanket, plunged in prayers, father Haralambie V. awaits the death. He finds somehow the means and the power to talk to us a little bit. Being a monk, he accepts the end with serenity but not without cares; as a sensible man who prepares himself for a long trip and knows it's not laughing matter, it's wise to think in advance of everything, to make the necessary preparations and to equip yourself, thinking that it is better to be plenty than scarce.

He grants me some time and looking at him, speaking to him, I am overwhelmed by the conviction that the sufferance has meaning, that life in its whole it's not possible to be meaningless. As always, I am obsessed with Sartre's formulation – We are doomed to be free – that is not without strength and truth, even theologically. And the correction given by Merleau-Ponty: we are doomed to give meaning to the things. Sorin Vasilie: not the reality is important, but the truth (which is something else) and the meaning. The patriarch Athenagora: What today's man hungers for? For love and meaning.

To father Haralambie – as to a saint – I dare to confess – he is the first – the two dreams I had at Jilava a year and a half ago, in the cell 25.

Once my mother showed herself to me in a dream – she was always going to Capra, to the church, and she was speaking Romanian so clean and charming – and, taking me by hand, she brought me to a wall of a House of the Lord. A huge wall fully painted with figures of saints and covered with icons. She was leading me toward the painted visages and she was prompting me to kiss them.

The second dream was more earthquake like, and I call it dream because I don't dare to call it otherwise.

It was very cold in the cell 25. The winter of '62 was tough, with huge snow heaps and yells of blizzard. Odobescu in Lady Chiajna: It is sad and ugly the winter in the countryside. Sad and ugly was in cell 25 section 2 too.

The chimney of the stove fell down, we cannot even make the poor fire of three chips that we could light between December 15th and March 1st. The soot covers everything with a thick, fat layer of black slime, continuously growing, adhesive. Shivering with cold, we feel overwhelmed by filth – and we are hungry. Because of the snow the supplies were probably cut. They distribute us only once a day and at irregular intervals a small piece of cold corn bread. We have no more water. The barrel is overflowing. Strange, the frost, instead of neutralizing the smell, it exasperates it. We wait for the arrival of the polenta like some locked animals whose feeding relies upon a forgetful master. The corn bread is an ice stone and is made out of baked corn meal, not boiled.

In the atmosphere of trembling, sorrow, ice and dirt I manage to be calm. The cell is composed only out of good and polite people. And we don't despair, between us we are gentle, joyful as only in jail people can be – premonition of the monastic hesychasm or of the heavenly happiness. A big bessarabian landlord, especially nice: Cimpoieşu, and others. Next to me slips a chauffeur – he is the very chauffeur of Cimpoieşu, sent to judgement together with his master and sentenced to a shuddering number of years. (Like Cherciu, the chauffeur of Alimăneşteanu, because he was bringing food to his master at the forced domicile in Bărăgan[116].) He behaved very well at trial, he followed his master to jail, the way the squires were following their masters in crusades, wars or adventures. The specifics of the jail regime, however, he cannot bear. He's nervous and – like most of the simple people – he suffers because of the promiscuity, filth and misery more painfully than the intellectuals and the members of the upper class. He is bothered by the – "horrible" – snores of a neighbor. With shyness he asks me to switch places: to move myself in his place, closer to the source of snores and him in my place. The distance that he can make this way is without any importance, but the man has illusions and in this case, where everything takes place in a neuropsychic plane, a simple displacement of a few centimeters may contribute to the process of calming down. We make the switch.

(It's easy for me because I stayed in cell 80 at Gherla with a kind and cultivated man, general C-tescu-Țăranu, the unbeatable snorer of all times and prisons. The noise he was producing was so invincible, so irresistible and terrible, that you couldn't even think about slipping in the same room with him. Especially because it was not an uniform noise, but an unending series of booms always different, always surprising – a true inventive gamut of an artist whose style would renew continuously. You would eventually come after weeks of living together to doze away, but only now and then – like those naval captains destined that neither after years to get rid of sea sickness. Nor barley did I manage to eat earlier than after three years of prison.)

Next day, toward evening, the chauffeur asks me with even more shyness: he wants, however, to come back to his first place: where he slept it's not convenient, there is air flow. We change it back.

And the next day the maneuver repeats.

About two o'clock in the night a new batch of people is brought, a big bunch, plenty over full, only them were missing. And how pitiful they look around, are they coming from less sinister places? We received them the way they didn't expect, in silence and making fun of sorrow. But where to accommodate them? Everybody crowds together to create new spaces – imaginary most of them, like those of the Riemann geometry. Some of them have no choice but to doze on the benches. One of them, big, exasperated and wretched – whose face expresses sufferance and fatigue

– I invite him to stay in my place, together we wouldn't fit; and, anyway, you can see he needs badly two or three hours of sleep. I spent the rest of the night on the bench.

Next night I fall asleep broken. And then, in that very night, a miraculous dream is given to me, a vision. I don't see the Lord Christ embodied, but only a huge light – white and bright – and I feel happy beyond words. The Light surrounds me, is a total happiness, and removes everything; I am soaked in blinding light, I float in light, I am in light and I rejoice. I know it will last forever, it is a perpetuum immobile. I am the light tells me, but not by words, but by the transmission of thought. I am: and I understand with the intellect and with the heart – I understand that it is the Lord and that I am inside the light of Tabor, that not only that I see it but I live in its middle.

More than anything else I am happy, happy, happy. I am and I understand that I am and I am telling it to myself. And the light seems more shining than light itself and seems like it is talking and it tells me what it is. The dream seems to last for ever and ever. The happiness not only that lasts forever but it is ever growing; if evil is bottomless, then good is without ceiling, the circle of light grows wider and wider, and the happiness, after softly embracing me, suddenly changes its tactics, becomes hard, jumps, falls on me like some avalanches that – antigravitationally – raise me; then, again, proceeds otherwise: sweetly, it rocks me – then finally, unsparingly, it replaces me. I am no more. I still am, but so strong that I don't recognize myself. [117]

(Since then I feel awfully ashamed. Of stupidity, of evilness, of filth. Of moods. Of guile. Shame.)

Father Haralambie listens to me attentively, he doesn't smile, he doesn't look surprised. Then he pronounces: he doesn't believe that the dreams or apparitions are suspect. On the contrary, he congratulates me. However he asks from me discretion and humble restraint. And especially – it is hard to understand, he says, still he asks me to do an effort – to consider them natural, something not extraordinary, something that shouldn't remove me from the common way of life. A good thought from my mother, like a greeting. And the mercy of Lord is plenty: when He passes, it happens that the hem of His coat to touch you'd wonder who.

We also make plans for the future, the father – like all authentic dying men – being one hundred percent convinced he is going to die and also one hundred percent convinced he is going to live.

But only few days pass and he has a strong hemorrhage. It knocks him down. The prisoner doctor, called on insistently, arrived late, shakes his head. The chief of the cell wraps father Haralambie in a blanket, and I bring him, with the help of another prisoner, next to the cell door from where, we standing with the face toward the wall and with the our arms covering the eyes, the guards – taking him from the floor – carry him to the infirmary.

I found out that he died next day.

–   Péguy, mobilized in August 1914: he went to say good bye to all his friends and to make up with all his enemies. He wandered through Paris from one end to the other. He apologized to all the people he wronged: he didn't forget a maid from the house of a friend, having the feeling that once he talked to her harshly. He left decided to die for the cause he believed, not to mention the universal Republic and the last of wars. And he was serious: he died in that very September, being overzealous, standing upright to command more precisely the fire of his people. Down, lieutenant, down… He didn't listen. But in the same time he asked his wife to buy and keep for him, during the war, all the journals he was interested in.

You know nothing about people as long as you don't keep continuously in your mind the simultaneity of the pluralism of the contradictory plans of conscience.

BUGGY MAMBO RAG

… "Corn" has three plurals, "coarne", "cornuri" and "corni"[118]… I was lucky to find at eighty-three many people who knew well The shirt of Christ: I heard it told in detail after that in other cells... Pa vu ga de ke zo ni... Marcellus tells to Demetrios...

October-November 1962

At that time many will fall from their faith; they will betray one another and hate one another. Matt. 24, 10

In cell 44, from Gherla, infirmary cell, I know the exact opposite atmosphere compared to that of tunnel 34 from Reduit.

The hate boils, the denunciation is at home, the envy and the feud installed their chairs, the demons are dancing and Beelzebub plays hopscotch as on his father's estate, he has no worry. Nettles, hemlock, belladona. After all, writes Bergson, why not suppose a life founded not on combinations of oxygen, nitrogen, hydrogen and carbon, but on combinations of cobalt for instance? And why would not be worlds where not the carbon dioxide but ammonia insures the photosynthesis and the growth? The anthroposophy of Rudolf Steiner describes besides our harmonic universe another one, syncopated.

In room 44 from Gherla there is a syncopated world, an ammonia world. Distrust and suspicion laid waste everywhere, like the scorching whips of wind in the steppe. Not only that people don't talk to each other politely, they don't even insult each other. The oppressing clouds of the electricity of anger meet the flabby clouds of scowling. A heavy haze, sometime disturbed by the throbs of spontaneous clashes.

Every patient is convinced that the others are just faking it. The medic prisoners notify the cops about the numerous suspected cases of simulation. Upon each kettle falls maliciously the searching envious gaze of those around. The little medication given to a sick man is weighted by the eyes and by the mind more exactly than a pharmaceutical precision scale.

It is the marsh phase of which talks the Booklet of the nest chief[119].

Colonel Marinescu, nervously ill, bursts into hysterical tears several times a day; he is considered a show off. The peasant Benea from Blaga's village is paralyzed and he must carried in arms to the barrel. Hardly I find someone willing to help me to carry "this crook". Păstorel, because he is distant, is ferociously hated. Dr. Răileanu, savant phtisiologist medic and biologist, indeed a very aloof nature, but also retired, they want to beat him. He is saved by general Vatamanu, who is considered a terrible liar because he recounts the aurocch hunts he participated to.

The room chief is a conscientious and he suffers from insomnia. When I happen to get descend during the night to go to the barrel, just my boots awake him from the drowsiness he achieved after long efforts. He curses me and he throws at me glances so heavy with hate that I loose my voice; of course I drop a boot a couple of times – with a thundering and stormy noise – which makes him right in the eyes of everybody.

The accusations of stealing are like a chain reaction. We are given a small bottle of about fifty grams of lactic acid and I am in charge with distributing it to those that belong to the category "digestive disorders" (most of them are cases of intestinal tuberculosis) where I fall too. I took the bottle from the peephole, I went directly to the ten sick people, I took from everybody their personal bottles, I put all the bottles (including mine) on a window sill and with the dropper I put an equal number of drops, rectifying and pottering about until I reached an absolute equality. The empty bottle and the dropper remained where I worked, and the others (ten) I restitute to their owners, for myself keeping the eleventh.

After a quarter of an hour the rumor is spreading that coming from the door I passed the tub with water (I couldn't pass through somewhere else), that I took water and I replaced the lactic acid with water that I distributed, keeping the acid entirely for myself.

The accusation is fantastic – as the characters of Moliére like to say: I didn't have the time to do the operation they attributed to me and I would have been seen by everybody, caught in the act.

It doesn't matter. The chief of the room and a bunch of professional inquisitors subscribe. I am in luck: nobody consumed the drops. I gather again the bottles, I pour the contents in the common bottle, without pouring the content of my bottle. I give it to the chief of the room to taste it; which he does making a grimace because of the sourness. I pour then the liquid from my bottle – and the common bottle is filled.

Although the proof is made, I don't convince anybody.

BUGGY MAMBO RAG

…What are you talking, it is a quote from Milton… My opponent was Istrati Micescu, and what do you think… Yes, blaireau[120], dammit… Von Steuben, the Prussian baron general, was close to be elected president of United States after winning the independence war… Oh, yes, it's from Goethe: Wärte das Auge nicht sonnenhaft so konnte es die Sonne nicht erblicken… Without butter and cocoa has no charm, just that the butter… Malaysia! Kuala Lumpur. Luang Prabang is in Laos… No, dear, forgive me for contradicting you, Leghorn are white, the red ones are Rhode Island…

–   The passion of envy is incomparably more active than the selfishness, benign malady. And the virus of equality prompts us to desire the bad for all of us with frenzy. Cioran: better everybody in hell and as deeper as possible, rather than someone to enjoy something more. I have seen the thirst of egalitarian hell in many cells, where a sort of version of the law of final utility of Böhm- Bawerk worked without fail: the envy is in inverse proportion with the size of the difference between the units that compose a human collectivity.

At Dante and Jules Romains is different. In the Paradise, those from the third heaven do not envy those from the fifth heaven: they are glad for the others joy, participate to their beatitude, and with their place in the inferior heaven are happy. Jules Romains in Les hommes de bonne volonté[121]: I prefer to leave in a small room in the mansard of a palace rather than in a salon of the same decrepit and devastated building.

The society of yesterday was made from selfish people, lead by their own interest; everyone was thinking of himself and that's why it was easy to be happy then. Concerned with his own well- being, the man didn't care about the well-being of others.

(Was the man indifferent to other's unhappiness? Answer: 1) no matter what is the regime, the man would still be indifferent to other's unhappiness: 2) but regarding the happiness of another he is not indifferent – he will be envious, using any despicable means to undermine it – except if he is enough preoccupied with a possible accomplishment of his own happiness.)

I keep my eyes closed in room 44: ah! how must have been those walks in Europe before World War I – Edward VII with the cigar in the corner of the mouth, incognito in the alleys and the cafés of Marienbad – and ah! (quote Galsworthy) Bucharest on a September day with a opalescent green sky: the Pantelimon highway, torpid in a day of August, September, and so many cold pubs on each side; the Armenească street, quiet as a patriarchal of Şt. O. Iosif, during winter time, when in the stoves the fire throbs…

I turned crazy and idyllic, these clichés are ridiculous, stereotype… Yet, where does it come from this persistent fresh fragrance of melilot, of wet soil, of warm bread? (Yo, tells me Al. Pal. after getting out of jail, you've become a sowerist[122], worse than Romulus Şeişanu, Timoleon Pisani and those from the "Universe" and from "The youth contest". I was told that your preferred author is Nicolae Densuşianu!)

Malmaison, cell 12

When the cop stops in front of the door, I manage to lift (very little) the black glasses; I use the hand that he doesn't hold tightly. It doesn't have any importance if you know or not the cell to which you are assigned, but I feel that any detained or convicted makes a point of honor in knowing it. The cop sees me and he hits me harshly. It is fair: the forms must be observed – the form is the guaranty of the law – we do our duty everybody, we are even.

Cell 12 must be very close to Plevna street because I can hear very clearly the bells of the church situated behind a small garden between the streets Ştefan Furtună (General Angelescu)[123] and Witting.

The bell creates a sonorous space of its own – a true universe. Who is in the range of its waves participate at the state of exaltation and fascination always and necessarily caused by any bell. Poe: Bells, bells, bells, bells. The comforting force enters in cell 12 where my colleague and I live like humans and not like beasts only when the unseen neighboring church sends us the victorious message of its bells.

The first effect of incarceration, accentuated by the bells: the feeling of guilt. Although we are here based on some phantasmagoric accusations, we fully realize a general culpability: toward ourselves, life and people. We are innocent regarding the accusations brought against us. Oh! how guilty regarding all the rest. We bear on our shoulders, on our back, soul, the sins of the world. And the suffering of the animals: Markel, the brother of Zossima: yes, because of our sin they come to eat one another and to be hunted.

(In Islam everybody is obligated to be, at least once in life, pilgrim. If one wasn't, then his inheritor has to fulfill the obligation. But not only the inheritor: anyone has to do the holy pilgrimage in the name of all those that did not do it, everybody is responsible for all. So do we.)

Jilava, February 1962

Bruder Harald, in the presentation of the life and the work of Martin Luther, quotes and comments the essential words uttered at Worms in 1517: Hier stehe Ich; Ich kann nicht anders. Got helfe mir. Amen.[124]

Words of a prince. Other thing than: "What could I have done? I signed." (The reasoning of the rebel monk is the opposite: as for signing, I won't sign, what I'll do we'll see, Lord have mercy.)

When I go at night, after the taps, to the barrel that is in the opposite side of the tunnel-cell and I walk the whole room until my bed – according to the disposition of sergeant Ungureanu it is near the door – all the others are in their places, sleeping: I prefer to remain the last one because my miserable guts force me not to hurry. I pass, therefore, as in a procession between the two rows of people prepared to sleep and I take care to wish good night to each and everyone. I am answered with fervor and amiability and I feel happy that I can feel their sympathy and that I act as I should.

Of course, I know that I act well and by this very knowledge I suppress the good. The existentialists are right here: since we have the conscience of the good we are doing, the awareness compromises without remedy. The awareness is annihilative, forbids candor, the serene and innocent performance of the good. It spoils any elegant action.

They are and they aren't right these existentialists. They go a little too fast, these prestidigitators. The awareness spoils but not without remedy. We are not pure children, we are not saints. But we also aren't – badabing – some bastards, some salauds[125]. Saints, no; of course. But maybe the next best[126], that is impostors of the good.

The saints are the limit. After them come the heroes and then the noble men and at the end, limping, the darers of the good, a bit ridiculous, kind of gasping, but they are useful too.

We know we are doing the good – and therefore we taint it – but we are doing the good and not the evil. We do not share the cleanliness of the saints, but we are still doing something that raises us from the ranks of the bastards. There is, I think, – between les salauds and those from cell 34 (and other impostors of the good) – a difference.

There is, here at 34 something else, different than the heat that torments the cowards, the squealers and the defeated. (And they always pity themselves and they lament: the mewing of the defeat and treason. And they are very proud of their surrender: the vanity suits not only the stupid but also the villain[127].) It is actually something easy to recognize, as a tonic, as an intense color. The nobility and the chivalry are not simple nostalgia, they are from a different domain (as the Christianity that they reflect): of the secrets or the happiness recipes.

– Maybe is pure blasphemy, but I have a theory of mine according to which Christ does not appear in the Gospels only gentle, kind, righteous, sinless, merciful, strong, and so on.

From the accounts of the Gospels – without exception – He also appears endowed with all the wonderful qualities of a gentleman and a knight.

First He stays at the door and He knocks. Second He trusts people, He is not suspicious. And the trust is the first attribute of the boyar and the knight, the suspicion being, on the contrary, the fundamental trait of the şmecher. The gentleman is the person who – until the categorical contrary proof – trusts anyone and he doesn't hurry, avidly, to believe the defamation against one of his friends. For the şmechers and the scoundrels the first reaction is always the suspicion and the incomparable satisfaction – to know that the neighbor is as dirty as they are.

Further. Christ forgives easily and fully. The şmecher never forgives, or if he concedes (without really forgiving), he is doing it with difficulty, forcibly and in installments. But the Lord: "I do not condemn you either. Go and sin no more." I do not condemn you either…

He is always willing and ready to help. He feels pity. The widow from Nain, the blind men, the crippled woman, He helped them without being asked. He knows how to graduate the appreciation, gives to everyone what belongs to them. To the Canaanite woman who showed so much perseverance and courage, he speaks more than to others that saves, He uses a complementary formula: You are a woman of great faith! (Only to her: only to her the exclamation and the epithet great.)

He is always – and especially careful about this – attentive and polite; friend he says to Judas. Never an insult or a despising word to a sinner. You cannot see from any text haughty morals, or hypocrite bashfulness. And there is no prerequisite condition imposed to the sinners, no discrimination: Who comes to

Me I will not send him out. He welcomes the prodigal son (but while he was till a long way off...) And when he gives, he gives, plentifully, more than required, like a boyar. (What can be more far from the petty accountancy and the Pharisee's precise reckoning and better proof of generosity than these words from John 3, 34: "Measureless is God's gift of the Spirit"? The economic, no, the word is too mild, the administrative worry of Judas for the money spent on unction shows, on the one hand, that the traitor lacked generosity, and on the other hand that God passed – like a boyar – over calculation and avarice (granted they are disguised in charity works) to taste the joy of squandering (which is the same as sacrificing) in moments of spiritual elevation. This is also a noble gesture, the aristocrat being always ready to sacrifice his life or to disperse his fortune. (The aristocrat will give his life sometimes in duel for mundane motifs or he will loose his fortune at cards – but his behavior, as everything that is earthly, is just an awkward imitation of the generous virtues; isn't the physical love just a pitiable counterfeit of the divine love?)

Trust in people, courage, detachment, goodwill toward the wretched people from whom you can't get any advantage (sick, foreigners, prisoners), a sure sense of grandeur, the predisposition for forgiveness, the contempt for the prudent and the miser: all these are traits of the gentleman and the knight.

He prompts all people to acknowledge what they really are: sons of the Father, of the master. From this point of view the book that is the closest to the Gospels is Don Quijote, since the knight of La Mancha tells to the customers of the pub that they are in a castle wihout knowing and he asks them to behave as the aristocrats they are.

Prince Myshkin, when the actions of Ganya are alike those of a lout and an usurer, how does he react? He feels pity and he's ashamed of the one who forgot (in anger and in his thirst for money) the title of child of God.

– The situation of the Christian is the same as the aristocrat statute.

Why? Because he has its basis in the most "aristocrat" attributes: liberty and trust (faith). What is the noble, the feudal? More than anything a free man.

What is faith? Trust in the Lord, although the world is wicked, despite the injustice, in defiance of the baseness, notwithstanding from everywhere come only negative signals.

The words of Tolstoi (in Anna Karenina, the scene of the election of the nobility marshal of the province): "This is why we are noble, to have trust."

BUGGY MAMBO RAG

The inhabitants of Besançon, do you know how they are called? What about Charleville? And Monaco?... Not because I was his minister, but you should know that Ferdinand[128] was not the blockhead your people[129] pretended he was. He was a noted botanist, a good polyglot, he knew Hebrew, was a theologian and a numismatist... I believe at Einsiedeln, yes, the black Virgin is at the monastery of Einsiedeln... they are called Bisotins, those from Charleville, Carlopolitans; from Monaco, Monegasques... yes, he liked gypsy women. It is in Baudelaire: Horloge! dieu sinistre, effrayant, impassible[130]... you have to acknowledge he was not the stupid man invented by you; he was very generous with the acolyte officers: look, the story of my brother: at Christmas everybody was receiving a cigar and a gold coin... Ah, I see you don't know, robin in English is robin[131], and wren is wren[132], let's see if you know birch tree in French... And Maria[133], how unjust you have been toward her... Marcellus tells to Demetrios...

1966

In L'Otage[134], Claudel state something extremely important, that all the experience of life and the world's spectacle since the end of World War II keeps confirming, piercingly.

"Let's see, says Coufontaine to Turelure, what will happen if the world of affection and trust will be replaced by the world of competition."

It might very well be that in the old world the comforting words affection and trust ended up by being emptied of their content, to become formal as so many others. But we saw what it means a world based only on competition, the world whose emanation, the dialectics, put the cherry on the cake bringing its followers, hate, envy and suspicion.

The great secret of all the misfortunes: the suspicion. The poison, the weed, the conflagration.

Not in vain for Bergson the time is a source of unexpected surprises and the evolution is creative.

Proof: who thought in the first years of this century that these would be our main problems: fear, generalized suspicion, almighty şmecher? Yet they are. For us the futilities– as Camus calls the problem of Copernicus and Galileo, the heliocentricism or the geocentricism – are the grave and naïve problems of the beginning of the XX century: the progress, the spread of the liberal democracy, the beneficial science.

We have other worries.

And among them the painful problem of the suspicion turned into an endemic disease. (Duhamel was asking himself in 1928 why it takes so much a dinner in a restaurant in

Moscow; and he was surprised finding out that the reason: the performing of the recording operations and accounting control for every kind of food. Mostly, this is the cause of the slowness and the expensiveness in the socialist economic system.)

For Christianity the suspicion is a grave and horrible sin. For Christianity the trust is the moral avenue for the regeneration of a person. Only the man forges his peers proportionally with the trust he gives them and proves to them. The

90

distrust is deadly like the infanticide; annihilates as a man the one to which is administrated. The man himself, created by God, transforms his fellow man in a person – through a secondary act of creation – by virtue of the trust he shows to him (Claudel).

Naming the animals, according to the divine command, the man arranged them in the frame of creation; loving his neighbor and endowing him trust, makes out of him a Person, another thing than an individual.

That's why the suspicion is so harmful. Out of a human person transforms the suspected into

–   into what? Not in a brute, it would be too good, in something much more evil, in the most abject, damaging, cancerous thing that may be – into a şmecher.

Corollary: when we reached the conclusion that an individual or a group of individuals enters under the attribute of scoundrel or scoundrels, another is the procedure (also Christian): the dispatched, unhesitating action – the eradication.

BUGGY MAMBO RAG

…She was passionate, that's true. But also how beautiful and magnificent… and how much owns to her Grand Romania[135] nobody knows… Yes, Stere and Marghiloman[136] were sophisticated and intelligent people, but you should know, the true heroes were on the other side, were the idealists and the polenta eaters[137] lead by your doltish Ferdinand and your whorish Maria… Do you know how it is called the style of Rimbaud? what about Giraudoux? The French campaign in Italy against the Austrians, in 1859? By the armistice of Villafranca and the peace treaty from Zürich… Yes, bouleau[138], that was easy, what about maple tree?… She never lost courage, hope… all the time, then in Paris at the peace negotiations – who, if not her?…

–   Biblical texts referring to the thesis: Christianity is a religion of courage:

–   many times the Christ's prompting: Take heart, my son, Take heart, my daughter (Matt. 9, 2; 9, 22; Mark 10, 49; Luke 8, 48), Take heart (Mark 6, 50; John 16, 33);

–   the encouragement Do not be afraid (Mark 5, 36; 6, 50; Luke 1, 13; 1, 30; 5, 10; 8, 50; 2,

10; 12, 7; 24, 36; John 6, 20), Do not be alarmed (Mark 16, 6);

–   on the list of those destined to the lake of fire, who are the first? The cowards (Rev. 21, 8); and the admonishing: Why are you such cowards? (Mark 4, 40);

–   and especially the disclosure of the great secret: "The kingdom of the heaven is taken by perseverance, and those that endeavor earn it" (Matt. 11, 12);

(In other versions: is taken by charge and the attackers are taking it. The old English Bible talks about violence and violent men, the new one says it is violated and taken by force. The Frenchmen refer to the force too. The Germans give the equivalent Gewalt but after that they use a more expressive verb: reisen es weg.)

The Christian is the one to whom God did not give the spirit of fear (2 Tim. 1, 7) and he can lead the unseen war (Nicodemus Aghiorit?); is a good soldier of Jesus Christ (2 Tim. 2, 3) girded with the truth, dressed in the armor of righteousness, the helmet of salvation, the sword of the Spirit.

A religion confessed by the physical courage of the martyrs (Phil. 1, 28-30: meeting your opponents without so much as a tremor... for you have been granted not only of believing in Christ but also of suffering for Him... your conflict is the same as mine...)

What does Paul says? I will not fear! (Heb. 13, 6) What about John? In love there is no room for fear; indeed, perfect love banishes fear. (1 Jn. 4, 18).

–   The constitutional law was in college my preferred subject. Insatiable and anxious to go right to the essence, I kept asking myself what is the ultimate secret of the subject I was fond of from the beginning. (I was helped to fall in love by: Manole, whose theory was that if we cannot live in the Lords Chamber and among crowned heads and the great figures of history, we can at least come near them by the constitutional law; and I. V. Gruia, my public law (?) professor in the first year, who I was going to answer and repay him in 1945 with such un ugly behavior.)

Any science has its basic secret that can be surprised in the moments of crisis. Of the constitutional law, only after the years of prison and after the baptism I came to understand is the physical courage in the face of death.

The constitutional law – no matter how sophisticated are the other definitions – I believe is the science of guaranteeing the liberty. (An arbitrary definition? The axioms are arbitrary too.) And the liberty cannot be guaranteed in the end by any law, any constitution, any court of justice or juridical procedure. The constitutional justice court from Karlsruhe, conceived by the German juridical spirit (another one than that of Ihering, for whom the law was not just a high science but also a live power), proved to be in 1932 an illusion. The Mexican procedure amparo, that seduced so many jurists, is a patch too. (What better proof than the fact that belongs to a country where the following presidential decree was given: Art. 1 – No one can be general if he did not serve before as a soldier for at least one year. Art. 2 – Our minister state secretary at War is in charge with carrying out the present decree.) Or the High Cassation French Court, did it stop the coup d'état from December 2nd 1851?

And the things cannot happen otherwise with any constitution, procedure, or justice court. It cannot be otherwise because there is the Michelson-Morley experiment.

The experiment of the physicists Michelson and Morley proved with certainty that inside a closed system you cannot make observations of the absolute movement of that system because the observer, being himself inside the system, is caught, hence rallied in the absolute movement of it. Therefore, he cannot "exit" from it to observe it from "outside" and to emit objective observations with non-relative value.

In the domain of the public law the things are identical. Every political order has its "year zero"; from that moment starts the respective legal system. A justice court made inside a political system does not have the ability to "exit" the juridical system created by the respective political system and to override it in order to sanction it with its authority of simple creature. The juridical control of the constitutionality of the laws can function only from the one year zero until the next year zero, it never knew how to stop the apparition of a new political era: it dies together with the entire mathematical series that reached its limit. A cassation and a justice court relate to the respective juridical system, closed as a galaxy. It can appreciate the validity of the regular laws of the regime from the point of view of their conformity with the principles of the system, but it is as impossible for it to defeat the axioms of the regime as it is for the observer to notice the absolute movement of the system that he is a part of and that carries him with it.

What is left then to insure the freedom? Which is the sure warranty? Only one: the physical courage of the individuals. Even queen Victoria and king Edward VII – given as examples of constitutional monarchs – tried to remove from the position of prime-minister persons that they did not like. The unwavering solidarity of the political parties made them, with politeness, check-mate.

These were cases when only firmness was required. In other cases, more serious, the guaranty that never fails is only the physical courage in the face of death. This is the final secret of the constitutional law, toward which lead me Manole and I.V. Gruia, and the Christian faith confirmed it to me later.

The great spirits found out this elementary truth (elementary, but requires attention) long ago. For instance:

Descartes: All the difficulties come from the fact that you lack courage. Henry de Montherlant: Courage! We always come back to this word: courage!

Saint-Just: The circumstances are difficult only for those that pull back from the sight of their grave.

Fr. Rauh: No matter the social morals, shoudn't you be brave?

To whom says he loves freedom, it should apply the words said by a French actress from the XVIII century (Sophie Arnould) in whose presence an old general (he was not hearing well) was repeating the word uttered by her: what? fear?... The actress toward a valet: bring quickly a dictionary, I used a word that the general never heard.

But the most unequivocal is Brice Parain, definitively: If we want to be free, we should not be afraid to die, that's all.

(Maybe Corneille was melodramatic and grandiloquent, but he knew constitutional law.)

–   The device of the French revolution (adopted by the republic too), as people know it today (Liberty, equality, fraternity) is false and truncated. The whole device of the revolution was another

–   and the difference is like from earth to sky: liberty, equality, fraternity or death.

The two dropped words represent the deplorable mutation from courage and tragedy and heroic sentiment of existence to a bureaucratic formula of a vague principle for whose sake nobody is willing to risk his skin. The way, says Péguy, is always from mystics to politics.

Liberty, equality, fraternity is a simple slogan while the French revolution was a catastrophe; liberty, equality, fraternity or death is something completely different, a Barthian ganz-anders: it is a determination that makes any adversary bows with admiration and utmost respect.

–   Maybe the skeptics are more elegant and more attractive than the "fanatics", but when the pest breaks at Bordeaux, the mayor – named Michel Eyquem de Montagne – leaves the city; at Milano, in 1576, in the same situation and almost in the same period, the archbishop, St. Carol Boromeo, returns hurriedly from his trip.

–   In our time people laugh – the decisive influence is of the şmechers – of those who go to death. A Romanian, Eugen Ionescu, protested against the intellectuals contaminated by şmechers. (Using the occasion of the film realized by T. Richardson about the war in Crimea and the inutile charge at Balaklava.) They were answered long ago by another Romanian, a poet, Ion Barbu, who understood what sacrifice meant and how clean may shine the blade pulled from sheath – le sabre au clair – for serving justice:

Shared washings? Renew Argents more baptizing

And the heart of the riders – burned By this righteous ascending day.

–   The Michelson-Morley experiment may be useful for something else too. To solve the great problem: since God is beyond good and evil, it means there is no good or evil and the doing of good becomes a simple illusion, a useless obsession.

That God stays beyond our notions of good and evil there is no doubt. It is said by a great theologian as Meister Eckhart, it said by the entire apophatic theology. (God cannot be defined based on positive attributes, but only on a negative way: He is not good, not bad, not big…), but especially is said by the Savior Himself: "The Father… causes the sun to rise on good and bad alike, and sends the rain on the innocent and the wicked." Matt. 5, 45; idem Luke 6, 35: "He Himself is kind to the ungrateful and the wicked.")

The answer to the question why – in these conditions – is still worth to do the good is given by the experience Michelson-Morley. We are parts of a close system from where we cannot make absolute observations of the moral fundaments of the universe. We are not in the situation of God, but in the situation

94

of the man, which actually cannot know anything. Who says he knows is wrong, it is shown by the Michelson-Morley experiment. We can know some little things, some trifles: that the sum of the angles of a triangle is equals to 180 degrees, that the heart has two auricles and two ventricles, that, on the international scale, from grade six up the earthquakes are devastating... and others of this sort. The great absolute truths cannot be known because of the experiment Michelson- Morley: we are inside the system, we cannot make any absolute observations nor have certitudes. What can we have? Just intuitions, clues, beliefs.

We can only believe, when it is about serious things.

And we believe that in this close system where we live the only way to approach the absolute God (the one that is neither good nor bad) is the way of good.

It is an intuitive belief, uncertain, relative, strictly empirical, naïve, childish. Yet is the only one.

Why do we accept it?

Because the good (and only the good) teaches us to do Christ in who we believe and who is our Mediator with the absolute Father situated beyond good and evil; who when He was incarnated, walked only on the path of good. And for another reason: our existential experience proves us that only when we do the good we acquire something the evil ones can never have: quiet and peace – the supreme goods.

(I don't know that it is so. I believe that it is so and I observe – experimentally – that it is so.)

God is not good or bad, but here, in our relative experience, in our close system dominated exclusively by the results of the aforementioned experiment, for us who cannot have absolute knowledge, here and for us, temporarily and relatively, the only way giving quiet and peace and access to Christ (who on this earth, as long as He stayed, did only the good and made us understand that for the time being only the good can lead us to the absolute) is the performing of good. We are asked in this matter also humility; the humility to realize that we are not in the situation of the divinity, but of the creature. God can be beyond good and evil, we can't.

– Al. Pal.: You see everything theologically. You became a theologian!

I: Of course. The human condition is a theological condition. This is the great specific trait of the man: not the laugh, the tears, nor the lie, the general category reasoning (Julian Huxley)... The specific attribute of the man is the theological reasoning.

– What lead to the establishment of the dictatorship in Germany? The cowardice of the social-democrats and of the Prussian minister of internal affairs, Severing, that let himself being thrown out from his office of chief of the almighty Berlin police by two unidentified individuals and the presence, (noticed from the window) of a so-called military platoon in the ministerial building yard. I surrender to the force, said Severing with pomposity. No way, he was surrendering to the nothingness.

What permitted the French republicans to annihilate the very popular and powerful general Boulanger? The courage of the prime-minister Charles Floquet.

On my list of favorite heroes in a place of great honor is this little known name; a man who was just a politician and he occupied just the little exciting function of prime-minister of the third republic. But a hero he was – and what a formidable guy!

He was president of the Chamber when the czar came to Paris, for the first time since the proclamation of France as a republic. They introduced to the czar the high dignitaries. Floquet shouted to his face: "Long live Poland, mister!"

Him, the civilian, did not hesitate to challenge the spruce general Boulanger to a duel; and not only that he challenged him to a duel, but he challenged the cavalier to a duel with the sword; and not only that he challenged him to a duel with the sword but him, the civilian, managed to wound his adversary.

(In these conditions of course it is difficult to take down the legal government.)

He knew also to confront and, if need was, to defy. To the one raising the voice he was answering by raising the voice more, talking from high. At your age, he shouted at Boulanger, Napoleon was dead. But what else isn't he doing? He moves Boulanger to the province, defers him the High Court, puts him under surveillance, retires him, discharges him for mistakes in the service. When the universal suffrage send the general back in the Chamber, the government obtains the invalidation of the election. The internal affairs minister of Floquet, a certain Constans, is just a policeman and he uses procedures lacking elegance, humanity (he threatens Boulanger with the arrest, prompts his mistress, Madam de Bonnemain, to run to Belgium). But if Boulanger concocts plans that are not in accordance with the strictest legality, then why would the government be ashamed of it? Equal weapons, this is a sacred principle.

Severing and his social-democrats didn't even try to resist. Their argument is that any attempt would have been useless. You never know! An act always stirs new series of possibilities: it is your duty to give fate a chance, time and probability are not perfectly predictable – and also the reaction of the people in favor of leaders who don't let themselves trampled under foot. There is also this disparaged word: honor.

It doesn't befit the statesmen to play the ingenuous under word of strict respect of legality (on the contrary, they were allowing it to be trampled) and of resignation in face of force (the so- called force) – the thesis of Severing; or under pretext of Christianity (very wrongly understood) – the thesis of lord Halifax. For the statesmen is fitting to defend the public institutions and the public order entrusted to them by the nations. Severing, at least, did not pretend to be Christian.

But the other was committing the grave and shameful error to mistake Christianity for imbecility and guilty weakness.

– Far from me of being a communist, but when I read that one of the ministers of the Commune of Paris, Delescluze, seeing that the cause is lost – May 19th 1871 – takes his top-hat and the rifle and goes to the barricade where is killed, I can't help but feel a shiver and take – at least in my mind! – the military salute position for "honor to the hero", as in front of Saint John Nepomuk, who, rather than divulge to the king of Bohemia the confession of the queen, prefers to be thrown in the waters of Vltava; or in front of monsignor Affre, the archbishop of Paris, killed too, during the bloody clashes from June 1848, also on a barricade. What was he doing there? He left his residence and found a high place from where he was trying to reconcile the belligerents. "The place of the shepherd is with his flock" – the words written on the grave of monsignor Affre at the Notre Dame cathedral –, since he proved them, are not a formula anymore, but a force-idea, energy, life. By their confession by men, the commandments of the Scripture participate from the essence of Cross, named "life-giving" not only because it ensures our resurrection from the dead but also because turns words in acts, the code in clear language, the patterns in live, structured forms, the ideas and the principles in seeds. The blood is fertile; the sufferer on the cross, whoever he is, suffers but he also enjoys a privilege: he is heard and he is not without followers.

Even not having a special sympathy for Protestants, who can say that was not moved, if he was in Paris, by the monument of Coligny on which it is written He remained still as one who saw the unseen emperor?

All is nice and good until proven wrong; then the cards are shown, then, as Paul said, you don't see as in mirror, guessing; but face to face; then remains only this: the courage in face of death. The rest, folks and brothers, the rest represents as the protestors say: not words but speech; not speech but idle talk; not idle talk but slogans.

BUGGY MAMBO RAG

The plural of formula? Formulae, with e... The white cats with eyes of different colors are all deaf, I had one, her name was Miss Puff... You see, these Hungarian nationalists, they are ten, all convicted for nationalism, not one of them speaks to us... like we don't exist... The best hotels in the world are Atlantic in Hamburg, Fontainebleau in Miami, where maître de bouche is a great French aristocrat, and at Taormina, the former transformed monastery... Do not be afraid small flock... The only one among them who speaks to us and treats us well and has pro-Romanian feelings is the engineer Bethlen, a count... not surprising since while in Europe the thirty years war was making ravages, religious war, his ancestor, Gabriel Bethlen, prince of Transylvania, proclaimed already in 1620 the liberty of conscience and the acknowledgment of all confessions... Georges, mon ami, maybe you know what are these aristoloches Gide is talking about in

Paludes? What could they be? They are some climber plants. The Greeks thought they ease the labor pains, wherefrom their name, from the Greek lokhos…

May 1950
Manole, came as never before in great hurry, brings me a sensational news: Marcel Avramescu was ordained priest and he is functioning at the White church. Let's go, says Manole, to see him; we shall call him "father".

He didn't find the new priest at the church.

– I ran into him myself much later, in 1953, when he was transferred at the church of the Mothers' Skete, in an ancient periphery district, in a scenery of religious establishment from past times.

I begin to go often to the now strictly orthodox priest (phenomenon à là Thomas Becket?), with the appearance of a saint painted on a glass icon, with hieratic gestures, hair bound in a tail at the neck and cloaked voice, arrived to us as from a refined Thebaid with mechanic means of transmission.

Acting? Then such a perfect acting that cannot be played except from a text composed by the actor himself. At this level sincerity and artificial become indistinct, as the elements that loose their specific properties and show new behavior close to absolute zero.

Room 18
The Chinese theory of ming presented by dr. Al-G. – the words by themselves don't mean anything unless their content is fulfilled – looks a lot like that of Brice Parain: words are just promises.

It's not enough to be biological father to call yourself father: you still have to behave like the model in which there are gathered in a archetype, the attributes of this title. And so on: the son, the soldier, the teacher, the civil servant, the scholar… (Maybe that's why in the past they were making a difference between teacher and scholar.)

The word is descriptive and virtual. The functioning and the existence of it are provided behaviorally by us.

Gherla, September 1963
Reeking himself cheap perfume (in order not to be blasted by the stench, they all perfume themselves), the "Korean", one of the good cops, enters in the cell early and asks who wants to go out for chores in the factory yard.

As "insincere during the inquiry", and bearer of the label "favoring Legionnaires", and as dystrophic, I was not given any chores up to know.

There are some planks to be carried, explains the Korean benevolently.

The proposition constitutes an exceptional event. It's an opportunity that should not be missed, we get out from of the crowd.

I made a good move, soon I make four years of cell and electricity; the daylight and the sky give the dull and dirty yard of the factory a fairylike aspect and – because of some little wagons that circulate transporting lumber – an aspect of toy store, of Disneyland; The doll fairy by Bayer, Through the looking glass! You feel like frolicking, singing, mounting the wagons; we spend a lovely day, we eat in open air, we speak loudly, we laugh, we almost think we are in a holiday trip.

There is also the joy of meeting new faces; I happen to be during the morning at a planks pile with an unknown that turns out to be Vasile Vasilache, the monk, the former elder of Procov, brother of Haralambie that I carried out with the blanket from room forty-four.

Father Vasile knows about the death of his brother in the prison infirmary and he listens thoughtful the details that I am able to give. Sometime later, another inmate came to help us, tells us that he is from high treason. Incidentally I ask him if he knows anything about Gigi Tz., that I suspect he is still in the ghastly Pitești. I talk to him about Gigi, the artist, the man… The inmate listens to me smiling faintly. When I finished the eulogy: Tz. Is here, at Gherla, in the same cell as him; he didn't want to get out because he has a poem to compose. (Gigi "writes" a lot in prison.)

Amazed and moved, I ask the cellmate of Gigi to tell him to ask himself out for chores next day (the Korean notified us on the road that there will continue to be work) so that we can see each other.

My name is known to the inmate; he heard it from Gigi. (His arrest in 1950 caught us after a quarrel. Ah! no matter what, one thing is sure: of enmities and quarrels I am cured for ever.)

I spent the rest of the day and the evening in a state of effervescence.

The first thing I find out in front of a new pile of planks from the yesterday man: today, first thing in the morning, Gigi was taken out from the cell, reprieved.

Reprieved, after fourteen years out of a fifteen years sentence.

–   Religion at the Spiru Haret high school I made it with the priest of Saint Sylvester church – bourgeois district of semi-center of the capital – a tall man, big red beard, owner of a good vineyard, old and steady liberal, lover of strong black wine and fancy dishes, and especially sarmale. The glances he was throwing at women, otherwise quite discretely, seemed not to remain purely Platonic.

He had sympathy for me; I was, out of four, the only Jew that did not come with a waiver request and certificate that I attend religion with a rabbi. In the superior course (he was our professor in all the classes) he liked to declare: rather than see minister of Cults one of Maniu's catholics, I rather see one of our Yids, a good guy, and he was saying my name.

I had always A, I was saying Our Father and I was crossing myself.

I loved very much father Gheorghe Georgescu, likable man, anytime willing to jest and kind. He might be far, very far indeed, from the model of the Protestant pastor or the Catholic cleric, he might have committed sins and he might have had weaknesses, but the anointed priest a little worldly never seemed to me – not even then, during childhood, when we are especially exigent and unforgiving – an agent of the sly one.

The anointed priest the sort of father Georgescu – otherwise fervent believer, with smart talk, exquisite speaker, always ready to forgive and to smile, with no trace of acidity in his soul without dark caches – represents one of the possible (if not recommendable) styles of orthodoxy; he is not a guidebook, but I am not willing – just like that, despite the moralists and to spite the evaporated church-going ladies and the pious parishioners -, for nothing in the world, to cast the stone at him. (The same way I am not willing for the sake of the zealot sectarians to mistake the papal Rome with the den of red Whore and the synagogue of Satan.) Maybe in the long string of miracles through which God lead me to faith – because for anyone (notwithstanding how little) the way is planned with an incredible meticulous care – there is a place for this countenance of priest that to many of the today's purists seems scandalous. (So much more since, thank God, their need of fanaticism and intransigence is amply satisfied by the state laic authorities.)

My dear children, the world is more complicated than you think.

–   **The stages of forgiveness.**

Our trespassers, we hardly forgive. Or, if we forgive, we don't forget. (And the forgiveness without forgetfulness is like a courtyard without a dog, like a mouth without teeth[139].)

We forgive ourselves even harder.

(And this remembrance poisons. To earn the inner peace we must go, through repentance, beyond repentance: to absolve ourselves.)

The most difficult is to forgive those that we trespassed. (Who can forgive those he trespassed, he really accomplishes a difficult task, he truly beats a record.)

Self-unforgiveness has a more grave character than one may think; it means lack of trust in God's goodness, the proof of our relentless and accountant-like evilness. It is the case of Judas, who believe neither in the power of Christ (that He can forgive him) nor in the goodness of Christ (that He wants to forgive him).

When the French say Dieu a crée l'homme à son image qui le lui a bien rendu[140], they envisaged this trait of the being, specific to Judas. To the One who created us in His image and likeness we pay in the same currency by imagining Him in our image and likeness: so evil and unforgiving that we cannot believe that God can forgive anything. No! We cannot think a power, no matter how almighty in the physical realm (the most fantastic material wonders we admit), capable of doing this unconceivable thing: to forgive.

On the other hand, as mister Perrichon (he hates the man who pulled him from the precipice, he adores the man he pulled out from the precipice), we love very little those who saved us from shame and bad luck; we readily love, however, those we had the opportunity to come to their help, to show them our power and generosity.

Gherla

They are described to me, in the same day, two scenes that I hope will remain imprinted on my mind as long as I live.

The first, recounted by doctor Răileanu: professor Paulescu, before starting the lecture, he was always saying Our Father.

The second, evoked by the admirable teacher Nicolae Druică:

The father of Vasile Pârvan[141], a teacher too, who supervises closely the education of his son, was coming to attend the lectures of the one who did not deceive his expectations. He was staying on a bench in the back of the amphitheater and he was rising together with the students at the entrance of the professor. Only after he was sitting and signaled his son that he can sit too and start teaching, only then Pârvan was sitting and after him all the other from the amphitheater.

BUGGY MAMBO RAG

…There is an extraordinary picture of Proust, toward the end: he is standing, wears black clothes and tall starched collar, he stays rigidly, with the cane and the hat in his right hand, as for a parade; the hat is oriented with the bottom toward the camera and you can see clearly the fabrication mark of the hatter: a double crown… At Trebbia, in 218, the Romans lost because they were forced to fight frozen, after they crossed the river… Then let's count them again, Thalia and Melponema two, Eutherpe and Terpsichore four, ă, Cleo five, so, Urania six… ă… Can anyone doubt the meaning?

The author, arrived at the threshold of the finish of his opera, is calm and as reward he ennobles himself; the crown from the hat shows that he understood: that a certain unknown and just force made him, finally, count of Illiers… At Trasimenus, in 217, they applied the method of luring the enemy in a strait place… Ă, ă… yes, Erato seven… At Canal, in 216, the Romans maintained a useless depth, and Hanibal used the regional wind, placing his troops with the back toward the wind while the Romans were fighting with the wind in their faces, blinded by dust and sun… Seven, yes…

November 3rd 1955

Ana retained me after she took farewell from the other guests (this evening fewer than usual). She talked to me at length. Mihai listened to us, thoughtful, silent. Ana explained to me that since I have the desire to be baptized there is no point to wait.

I leave without uttering one single word; undecided, entangled. It's very late too. Mihai accompanies me to the gate; I receive the advice to stop saying pseudo-Dionis, but Saint Dionysius the Areopagite. Too many French Catholic readings.

At security, July 1961

Sleep interrupted by nightmares. I am first awaken by a guardian because I yelled during the sleep. Then a few more times because I sleep with the face toward the wall or with the hands under the blamket.

Questions. Remembrances.

Can one resist during the investigation? Are the full acknowledgment and the avalanche of confessions absolutely inevitable?

The thick volumes published by the Soviet Justice Department in 1937-1939. The judgments of the "right wing and the Trotskists". Read at length, intensely discussed with Manole. I recognize all the old conspirators of the insurrection, all the revolutionary elite. There is also a sort of compromise solution, tenebrous: Radek. The ceremonial formulae; the bailiff: the court, please rise. This care for the repetition of the formulae to create an atmosphere of objectivity. And not one single material proof, absolutely none, a document, a weapon, something… Only words. Precisely as in Hamlet: words, words, words… If at the confession the repentant can say: these and worse than these I did, in the court it gives the impression of fake. And all the long introductions of the lawyers that first defend themselves, specifying that they represent the defendants only as auxiliaries of justice. It is not a debate but a ceremony, an oratory where everybody plays his role and sings his part for the general melodic compound. Trotsky: super-bandit. The others are just bandits. This super is superfluous, suspicious. And the attribute debauched-Trotskist is in contrast with the objective politeness, with the bailiff, with the special respect for the insignificant details: the tip of the tail of the wolf disguised as granny.

London 1937

In order to arrive at the address provided by Nuți L. I had to wander through a long string of concentric circles: all alike streets, only little villas, little gardens, lamps the type Belisha beacons – shaken by the rain and wind that for three days reigned over the city.

On the streets, toward the evening I don't see anyone, only wind rain and lamps, desolation enters in my bones, so that the modest room where I find Nuți seems a haven: in the hearth shines purple an electric fire, the lamp by the armchair has a green shade, on the table my eyes are attracted by the tea cups.

The contrast between the British comfort based on simple elements (heat, water, temperate light, an elixir: the tea leafs, the rum bottle) and the autumn landscape of outside is so striking that I cannot but feel a sentiment of tenderness. Maybe in essence life is just this: a wild forest haunted by beasts, full of potholes and traps, shaken by lightning and gusts of rain and, at the edge, one single little house lighted and warm, from where the inhabitants will have to leave all before the implacable dawn?

For now in the room everything is simple and fleeting, sweet and gentle. Nuți pours the tea in the cups, the radiator keeps the place of the traditional logs and it is heating us enough; on a frying pan appear some fried eggs. Poor human fight against nature and reality, in which the Englishmen are masters. How much I wish to can sink in the delivering comfort, to forget the adverse forest that waits for us and surrounds us. Who plant it there, God? Or maybe God is the constructor of the villa on the outskirts? Saint Chesterton, pray for us. (After Saint Socrates pray for us of Erasmus.)

– Can one resist?

The lawyer D.P. Experience of defense attorney in numerous political trials. He was noticing (1957) unclear points even from the dates of the reports and statements. He thought he can make out certain faint signals. On a statement from an interrogatory were written the date and the time at which started. The accused was asked a simple and apparently dull question: how should be considered the behavior of the civil servant who speaks without controlled reticence with his friends about matters concerning the state? (The solution of the riddle: it must be considered as infraction and treason.) The time of the ending is an amazing figure: it follows that the accused was retained at the interrogatory eighteen hours. The answer was not satisfactory.

Next day the same question. This time the interrogatory ends after five minutes, the answer being the correct one. The explanation, the only one possible: meanwhile they applied a different procedure.

The lawyers – and this pains D.P. who is a talented lawyer – are locked in the file; they cannot plead otherwise than according to the statements from the file, considered definitive and universally valid. As a scientist who would not be allowed to question the principles even if the experience contradicts them. Let us read in Aristotle to find out if the oil freeze in the winter or not. The conclusion of the new scholastics: the lawyer is not a defender, an intercessor anymore, but just a dummy.

In cell 18, X. was inferring: you can never avoid the conviction. However, some acknowledgments can be avoided. You need only a bit of self-control, a bit of courage. And especially an utter mistrust. (The rule: unlimited trust in people, as persons created by God and absolute mistrust in the father of the lie and his followers.)

The other confessed everything. We know everything but we want to hear the truth from your mouth too. If you are sincere your situation will improve. Be sincere.

X.: Do not be sincere! (An advice especially good for intellectuals, sensitive people, easily attracted by the magic of this noble word.) Do not be sincere! This above all[142]. And deny all the time, you have plenty of time to talk if and when you will be tortured. Do not be hasty. There is plenty of time, thank the Lord. And when it is about something that only two of you know, keep denying: give to the other the possibility to decide, it is his secret after all.

BUGGY MAMBO RAG

We, general, have seen old Bucharest with gardens and Oltenians…, and courtyards with multicolor globes, they were terrible, but they had their charm, and people were eating in the courtyard, as in the countryside, under the biggest tree… The best creation in prose of the Romanian literature, professor… To eat from spring to fall under the walnut tree was, I would say, something few peoples in the world had, a happiness that enters in the corolla of wonders of the world, let me be forgiven by Blaga or his spirit if the poor man died… The first makes of automobiles? Let's see… De Dion-Boutton, Lancia, Isotta-Fraschini, Pierce-Arrow, Panhard-Levassor, Benz, De Launay- Belleville… Franz-Ferdinand at Sarajevo was killed in a De Launay-Belleville… But also at Dragomir's, if I remember well… the faience sinks with piles of ground ice and the caviar cans… and the little kegs with olives, with bluefish, with Mercur cheese and the planks with ham slices and the Martini vermouth and the cognac: Martell, Courvoisier, I always preferred a fine champagne, and even ours, the țuică Cireșeanu, the wormwood wine Bazilescu, the vermouth Duqué…

1959

From Apennines to Andes, the story from Cuore, with such an euphonic title, is evoked to me by the passing of the Avramescus from the Mothers' Skete to the church Udricani in Văcărești. Or Jerusalem of Dalecarlia, ideal conceived by the Swedish peasants of Selma Lagerlöf and Jerusalem of the Holy Land, with the same peasants, this time just immigrants overwhelmed by worries.

The foundation of the High Steward Udrican didn't bring too much luck to Mihai and Ana. The Port Royal spirit didn't subsist in Văcărești. The outskirts, the passion to destroy and self-compromise got both of them. The underground, the germ of self-derision. The priest is cheating on his wife, but not physically and in hiding, which happens, which people might even be able to forgive (we're just men, mister), but Platonic (apparently), with dramatic scenes, complicate turns, thirsting for justification, which stupefies and alienates. The priestess is not better either; lacking any feminine humility, instead of enduring her husband's whims, even to meditate upon the brutal Lipovenian[143] formula of the perfect man (he strongly believes in God, drinks heavily and beats his woman in earnest), to follow the example of Lady Acarie (she listened the advice of her confessor – and what confessor! Saint Francisco of Sales: as long as you are married you don't think of chastity, you have only one duty, you obey) what is she doing? She fills the town with laments, goes to the Patriarchy and the Cults Department with complaints over complaints and long written petitions.

– Come to think of it, before the baptism, the most important event in my life was the friendship full of admiration that I had for Manole.

I knew him in the first days of college. He was, like Mihail Sebastian[144], a man from the shores of the Danube, not from Brăila, but from the tinier Olteniţa. Brăila: international port; Olteniţa: well-to-do town. Capital difference. His father died young; they were three kids raised by a dark- haired, beautiful, energetic mother, once a merchant woman in Obor[145].

My respect for him was from the beginning whole and unconditional. All I was thinking and telling then, he quickly turned to bits and then he started to build from the foundation.

Maurassian spirit, clear and balanced, sharp and enemy of extravagance of any kind, he was despising the generalized optimism and the leftist politics from Sărindar. Liberal in thinking, skeptical in religion and conservative in politics. He wouldn't believe entirely in any doctrine. With his whole heart he was only with the Junimists[146], they were his ideal.

As a Maurassian, he was not interested in mystics, he was preoccupied, however, by the social and political function of religion and the latter we asked ourselves how to fulfill.

The rationale of Manole was simple: we were born Jews (he wouldn't say Hebrew for nothing in the world), we therefore are Jews. Let us be what we are.

Well, that's not enough; to be Jew you must do as everybody else (any singularity is suspect): to belong to your tradition, which is the Judaic religion.

We started looking for a rabbi. The first steps turned out to be quite difficult. The first address given to us turned out to be of a kosher butcher. Manole made a lot of fun; an anecdote by Theodor Speranţia, no more, no less. But we found out a colleague, son of a rabbi, conservative too, very anti-progressive but of nuance orthodox mystical Jew. He consented to listen to us, disapproving the arguments, not the conclusion; some surprise, no hostility.

Then he consented to introduce us to his father, who listened to us too, gently, he searched us with deep glances, understanding us only in part. We read then also The prophet child by Edmond Fleg. After that the things got complicated.

It seemed that in order to be Jew, at least as far as concerns the integration in a system of social tradition, it is necessary to go to the synagogue Friday and Saturday morning; that you need to buy phylacteries and, of course, the white shawl with the Hebrew name talit – learning the ritual of using it and, this above all, you must learn Hebrew. Hebrew, which is the ivirit(?), another novelty. The solution of reading the text of the prayers in Latin letters, I couldn't apply. There were, apparently, this kind of books, but I couldn't find them. Once, in a velvet-like fall afternoon, somewhere on the quay[147], we stumbled in a courtyard with many fowls on an old man about whom we heard he had what we were looking for. He came out of the house barely awake – he was wearing an immense robe – but he didn't understand what we wanted.

Manole didn't think these rules are excessive, they were in accordance with the discipline and the effort that any society rightfully asks from its members. Anyway, the savage tribes have their own initiation tests too. We started therefore to work, to buy, to frequent regularly the synagogue (where the father of our colleague was officiating), and I got the more difficult part of learning Hebrew, where, on the road, I made some more discoveries: that it is not enough to know Hebrew and its alphabet, it is also necessary Aramaic, the latter having in its turn for commentaries a different alphabet, of the scholar Rashi, which in its turn was commented in another alphabet... In short, I was repeating – life, of course, imitates art – the experience of the little hero of Fleg and I was noticing that I am in trouble...

Learning Hebrew wasn't so bad, Aramaic seemed to me more harmonious (its genitive
protects it from the excessive hoarseness of the former) but I couldn't get along with frequenting the synagogue. I thought that the synagogue is a church. No way, it is a place for reciting some texts regarding the exegesis and fulfillment of some rituals. The Jewish religion is a religion "in suspension" and without sermon, and the synagogues are just "memorial houses". In essence, the Temple being destroyed and animal sacrifices not being possible, everything is reduced to the reading or the utterance of the rules and prescriptions. It is a memorization, and a type of absolute structure, where the virtualities are not configured (?).

Our rabbi was talking fluently, but in a fantasized Romanian that was often giving the impression of anecdote pulled out from the collections of Theodor Speranția. Both the details and the ensemble were appearing to me as something cold, dusty, far away and stubborn. I was longing for the church from Pantelimon, of the Saint Sylvester church and its vaulted belfry (through which you can cross to Oltarului street), of the little church from Clucereasa. The cherry on the cake was put by the rabbi, linguistically, expressing himself on a Saturday: and he made a hole where es sint heraus gekimăn flacărăs[148].

The Maurrassian experience of assuming the religious tradition for integration in the social community worked for a while but I had only a relative gain in knowledge of the Hebrew elements (I had though the chance to read the Old Testament in original, with the dictionary and the Romanian text by my side) and the conviction that it is useless. At which it was added a respectful sensation of definitive farewell to the synagogue.

I tried, in good faith, with good faith. For Manole this was mostly a let's say psycho-social experience, for me a more from the heart, febrile endeavor. I tried.

Gherla, October 1962

My first teacher, a governess, represented by her very lineage, but also by her marriage, an anticipative summary of the European idea. After father she was German. After mother French; her maternal uncle, Auguste Molinier, was a university intellectual and published an edition of Pascal. There was also a Swiss grandmother and a northern ancestor. Lady de Branszky was the widow of a Hungarian nobleman, a great drunker and a great scoundrel, born of a Polish mother, daughter of a Russian boyar. I don't remember how my teacher came to stay with us, but I know one thing: I had the incomparable luck to receive the notions of culture from an extraordinary woman: a brilliant intelligence, tremendous knowledge and an admirable character.

She hated the Frenchmen and she admired the Germans. She despised the Catholics and she tolerated the Reformed. The cathedral Saint Joseph, where she was attracted by the concerts, seemed to her a museum with conventional works; in the Protestant temples she was entering without repulsion but without pleasure also. At least they were not open all the time (as opposed to the Catholic churches, insatiable; but where you could always find refuge in case of rain). Her true religion was another one, that – although at the beginning I couldn't understand too much of it – she confessed it to me right away: it was the faith of the general Ludendorff and his wife, der Norddeutscheglauben[149].

Lady de Branszky didn't talk badly of Jesus Christ – more moderated than Nietzsche –, at least the way He was seen by the Lutherans, because the Catholic idol, sculpted and flourished and the cult of the Virgin were stepping on her nerves; her enthusiasm was kindled only when she was talking to me about the deities of Valhalla, when she was detailing to me the song of the Nibelungs or she was reading from the texts of the lyrical dramas of Wagner. She was always praising Etzel, which is Attila and I believe that in secret she was adoring the walkyra Brunhilda.

Lady de Branszky, like Manole later, was a hard-core monarchist and as far as she wanted to consider her French origin and to occupy herself with the history of France, she inoculated me a profound respect for the idea of legitimacy; she made me read all the French monarchist literature and she made out of me – I was eleven years old – a fervent partisan of the count of Chambord (dead in 1883) and of the house of Bourbon. To her I owed my being looked over with annoyance (or at least with amazement) – whenever I was reading in the park or at the hotel the newspaper "l'Action Française", the organ of the monarchist movement – by some of the Frenchmen among which I used to spend about a month when I was going with my parents at Royat, for my dad to take baths in carbonic acid.

(There, at Royat, I saw a thing that I didn't forget and I told it in prison: Vintilă Brătianu taking the tramcar only at the second class if he was going in the neighboring town, Clermont-Ferrand.)

Of Ludendorff and Norddeutscheglauben I had part also at Gherla, due to the person of colonel Traugott Broser, from Brașov, former officer of the Austro-Hungarian army, in whose ranks he fought during world war I on the Italian front. Broser, massive like a mountain and very retired, became close to me because he had the chance to talk German with someone, then because he had sympathy for me. He warns me sternly about the great risk that I assumed passing from Judaism to Christianity: to remain suspended in the void between two spiritualities.

He is recounting to me the credo of Ludendorff too, noticing with great surprise that I know it. About Ludendorff – the true leader of the German army between 1914 and 1918 (Hindenburg – die grosse Null[150] – Broser can't stand him) – I find out marks of greatness; how he conquered the city of Lettich (that is Liège) just by an act of dare and prestige; the supreme courage he showed during the putsch at München in 1923, crossing the bridge – in its general uniform, with the sword in one hand and the revolver in the other –, going straight toward the forces massed on the other side who could have filled him with lead in one volley of shots – but they don't do it, only because they are under the influence of its prestige and its indifference to death. But especially something that I take upon myself to make a rule out of it. In the military school, Ludendorff and a colleague of his, from a princely family, of royal descent, are persecuted by a sort of Moș Teacă[151], a bad and imbecile non-commissioned officer. For the prince would have been easy saying one word to obtain either their transfer or of the imbecile to another squadron. And he wants to do that.

Ludendorff stopped him: if we want to be officers and to command we have to learn to suffer the absurd meticulous stupidity too. They didn't ask the transfer and they endured till the end.

From Broser I find out remarkable things about Wilhelm II, so much hated, to whom the Frenchmen made an infamous reputation.

He was a talkative man and of a limited intelligence but full of good intentions. Proofs: a) his behavior during the Dreyfus affair when, against all diplomatic usage and tradition, gives through Conrad of Hohenlohe the statement by which he solemnly specifies: the accused was never used by the German intelligence service; when he instructs the German ambassador in Paris, count Münster, not to hesitate out of prudence and national interests considerations to help a comrade officer in order to reestablish the truth and the honor of an innocent.

Normally, after the declaration made by the German emperor, any pursue should have ceased. Its disregard, unprecedented affront, constituted by itself a casus belli[152]; Wilhelm, pacifist, closed his eyes;

b)   his splendid affirmation: as a head of the state I answer not only to the parliament but also to God;

c)   the abrogation by which he stopped the corporal punishment in the army, unique in the world and history, the most democratic, because it gave to everybody the possibility to behave like an aristocrat, and perfectly efficient because it stipulated that from the date of the publication of the abrogation any inferior military rank has the right to slap – on the spot and right away – the superior that hit him;

d)   his European feeling, especially evident during the boxers revolt: the coalition of the European troops was put under the command of a German, general Waldersee.

(From his booklet about Wilhelm, one can see that Rathenau knew something.)

–   Saint Gregory of Nazianz: "The word of God was incarnated so that I could be as much God as He was man."

–   Again and again: Christianity does not mean stupidity.

Lo that Jacques Maritain too tells to Jean Cocteau: we must have a tough reason and a gentle heart.

Love implies forgiveness, gentleness, but not blindness and stupidity: often identifying itself as great malice, the weakness toward stupidity is the same as giving free hand to the villains.

There is another very spread prejudice that was noticed by the cardinal of Retz: we are tempted to link necessarily the intelligence and the malice ant to give to the whole, with great respect, the name of Machiavellian. Retz: the evil ones are not always and not necessarily smart. The evil ones might be stupid. The association of ideas: malice, therefore intelligence is a prejudice.

Gherla, November 1960
> You have no use in the belief of the forgiveness of sins if you don't believe,
> with full conviction that your sins have been forgiven.
> Luther

> Sed adde, ut credas, et hoc, quod per ipsum peccata tibi donantur.[153]
> St. Bernard from Clairvaux

We suspect, because of the fog that entered the cell that a storm is approaching.

Almost nobody talks.

To some people around him, the Catholic priest Traian Pop, whispering, gives them the advice to be lenient toward others and severe toward themselves.

But he adds right away:

–   Not too severe with ourselves. The devil must be sometimes laughed at; do not give him the prestige of tragic grandeur. The great Spaniard mystics – St. Teresa from Avilla, St. John of the Cross – were mostly cheerful. This comes from the power to be lenient toward ourselves; let us know how to forgive ourselves and how God forgives us. The way we should not be angered by the fact that we were angry, the same way we should not perpetuate the evil in ourselves out of lack of mercy for our self.

In the cell where is more and more dark, a sewing machines repairman which also plays the accordion, recounts dirty stories and memories from the weddings where he "performed", and a voice started to sing in undertone a worldly song, stressing the strange threatening refrain: woe what a rain comes from Cluj!

BUGGY MAMBO RAG

… Wagtail is bergonette, but let the devil take me if I remember how to say lovage… Fotiade got me crazy with the birds, the vegetables and the flowers. I don't know them anymore. Only some of them. Some I do, some I don't, it's like they fell down in voids of darkness, the nothingness swallowed them, the disintegrated like the nylon socks break. Still, I knew them all… Ah, lovage, wait a minute… I wrote nothing, absolutely nothing against the regime. In every letter I wrote to him: it's good, it is good, I'm healthy, I earn, praised be God, as much as I need, we are healthy, we don't lack anything, it's good… Then how come?… Him, my brother, he wrote me. I was telling him that I am happy, happy, happy, but him: I know better, you are talking nonsense, we know what is going on… I understand the truth is the upside down… It's in Romans 13, the text is categorical, mister Ioaniţiu, whether we like it or not, the text is clear, I wonder how can it be contested by a Christian… Do you have a brother in Athens? I say: yes. He says: do you write to him? I say: yes. He says: and do you complain about the regime, are you slandering the country? I answer: no, God forbid… Read the letters!… Very well, it's very good that you have them, let me show you, here: I am happy, I earn, it's good, good… But what he says?… Well, that's his business, I don't know, look what I say: it's good… What about him?… It's all right your Grace… Livèche, dear, livèche, I finally remembered… What he says is his business, I don't know, look what I say: it's good… What about him?… I don't know, I didn't say it, him, my brother, not me, not in my letters… Yo, you're jerking us around, you scoundrel, you rogue, you jewel, you Greek, we know better… Eh! If Alecu would have lived… Tătărescu[154] couldn't hold a candle to him, what a difference, a chasm between them… When Ferdinand and Maria sent Hiottu to Paris, only him said they are doing a bad thing. Then he proposed to send Baliff, for whom Carol had sympathy, instead… I say: him, not I. He says: you think we don't know that you would like to be in Athens with him, otherwise he wouldn't write this way… And he grabs me… Marcellus tells to Demetrios…

– The Protestants who laughs at St. Anthony from Padova seem to me very little understanding. In St. Anthony of Padova they see a patron of lost keys and lost doggies. It is bon ton to smile when you hear of a saint specialized in such

110

trifles, who recruits his clientele among deaf crones, forgetful, maniacs, diabetics... Even some of the Roman church faithful avoid him, preferring the society of Augustine, Thomas d'Aquino, Jeronimus... St Francisco of Assisi, with all his protestor and hippie features – he stayed naked, he spoke to the birds, lived out of begging – is better seen because he is picturesque (birds are poetic), but what can you think of a saint who takes care of such little attractive and interesting beings like old men who can't find their keys, who lost their dog, who forget what they forgot?

What blindness and narrowness! St Anthony is especially worthy of admiration because he is so good that he feels pity even for some poor beings of which everybody finds appropriate to laugh at or to look upon them from above, with irony and condescension. But the loss of the keys might be the cause of violent sufferance (more embarrassing because it seems ridiculous), and the death of a loved doggie is a tragedy for who is alone in the world and weak in life. There are snobs of the compassion: only for heroes and solemn events. But St. Anthony dares to pity lesser pains and to turn merciful toward the wretched in black clothes, the mocked and the lovers of cats.

There is here an overflow of kindness, a subtle mercy: a sort of missionary not in the remote islands of the south seas but in the most modest regions of the psyche, at the crossroads of ineptitude and resignation. The vanquished, the confused and the unlucky have their right to comfort, don't they?

On the other hand, some Catholic commentators show that St. Anton does not help retrieving some lost objects, but the lost faith... Of course. But the explanation of the commentators deprive St.

Anton of what seems to me amazing about him: the care for those a bit ridiculous, that are called upon by Christ too, that suffer in this world too, that – to our knowledge – are not excluded from the banquet.

– Christ, as gentleman and knight.

At the accountant-devil there isn't even the slightest erasure. Christ, at once, erases an entire record of sins.

Christ, a boyar, forgives everything. To know how to forgive, how to give, how to forget. Christ not only forgives but He forgets too. Once forgiven, you are not anymore a servant of sin and a son of slave; you are free and friend of the Lord.

And how This One addresses Judas, which He knows who he is it and why did he come? Friend, He says. This friend seems to me more poignant than even the forbidding of the use of sword and than the healing of the ear of Malchus. It expresses what among us, humans, is called the supreme refinement of self-restraint in the face of danger – supreme virtue required of the samurai. Maybe peaceful words (don't draw the sword) and compassionate gestures (the healing of the wound) could have been said and done also by a saint. But friend implies greatness and serenity that only coming from the divinity, don't give the impression of non-reality.

(The truth is that a simple man, and a very sinful one, king Louis XV, reaches an awesome height when, touched by the knife of Damiens, shows the perpetrator with these words: this is the gentleman who hit me.)

According to the story of the nobleman to whom comes the tailor with an IOU. The nobleman refuses to pay. Then, in the presence of the tailor with the script in his hand, he orders the servant to bring two thousand ducats to the one who, yesterday, won from him on word of honor that sum at a card game. To the tailor who expresses his bafflement, he explains: the honor debts must be acquitted because there are no proofs. Therefore, right away, the tailor throws the script in the hearth fire.

Here the anecdote ends, the nobleman having paid the tailor.

But it's an imbecile end and reeks falsity. Of course the noblemen would have paid him! This goes without saying. Even a brute would have done the same. But the nobleman – if he is a nobleman – does something else, and this is the authentic version of the story, he says: have a seat, sir, and I will pay you in a moment the sum that I owe you. This have a seat sir is the proof of the boyarhood, and not the payment itself. It is an acknowledgment of the power of the man to transfigure himself. We can always transfigure ourselves and become at lightning speed worthy to be invited at the royal wedding banquet. (Otherwise, how could the Lord dine with us and how could be understood the words: Come, you, blessed by My Father?)

Except that not everybody is capable of recognizing the transfiguration when he meets it. The şmecher for nothing in the world would believe it; and also the Pharisees and the accountants. In their bio-mind-sphere that they carry always with them, in their magnetic field, anything that is not in accordance with their creed doesn't penetrate. The play of Franz Werfel, Paul among the Jews; the most atrocious anguish of the confessor was caused by the sneer and the stubbornness produced on the face and in the minds of those he beseeched to believe that now he is a new man.

–   Among the books of the Old Testament, the most opposed to the New Testament is the ghastly chronicle of Ezra, an accomplished moment of intolerance and racism.

What were supposed to do the Jews who were coming home from a long and burdening slavery? To sing and enjoy? Not at all. After the help from the neighbors was rejected haughtily ("It is not for you to share in building the house for our God; we alone are to build it[155]"), Ezra talks to his kind in the most eugenic, most Rosenbergian possible manner. Because the Israelites married foreign women and they mixed the holy race with alien populations, they must proceed, first and foremost, to cut off the chosen ones from the abomination and the pollution of other impure peoples in order to put a stop to the iniquity of the mixing.

He didn't even allow them in the city; he keeps all those wretched people out in the rain for days so that they can make the lists of Israelites married to foreign women.

And it starts the long and duly job of making the lists by specially appointed committees. It is the grand day of the triumph of Bureaucracy. And after the racist bureaucracy – in an atmosphere of inventorying and concentration camp – finished its work, the foreign women and their children are chased away.

Only then allows Ezra the people to enter in the city and to find shelter.

Those who have difficulties understanding the words of Paul – we are free from the curse of the Law and we have entered under grace – could use the reading of the first book of Ezra. Also those who ask why the teaching of Christ is called the "good news", those who look for the origins of the racism and those who are interested in prototypes of Bureaucracy.

BUGGY MAMBO RAG

… No, I'm sorry, the first person of the imperfect of the subjunctive of apercevoir[156] is apercevassions… You keep pestering me with the subjunctive of the French verbs, but let's see how you are doing with the conjugation of the Romanian verbs… Ah, you pretend you know them, then tell me the simple perfect of to sew, to saw and to sow… Right… Oberth[157] was a high school professor at Mediaş, where everybody was laughing at him, were pointing him with the finger and they were calling him the man from the moon… He was the son of a medic from Sighişoara and he was considered a nutcase, until Hitler made him professor at Vienna and he became the first collaborator of Werner Von Braun in America… How about the four idols of Bacon, which are they?… Colonel, do you remember when was the battle of Manzikert?.. Let's see, for sew we have sewn… NO! NO!… The capital of the British Honduras is Belize and of the Honduras isn't Tegugigalpa?… What about to sow? What? Also sewn[158]? What are you talking?… Voichiţa of Radu the Handsome was the fourth wife of Ştefan the Great[159], Maria of Mangup was the third, and The Frenchie gals was not written by Ventura, it was written by Facca… From Danube to Seine, From Carpathians to Pyrenees/ The noble Latin nation gathers its children[160]… See, you don't know… Que nous nous enlissassions, que vous… Of Turţ is the one from the Oaş county[161] and it has up to 65° Celsius… About 1070 I think…

Jilava, at the infirmary (May 1962)

La cour des miracles[162]

In the first bed, on the right hand side, I don't remember who was lying. A man silenced by sufferance and filth.

In the second bed Aurelian Bentoiu, cadaverous, unrecognizable and excessively tall. Recently operated (prostate cancer), left in abandonment with bandages that stink he is stirred by acute pains, tormented by the feeling of injustice and he's afraid. Sparklingly intelligent, with an urge for conversation, for remembering and predicting, he is also always ready to quarrel.

Quarrel, thank the Lord, he has more than plenty. As in all infirmaries here too people are morose, acid and irritable. (On the sections, where it is much more difficult, on the contrary, the self-control and resignation are the rule.) In the left bed in the back, paralyzed from waist down due to a hemorrhoid operation superficially performed in a jail without hospital, Radu Lecca. He hates Bentoiu; most of the time he attacks him violently, he is swearing and cursing terribly. Bentoiu answer him rarely and then with the same cursing and insults of a gypsy, a coachman, a market man.

Otherwise, Lecca shows an example of remarkable strength of character: he doesn't accept help from anyone. He goes to the barrel alone, crawling, hitting himself, using the bed bars, as an ape upon which were made some Pavlovian or Lorentzian experiments, with gestures evoking that missing link between primates and anthropoids hypothesized by the evolutionists.

A third one paralyzed is the journalist Al. Leontescu., completely immobilized on the mattress. More quiet than the other two, he is sometimes taken over by angers generating curses and imprecations that are not left behind by those of Lecca and Bentoiu.

The paralyzed man in the back on the left-hand side is silent and utmost quiet. He doesn't ask anything, he doesn't want anything. He indisposes however everybody by his refusal to make any movement and to respect the elementary hygiene of the human beings. He defecates in the bed without asking for a pot, drinks and eats from a dish in each he also urinates – from time to time he overthrows its contents in his head – and to all reproaches and appeals he answers with a modest smile.

Professor C. Tomescu, theologian, Vlad Stolojan (nephew of both Nicolae Filipescu and Ion Brătianu[163]), a former captain and a few silhouettes that are clouded in my mind complete the room dominated by Lecca, Bentoiu and Leontescu. The last two compose poems; poems they recite and that move us deeply.

My arrival in the room causes, I think, certain uneasiness to Radu Lecca, and professor C. Tomescu, the latter having been state sub-secretary at Cults in the Goga-Cuza government[164], until, fortunately, Vlad Stolojan – who knows me from Jilava – sketches for me a biography more than benevolent and the ice melts. Lecca, however, watches me with eyes full of distrust, not of myself, but of my ability to forgive him.

Gradually he gives in and he listens to me charmed whenever I talk without gloves about the French revolution (lady Branszki is in my side) and I quote the book of Ludwig Klages, Geist als Wiedersacher der Seele, specifying that if the spirit could appear as opposed to the soul, what would the author say seeing that in our days the soul is opposed not by the spirit but by the baseness, the most ordinary trickstery (and I am glad that I can tell it in German: die niedertrachtigste und gemeinste Schlauheit), the grin satisfied with itself.

I express my hope that when leaving the prison we'll find Europe unified by democrat- Christian parties, a place where the old spirit of the chivalry could be reborn this time to an incomparable higher number of people.

Although the way Radu Lecca talks to Bentoiu revolts me and his incessant attacks against the liberals are tiring; although he is an adventurer, in his eyes shines something from the heroes of Karl Maria von Weber, from the Teutonic sentimentalism, from the nostalgia for wandering in search of exceptional facts.

But how far are the trumpets and the horns of the knight von Weber from us and from our times and the place we are! – still how much they are close to us because of our conversations and pranks in this cell with so many common traces with a medieval jail.

(Then let me tell you so that you'll know: the past tense of sew is sewn, of bake is baked, of mow is mown... Sewn? I'm not convinced... Maybe you're not, but that's the way it is, see, you don't know Romanian...)

I get along wonderfully with professor Tomescu, I soon earn his trust and friendship; he was going to stay at my side in March 1967 during the funeral of my father, we were going to prove to the skeptics and the fools that reconciliation and forgetfulness are possible. (Sandu L., I wasn't going to see him again, the scene in the van remained only as a remembrance of ours, common esotericism.) Leontescu is grateful because I speak with admiration and respect of Nae Ionescu, that he idolizes; the most prestigious shadow profiled in the Tracian sky since Zamolxe[165]. I feel connected to Bentoiu by a sort of psychoanalytical pity for his solitude of wretched sick man; in captain Gy., with clever hands of qualified nurse, I find a devoted man skilled in easing the pains and especially the feeling of abandonment to Bentoiu.

After ten days of insistence and recriminations, Bentoiu obtains, finally, to be brought to the medical office, where we are accompanying him, the captain and me. In the office we meet the deaf doctor. Her glances are extremely bored and hostile. Bentoiu is ordered to lye on a couch, I – kneeled – keep a basin and Gy. the long tube through which the permanganate will flow. The basin is still perfectly clean when, trying to avoid being in the way, I touch with its brim the tip of the doctor's shoe. She kicks me with her leg, violently, the way you would kick a dog, a ball, and overthrows me together with the basin. As reprisal she wants to send the sick man back not bandaged. A twice horrible perspective: I made an immense bad and I earned the victim's hate forever. Inspired, I avoid apologizing. We all are silent for a long time. The doctor wraps all three of us in a silent volley of anger and despise. She is so mad, that if she could she would annihilate us, she would crash, volatize us, with movements of vintager that squeezes the grapes in the press. However, after a long hesitation, she changes carefully the bandages of Bentoiu.

Once back in the cell, the sick man recite to us from his poetry. He is a the son of a peasant, from Fălticeni, on Borcea and in his idyllic verses the heart of the city lawyer softens:

O, immaculate flower of acacia! Priceless symbol of modesty

You come late in the dance of spring Stepping with the shyness of a virgin That in the end of April in the evening Would dance for her very first time[166]

Then, with the feeling of relief and euphoria of the patient with the bandages changed, he talks in great detail about Constantin Brâncoveanu[167] that he studied in an erudite manner. In Brâncoveanu he sees the most striking example of the politics of duplicity, even triplicity that the Romanian people was forced to have along the centuries. He defends him. (And what curious details: the ruin of the voivode obtained from the Turks, who knew very well for a long time the character but they closed their eyes, by the ambassador at Constantinople of the Sun King – the one celebrated as the patron of a golden age – and by his own uncle, the scholar High Steward Constantin Cantacuzino – who now boasts that he poisoned his brother Şerban out of loyalty to the Porte because he had discovered his treason. Then the presence at Constantinople, in 1714, beside the martyrs, of Văcărescu, as determined as them.)

Toward the evening, Lecca, more relaxed, tells us in great detail about the last days of the Antonescus and of those sentenced to death with them: Pantazzi, Piki Vasiliu, professor Alexianu. The marshal was deeply upset by the overwhelming fear of Ică, his refuse to take communion, the state of stupor he was looking for and obtained by using barbiturate. He was making himself hard reproaches. Few steps before the posts, Pantazzi and Lecca are detained and informed about their reprieve. Ion Antonescu died the way he lived: bravely.

Lecca is imprisoned since August 23rd 1944[168]. Until a while ago he didn't know if his wife lives or not. By chance someone who met her quite recently came in the cell. Lecca doesn't believe, he suspects that out of feeling of compassion they tell him lies. A certain detail convinces him: that his wife was taking out of her purse pieces of sugar that she was crunching.

Taking care of Bentoiu consumes all my time. Although an unbeliever for a long time, he made up with the church. He asks me to say prayers and he prays too. I convince him to learn verses by Gyr. He talks at length with professor Tomescu.

Carol II is attacked by Lecca. Antonescu is criticized by Bentoiu. In my opinion, Carol is the most devastating calamity that ever fell upon Romania; worse than the Huns, the Avars, the Gepidae, the Petchenegs[169], the Tartar invasions, the Polish szlachta[170], worse than the flood, the hail, the drought, the invasion of Carol-Robert[171], the pest of Caragea[172], the incursions of

Pazvantoglu, the Turkish punishment expeditions, the pasha from Silistra[173], the Cossacks, the love of the protecting power[174] after 1774, the fires, the earthquakes, the locusts, the deforestation, the territory losses, the fall of moraines, the tax on chimneys, the landslides, the levee breaks, phylloxera[175], the lady-bug, the Austrian and Russian occupations, than the poisoned wells, the women raped by invaders, the children taken as Janissaries[176], than the fall of towers, the defiled churches, than Mohammed, Baiazid, Suleiman and Fuad[177], worse than anything. Ubu roi in person, we came to pluck them of money, to tie the ass by the fence and then to make ourselves scarce. Out of respect for Bentoiu I refrain from talking too openly. About Antonescu, however, I cannot help but to show that, anyhow, he was the only one in Europe that dared to oppose Hitler, to confront him in a matter of pride for him, a matter in which neither Pétain nor the cardinals dared to say no. While the cream of the German aristocracy, the marshals and the field- marshals covered with medals and decorations were staying put and were trembling, and Hitler was foaming at mouth and was running from one end of the room to the other, Antonescu resisted him in his own den at Berchtesgaden; firm, with becoming modesty, he saved from death hundreds of thousands of Jewish souls.

(Lecca: With the price of a couple of rags, a working day of eight hours and sleeping home, a few apartments... Göring agreed, he told me: just make sure Hitler doesn't know...)

And, no matter what, king Michael could, had to remove Antonescu from power, if necessary to arrest him – although the solution of sending him abroad in a plane would have been more noble – but he shouldn't have him delivered to a private citizen, to Bodnăraş, to be brought to his house, worse than the insolvable debtors in the old Roman law. The king could have kept Antonescu arrested in the palace, ask him to commit suicide – and it is acknowledgeable that Antonescu was guilty of mistaking his personal honor with the right to life of the nation, while Bismarck was distinguishing the duty of the sentinel to die at his outpost from the duty of the leader to sacrifice, if necessary, for the salvation of the country even his honor – but no matter what the king shouldn't have agreed that Antonescu be taken to a private house and delivered to a foreign power. The royal gesture, better said of the counselor of the throne[178], has no excuse.

When I am taken out from the cell to be sent back to Gherla, I say farewell to all. Bentoiu, smiling, thanks me. Then, he starts to cry. Lecca, suddenly, kisses me. They died, soon after that, both of them.

–   At last, I learn from professor Tomescu the evening prayer, Gladsome Light, whose ineffable charm conquers me at once.

How can those who have it available since always prefer the Indian incantation formula om manî padme hom?

And by the way, how can they place the theosophy, the Zen, the tantrism above the gospel?

Lumina lină a sfintei slave[179]: is there another verse alike in the Romanian language?

In 1937 when at Christmas the government was formed, Tomescu sent to all his colleagues a

Bible.

(At that time, out of spite, I was sitting sick in bed. It was snowing incessantly.)

December 1970

Hardly would anyone die for a righteous man; yet for the kind man maybe someone would accept to die.

Rom. 5,7[180]

Much, much, much better were the youths in the prisons than the elders were.

Because it is easier to give up life when you have plenty of time to live? Because at young age

passions are more fervent but the spiritual vigor lest tainted? Because they didn't experience the rancor, the prejudices and the enmities of the old generation? Because they were less obsessed with the sourness and the outbursts, less burdened by the annexes of the passing of time: disfigurations, failures, disappointments, confirming thus the theory of Robert Brasilach according to which it is better to die before being defiles by the muddy march of the years? I don't know. They were better.

There was not one cell where the youths – and especially the Legionnaires – not to come to my help and not to give me the morning "coffee" and the biweekly piece of bread – priceless treasures for one sick at intestines – in exchange for the soup of putrid pickles, for the uncooked beans, for the potatoes boiled with peel and soil together or the raw cabbage at which even the beast look nauseous - –he only aliments that I could offer.

Until – and there have been more than three years – I learned to eat barley, they kept me alive. And without any ostentation.

Just by chance, Dinu P., from father Todea, finds out how his father-in-law, the social democrat Gh. Ene Filipescu died.

At Târgu-Ocna, tuberculosis hospital for the political prisoners until 1956 (because after that there weren't anymore hospitals for political prisoners), Filipescu proclaimed his socialist and atheist convictions in a cell full of Legionnaire youth. It's true, he was admonishing the guardians too, "children that abuse their parents". (Rubashov in Darkness at noon or The zero and the infinity).

He was more and more ill – the disease was advancing quickly – and he suffered (his breathing was painful) till death.

The young Legionnaires treated him so good, so carefully, so selfless and with love and with such a deep respect showed to the eldest among them that finally they softened his heart.

Before giving his soul – with great difficulty, because every breath was a spasm –, Filipescu embraced the one who especially was devoted to him, then all the others, he confessed to father Todea and died after taking communion. After few weeks died also the boy that took care of him like a son[181].

Psalm 39,13: "Let me rest before I go and I am no more."[182]

October 1958

The lines in which the Jews wait for applying for immigration in Israel start at three o'clock in the morning, than at two, one, eleven o'clock in the evening.

They are made out of small ruined merchants, old men and old women left alone in the country, but also party members, directors and general directors of ministries, superior office holders from state central institutions, cadre from the political establishment, militia and security organs.

The impression made by the lines is strong. I am a Jew, still strange feelings begin to smolder in me. And dad thunders with rage. Dad, actually...

(But this is another story. The house where we lived, not ours, was bombarded on April 4th 1944. After August 23rd we were accommodated in her house by the daughter of general Butoianu, nea Mihai, former classroom colleague of my father at the real high school Nicolae Bălcescu in Brăila. From the back at the Olari church up to the Moşilor way, where the Russian columns start entering from Colentina there are only a few yards.

At August 30th I was staying on the sidewalk and I was looking at the tanks. I swear I was not smiling, not saluting, not applauding, not exclaiming; I was staying and simply looking, just like that. I felt suddenly a tight grip on my arm and blessed with an IMBECILE pronounced clearly and stressed – you stay and look, cretin, you all stay and look and you don't know what is in store for you, look at them how they laugh, they will shed bitter tears and you will too... Let's go home... I take my father prudently by hand and we go quietly toward the Butoieni's house in the Olari street.)

–   This gesture of pulling the passport from the pocket has something of a trick, legerdemain, jokester. Or of a spoiled bad kid. I don't want to play anymore. I want my mamma. Mr. Goe[183]. Like the kid who when he doesn't like the play, when is not convenient anymore, retires, leaves gloomily for home. Or the winner who leaves the table after he took all the money. I want my mamma. I want home. I don't want to play anymore. You get everybody ready, you rouse them, call the singers, warm up the party, call the shots, you are their man – then you drop everything, you leave them in the lurch. Adios. Bye, bye. Nothing to say. He vanished. Edgar Goodbye. Come again. Jozefini trio. Doktor King, fakir seances. Mafalda, 43 Dorobanţi boulevard. The bullet paper pulled from the vest like the ace of spades from under the sleeve. Laila, the famous medium, 373 Grivița boulevard, tramcars 12 and 24, in the back of the courtyard, from 9-13 a.m. and 17-20 p.m., in my absence my husband, professor Theodorescu will receive you. The trickery, the swindler, the cheat, the hoax. They deserve it, the fools.

Some wise men are disgusted – some others smile. Simple people are taken by hate, spite, envy of the enduring kind.

(Cervantes in Algeria, after years, manages to organize with some others an escape. At night, they all meet at shore. The hired ship is there, ready to go. One of them is missing, though. They wait for him. The time passes. They decide to leave without the one who's late. But Cervantes insists: let's wait for him, imagine his despair when he will arrive and he will see the ship at large... They wait with anxiety, finally the missing one is coming... He was the squealer. They are all caught and brought back to slavery.

This atrocious story – where Cervantes appears so noble, proving that is not by chance that he wrote Don Quijote – is resurfaced in my memory, with no apparent connection, by the sight of the lines for immigration.)

–   Again through an association of thoughts that, at the beginning I cannot understand (but later I do), I remember the (pseudo) memoirs of Ciano, read around 1946-1947.

After 1942, suddenly, the tone of Ciano's memoirs changes: now he talks like a European, an aristocrat, a gentleman, a liberal; the Nazi horrors disgust and terrify him. He wants peace, quietness, he wants le bon vieux temps[184]! Look at him! No more the empire, the violence the castor oil; Ciano, himself, everybody knows, he is only a diplomat, like Talleyrand, like Vergennes, like Metternich. He didn't eat any garlic[185]. He didn't stain his hands with blood. He is a society man, with sins, of course, but he always wears white gloves.

And in his memoirs appear new characters: God, the pope, the king, prince Umberto. But when? When does Ciano remember the little king, the pope, Talleyrand and Europe? When he is cornered by the fear, when it became clear that the troops of Germany and her allies will not win the war. Not before. Only then the old wholesome fear recognized her child: good mother. Only then appears again il conte and he starts polishing the values of the old liberal civilization and the candelabrums of the European saloons.

Also at Jews we see a return to the past and repudiations: but repudiations due not to an evolution or a shattering discovery but to very concrete external factors.

–   The hierarchy of sins.

The church divides them in: venal, capital, crying to high heaven and against the Holy

Ghost.

Prison knows only two categories: those that are forgiven (contraband with hard currency

and gold, illegal crossing of the frontier, theft, murder, lust, homosexuality, parasitism, vagabondage, defamation of the state institutions) and those that are not forgiven (blackmail and squealing).

(We, humans, don't forgive them; when there is trembling repentance, God knows what He does; in The trial of Jesus by Diego Fabri, the Mother of God with her poor woman kerchief covers the head of the traitor trembling with repentance tears.)

– Division of work.

The occidentals: (Beckett, Ionescu, Cioran...) are unhappy for us; and we – we who know what a piece of sky can be, a piece of bread, a personal bed, a nail, a pencil – are happy for them.

April 1960

After one month we all from cell 18 are taken out and spread into other cells. I am lucky to be taken together with my godfather and brought to 24, where the first man we met is the monk that christened me and who was taken from our cell two days after the baptism.

In the new cell the atmosphere of exaltation and burning interest for exchange of ideas does not exist as in the other cell. The sun set and the moon rose. After the period of the spirit and the fire, follows a period of getting used to the ordinary life. The sudden difference of spiritual and energetic level seriously elicits me and makes me understand that the hard thing is not to answer to a fierce situation, even a tormenting one, but to learn to resist to the daily friction of the triviality. Mauriac too, quoting Charles du Bos: to believe even without the uninterrupted sound of music. Yes, that's exactly how it is: suddenly you cannot hear the music anymore, as if you passed the corner of the street. Now is the real challenge! At the investigation it was a fight, an absorbing and in its way enticing whirl, but now, in the boring gray of the program (even the exceptional program of the jail that, no matter how different than the outside one, it is still a train-train de vie[186] – and how purposely empty is: the Individual, the Time and the Others) what else is left? That which is more personal, that what you are: the strength, the fat, the gray matter, the hormones – YOU!

Fortunately I have for support my godfather and the reverent Mina. The monastery life (he wears the frock since he was a lad) prepared him wonderfully for prison and taught him what is essential for patience: to know to be silent, not to be amazed or upset by anything, to be deaf, determined to endure everything, without protest, with a blind and stubborn equality having for an ideal the disregard if not the insensitivity. And among these the greatest are: the silence and the disregard. The biblical text (James 3.2) – in which it is said that a man who never says anything wrong is capable of controlling every part of his body –

has a scientific and experimental character by no means inferior to, say, one of Claude Bernard's.

The godfather, here, shows himself more and more "spiritualist" which, in the intellectual language of the room means a mixture of necromancy, parapsychology and metempsychosis. The necromancy leaves me indifferent. Mihai Avramescu and Pavel Sim. gave me to read Guénon, who pulverized necromancy –, but with me there is also a personal repulsive reaction; regarding parapsychology, at its place of justified psychological branch, based on evidence, cannot be contested. After they laughed so much at the bio-currents of Dr Giurgea from Militari, now they are in the public domain of science.

But even necromancy (to be found where you wouldn't expect: the gendarme captain M.D. has a friend who was the king Louis-Philippe and he knows a woman who is the reincarnation of queen Elizabeth of England) in the dry atmosphere of the cell, because it is something else than the odious daily routine, the known in detail utilitarian objects (niche, barrel, sink, table, pitcher, kettle) and the brutal light of the bulb, seems to us enticing. In any case, it evokes rooms with superfluous furniture or with a turned off lamp and this is not little thing. In the cell every mystery disappears: the scarce of the objects, the thorough knowledge of the habits and the character of the people around, the absolute invariance of the passing of time. And it turns out that among other things – but not far from water, sleep, toilet, vitamins, exercise – we have an absolute need of shades, a bit of mystery. Any kind of spirituality is welcomed and purifies us. So that I listen without being upset many recounts about white, red and blue spirits, about Ketty King and Sir William Crookes (Ketty tricked Sir William: in his home she was appearing to him, but when the illustrious physicist wanted to repeat the experiment at the Royal Academy quarters, she didn't come; why? He asked her later and he received the answer: so that they would laugh at you, honey; tricky, isn't she?) and I get familiarized with Alain Kardec, Léon Denis, Raoul Montendon, Gabriel Delanne and Sir Russell Wallace. Files of fragile shadows sneak shyly into cell 24, apparently aware of their inconsistency but full of goodwill, poor dears, (even Ketty King – with her baggy dress from the XVII century, – she doesn't play tricks anymore, out of pity for us) and they sweeten a little the draught of the matter with drops of illusion.

(In this second prison cell something happens that seems to me similar to what must have happened in the road to Emmaus. The Savior is not among His people anymore, the groom left. But it is incumbent to you, as a man, to emanate fidelity and a new kind of happiness, in undertone, and to discover the reality of the presence of the Comforter in the most unexpected and bare place: in yourself. You must give more yourself, you are not anymore a simple spectator, a guest at the wedding, but participant with equal rights, associate, constructor of happiness on your own. You must prove something very difficult, that not only the beginning – the wedding – is pure, but also the daily living maybe maintained at

122

an acceptable degree of relative noblesse and dignity. The same as the beginning is not: and it hurts. But this is precisely the difference between childhood and maturity: the accepted and endured pain, the acceptance of the inevitable difference of level between the purity of the wedding and of the celebration and the impurity of the common days and of the lean years. [187])

Jilava, March 1960
The error of Nietzsche, proclaims Al. Pal. in the deafening noise of room 18 (Who registers for the barrel? Where did you put the pitcher? Vexillum in French is oriflamme, abassourdi in English is flabbergasted. Watch out, those who go to the barrel, there is very little water left! I don't remember how do you say dropper in French, do you remember, prince, how is dropper in French?) is that he despised the most virile feelings and among them the one especially virile, that so frequently show the Homeric heroes or the medieval heroes: mercy. Tears are also the attribute of the warriors in Iliad.

(Mercy, I was going to read after discharge, in Eugen Ionescu's works, mercy is not sentimental, Nietzschean gentlemen, but humane and masculine. Al. Pal. said this before any of us could read these words of Eugen Ionescu.)

1934
Manole about madness: the most pertinent thing about madness was said by Sholom Aleichem: the madman does not break only the windows of others.

Therefore, we can know anytime and anywhere if the madman is truly madman or a fake. If he breaks only the windows of others it means he is not sincere, but if he breaks his windows or his and of others then he is without doubt an authentic madman.

Authentic madmen: 1948, Radu Cioculescu: he doesn't give to the Security the names – not known by that institution – of those (I am one of them) who helped him to write and to send abroad some memoirs. 1950, A.L. Zissu: he refuses to sign the appeal for peace for Stockholm; he tells to those come to him with the petition that he is for war, he scorns them, he chases them – and the poor people, frightened, ran away realizing that because they are three they are forced to denounce him[188].

Cernica, 1965
Father staretz Roman: the great guilt of the Pharisee is not the pride as much as his conviction that he is self sufficient, that he can justify himself, that he doesn't need God.

Again about time: the Christian is the one who lives not in the past, not in the future but only in the present. The past does not weigh on him, and he doesn't worry about the future.

(Maybe especially for the Christian is true the verse of Mallarmé, one of the most beautiful of the French language: Le vierge, le vivace et le bel aujourd'hui[189]?)

September 1940

I read with strange feelings of satisfaction (only Cassandra knew how painful is to see you were right), glued on walls and posts, manifests of the Legionnaire movement against Carol II. It is the right to critic that the authors of the manifests earned it through sufferance. But, after only a few days, certain statements and articles reek revenge and the art to use the direction where the wind blows. Overwhelming the title of a short article by Iorga: Let us not be insolent.

Jilava, cell 0, december 1963

Professor Vasile Barbu, former chief of the Legionnaire organization of the Vlaşca county:

I'm telling you the truth, I speak to you as to a comrade, the Captain, truly, was above any believer. If he had lived, the Legion would not have become what has become: the fifth German column.

Christian and Romanian was the Legion for its founders and leaders, all killed by orders of Carol II. The ideal of Codreanu was the Icon and he would have run the country accordingly, not according to the Nüremberg program. But since there were left only a handful of yesmen and around them only some hotheads...

–   To the European spirit Dr. Al-G reproaches the ferocious, animal attachment to life. The European is almost incapable of suicide: proof of cowardice. The Asian is more detached, not so pitiably enslaved by existence. In Christianity (he doesn't contest it) prevails the cult of the eternal life, but at the European, at the white man, he sees something different: a base fear, a clinging at any price, with the price of any baseness, any crime, to the verb to live. This clinging to life of neutered dog, of paralytic blind, of cancer sufferer maddened by sufferance but still sucking vitamins, of traitor who for escaping death sold his entire kind and his comrades, it is best expressed by the neutral

non-reflexive pronoun of lack in French: On veut vivre or in German: man will leben. The most depressing formula: es will leben, applied to the man.

July 1952

Father is at the glass factory in the Black Forest, in the remote Bihor county. Making eleven months in the same factory, (almost unbelievable) I finally get a leave of twelve working days. I decide to spent it at Timişul de Sus (Upper Timiş), where the Augustinian mothers still keep a pension. (Manole: all the Yids were taken by a great love for monasteries and Catholicism.)

The building facing the road of the institution being full, I am lodged in the annex close to the chapel, where permanently lives the widow of minister C., who played an important role in the making of the Timiş locality.

Right away after arrival I ask permission to pay my respects to Madam C.; she receives me with joy and she remembers well my father.

After a few days I get sick quite badly; my neighbor brings me toasted bread and tea. She wears – like Alexandrina Cantacuzino and the other ladies from the National Association of Romanian Orthodox Women (sometimes even queen Maria) – a dress of dark velvet; the dress goes up to the chin and around the neck stays a long necklace from which hangs a massive silver cross. Every time she brings me toasted bread and tea, Madam C. makes the sign of the cross on my forehead.

February 1971

I have come that they may have life and may have it in all its fullness.

John 10,10

The yesterday sermon of father G.T. and the letter from Ottawa of Toma Pavel almost coincide; as date and subject.

In both of them is about the theme of the feast in all the teachings of Christ.

The Lord uses any opportunity for feasts and enjoyment. There are dinners given for bodily healing (Matt. 8,15; Mk. 2,15; Lk. 5,29); in the case of the prodigal son or the tax collector Zacchaeus, the great repentance is what justifies the splendor of the celebration. The Lord blesses and multiplies the wine at the wedding of Cana; Mary anoints too during a dinnerl at Bethany there was great feast since Marta was so concerned and overwhelmed by work.

Not only that He does not refuse the invitations of the sinners, but even the Pharisees are not rejected by the Lord. The heaven is compared to a feast (Matt. 22,2; Lk. 14,16; 22,30) and what is promised to the man who open his heart to Christ? The one who until then was staying at the door knocking, now says: I will come in and he and I will eat together (Rev. 3,20).

These unending good mood and will of the Lord to celebrate the joys by feasts appear projected over the course of all the years of preaching; the texts: "For John came neither eating nor drinking, and people say, 'He is possessed'; the Son of Man came, eating and drinking, and they say, 'Look at him! A glutton and a drinker, a friend of tax-collectors and sinners!'" (Matt. 11,18-19) and "For John the Baptist came, neither eating nor drinkingwine and you say, 'Look at him! A glutton and a drinker, a friend of tax-collectors and sinners!'" (Lk. 7,34) are clear.

Paul, following the example of his Teacher (Acts 6,34) after a victory of the good (the baptism of the jailer from Philippi), he set out a meal too and rejoiced with his whole household.

125

– A. Schmemann assumes the materialist formula of Feuerbach: "The man is what he eats" and he says this is a strictly biblical and Christian formula.

Whoever does not eat My body and does not drink My blood...

Again Schlemann (who is Orthodox): the world is for the Christian a feast, the image of the feast appears all over the Scripture and it is also the finale, its coronation: "so that you eat and drink at My table in My kingdom".

BUGHI MAMBO RAG

...of the type eintretten, tratt ein, eingetretten, ...from vivre is je vécus, tu vécus, il vécut..., from voir is je vis, tu vis, il vit... Spanish has two separate words for to be: ser and estar. The present of ser: soy, eres, es, somos, soís, son, the present of estar: estoy, estas, esta, estamos, estatís, estan... nous vécûmes, vous vécûtes... the Sanskrit declinatio however has eight cases: nominative, accusative, instrumental, dative, ablative, genitive, locative, vocative... of the kind erkündigen, erkündigte, erkündigt... the preposition follows the verb and can change its meaning, creating this way new words, for instance to speak up, to give up, to wash up, to drive up...

– The Lord – it follows up from everywhere – blesses, fertilize and multiplies: bread, wine, fishes. He does not appear as a God of the desert, the wasteland, the tundra, the sterility, the dryness but of the richness, the fullness, the feast and the enjoyment. Whoever wants to come to Him will find the joy and the feast. Not only at Socrates and Plato. (That one is just a preliminary image; as much as possible.)

The blessed Augustine: Marta worries and endeavors while Maria is partying.

Among the reasons for which God refers so often to feasts and entices with well garnished tables (the calf is a lot...) I deduce:

a) The one invoked by the skilled theologians; the skilled theologians do not value too much the argument invoked by their less skilled colleagues: God created man so that He be worshipped by him. They formulate in a completely different manner, a manner worthy of the greatness of the divinity the purpose of creation: to give to man the chance to participate to the huge, euphoric joy of living (life as it is, says the Catechism of the Dutch Catholic bishops, is a miracle that takes your breath away). Etienne Gilson expresses clearly the reason why God created the world and the people. Only to magnify Him? It would mean we know Him very little. "What God forges are not some witnesses that prove His glory, but beings that enjoy it the way He enjoys it and who, participating to His being, they also participate to His beatitude. Therefore not for Him, but for us is the Lord looking for His glory; not to obtain it, because He already has it, not to increase it, because it is beforehand perfect, but to share it with us."

(Not in vain I keep insisting, pestering that Christ God is a nobleman, a gentleman, a boyar.)

126

b)   The one upon which I like to ponder at length: that only at the feast the man enjoys the joy of the other, more, he needs this joy: the more the guests are happy, the more the feast is beautiful and successful. The feast is maybe – in a paradoxical way – the only place where the joy of another is not envied. And where there is no competition, numerus clausus; the more the merrier: the increase of the number of guests far from being a stumbling block, a danger, it multiplies the joy of anyone and of everyone. If so, then the feast realizes the paradisiacal condition: it supposes first the ability to enjoy other's joy, to commune it.

Jilava, room 50 (tuberculosis infirmary)

The Adventists in the cell, and they are quite a few, despise openly and hotly father Petcu from Năieni, country priest with no superior theological knowledge, whom they easily defeat quoting – copiously – biblical texts specifying chapters and verses, peremptory proof of a great familiarity with the Scripture but also habit of procedural parrot. They look down on him because he gets entangled and also because father, worn down by boredom and misery, takes comfort in the remembrance of the Istrița wines – prize winners at international viticultural contests – and the parties of a village of hard working farmers.

Indeed, the spectacle offered by the Adventists takes oftentimes a dramatic display: if the food is made with a trace of fat or horse meat – at the tuberculosis infirmary it happens sometimes – they reject it, raise their arms and they bring their offering as a tribute to the Almighty. It seems artificial, rehearsed, but coming from people transparently lean, with frequent hemoptysis and hungered after long prison years the gesture takes a very concrete character. Meanwhile, father swallows hurriedly as the rest of us. Suddenly he is put in an inferiority position.

Deciding to defend the poor man, very nice otherwise, I start by learning by heart the texts that are contrary to the Adventist interpretation (objective and honest, they indicate and they teach us these texts) and we arrive, the priest and I, to battle them on their own scriptural terrain. To the blind observance of the Sabbath we oppose the fundamental passages from II Cor. 3.6 (the letter kills but the Spirit gives life); Matt. 12.8; Mk 2.28; and Lk. 6.5 (The Son of Man is also Lord of the Sabbath); Mk. 2.27 (The Sabbath was made for man and not the man for Sabbath), Rom. 14.6 (He who observes the day observes it for the Lord; and he who does not observe the day, to the Lord he does not observe it), 17 (the kingdom of God is not drinking and eating) and 22 (Do you have faith? Have it to yourself before God. Happy is he who does not condemn himself in what he approves.); I Cor. 8.8 (But food does not commend us to God) and 10.27 (If any of those who do not believe invites you to dinner and you desire to go, eat whatever is set before you…); Col. 2.14 (And he wiped out the certificate of debt with its requirements that was against us) and 16 (So no one judge you in food or in drink, or regarding a festival or a new moon or Sabbaths).

Especially with this last text we make wonders among the colleagues who watch the dispute carefully, glad for the victories of Orthodoxy but also admirers of the strength of character of the sectarians.

When we are taken out for bath, on Saturday, the Adventists do not agree to wash their body. The hands yes, even Saturday; but not the body. The spectacle that repeats itself weekly (we are in a period when the penitentiary direction allows the application of the rules of hygiene) brings into open two naïve forms of stubbornness and proves once again that everybody is a bit right. The Adventist clenching, illogical, legalist, Talmudic is – bearing in mind the sufferance and the insults that causes – also admirable. But the guardians aren't wrong either asking the inmates to wash themselves. But why isn't given to the Adventists the possibility to wash themselves another day? Because Saturday is the bathing day in prisons! Malice you can still fight but bureaucracy is undefeatable. First father Petcu, then all of us, are asked to soap forcibly our comrades who stay naked under the shower, with their arms crossed across the chest, smiling seraphicly, waiting the martyrdom. They are pathetic, silly and profoundly respectable. The priest refuses firmly the opportunity offered to humiliate his unforgiven adversaries. (And the guardians who know well the affair, find hard to believe that the priest does not want to avenge himself.) We all refuse the offer now addressed to the entire collective, then the order that is given. Finally the cops don't insist and the scene ends as the Frenchmen say in queue de poisson[190], takes a rain check like the wooden gratings installed under the showers. While when the right-worshippers are in unanimity they are barely given the chance to soap themselves in a flash and to rinse even more instantaneously, when Adventists are present, the guardians, to provoke and to annoy them, to spite them, they prolong on purpose a lot the staying in the showers, and they give plenty of hot water: the right-worshippers leave satisfied of cleanliness and truly bathed.

With the little water we receive in the cell, renouncing any washing, we help the disciples of captain William Miller to wash themselves on their turn Sunday morning.

–   Traian Crăcea, young Transylvanian, fiery and skillful Adventist preacher, is the only one of his kind who admits the possibility of salvation for those who are not part of the sect. (The Jehovah witnesses are even more exclusive, at them the saved ones are numerically limited.) Crăcea talks about Christ with tears in his eyes, real tears, not like those of the Balzacian hero who was mourning for his inaccessible loved one, lost behind the bars of the monastery.

Jilava, room 13

Nemo's theory and mine about Doktor Faustus of Thomas Mann. I summarize it to Nicolae Balotă who listens with great interest.

Doktor Faustus is a book conceived on three plans, out of which two are initiatic.

The first plan, of the naïve lecture: Serenus Zeitblom is a nice and normal man, Adrian Leverkühn is a madman. These artists are actually demonic. Art is dangerous.

The second plan, or the first degree initiation: Serenus Zeitblom is an uninteresting dolt, Adrian Leverkühn is the artist in all his truth, art supposes a measure of madness, only this way can it be creative and justifies the insipid existence of the world.

The third plan, or of the second degree initiation: Serenus Zeitblom is right, but not in an fastidious manner, but paradoxically, frenetically, Kierkegaardian. Adrian Leverkühn is truly a madman, the ideal is an effervescent Zeitblom. Then the faith of the crones is good? Is it good to go to church and light candles? Of course. But in a crazy manner. Zoom effect: the normal, if it is practiced with enthusiasm is superior to dementedness. The decent life considered as one of the fine arts[191]!

I remember the theory of Manole about the necessity to create a party of the violent moderates (or the conservatives in trench-coat) with the purpose to defend with – Sorelian – vehemence the equilibrium, the reason and the decency.

February 1931
Tea at Anetta, with several guests. Manole agreed to come too, after long insistence from my part. He declares that he is not interested in a gathering of pro-communiste or vague leftist little Jews. During the dinner (cold refreshments) he acknowledges that there are honorable things that can be said about Karl Marx. What are those things? wants to know Bellu Z., a little bit curios but especially despisingly patient. (It's obvious that this bold young man is not enlightened. Let us help him – enlighten him.)

For instance, says Manole, the fact that he married a fat German lady of very good family. When Engels wanted to marry a working woman, Ms Marx threatened him not to receive him in her house anymore. Then Marx had a splendid beard and was a handsome man. And he was drinking seriously, true, mostly bear – observes Manole with regret, like the man forced to acknowledge the defects of an otherwise perfect personality – but he was holding his liquor and one day a drunk Englishwoman fell in love on the imperial of an omnibus with him and his beard.

Bellu Z. boils. (Provocation!)

That he liked to stroll in London in the omnibus, preferably on the imperial, Manole continues. And regarding Lassalle, a very honorable thing was said. By

Bismarck: he is an adversary to me, but I would like to have him as a neighbor on my estate.

All the leftists turn their head disgusted and – after a moment of heavy silence – they redirect their attention toward sandwiches and bottles.

1969

At the bakery exit an old, small, discreet beggar. I give him three or four lei.

He takes out his hat with respect and he thanks me babbling for long.

I don't know why – the remembrance of my father, the physical resemblance (little and stooping), the so polite gesture, the shame of being saluted by an old man for a few lei, the invasion in the memory of scenes from prison revealing the poor human condition? – but I start crying with bursts of tears in the middle of the road, like a madman.

Gherla 1962

Virgil B., with squirrel eyes, small, thin by his nature, now like a skeleton, stopped in his development, whom the infectious hepatitis left with wax like skin of green hue, is a prisoner since he was seventeen. When I met him he was twenty-five. The glances, the movements, his briskness, the gestures of spinning top, the thirst for knowledge, the angers for surprising reasons are those of a child. He knows incredibly many things, some of them belonging to the encyclopedic column of science and technology magazine for youth. For instance the entire table of Mendeleev, by groups, subgroups and periods, symbol after symbol. I learn it too, together with major Ilie Șerbu; to this one, the age did not stopped the inclination for learning; and it didn't kill the will of good.

Virgil developed a passion for existentialism, about which he heard before; I explain it to him again and again. I recount to him the plays of Ionescu: they charm him. Although he lives isolated from the world, inside the thick walls of the former fort Jilava, or inside the Teresian building (or Martinuzzian) from Gherla, to Virgil the spirit of the generation and the atmosphere of the time (wherefrom the wind of the century blows) gives him special antennas that facilitate the comprehension and helps him guess by skipping.

While talking to him about existentialism and looking around (we are in a bad cell), I formulate the opinion that – descriptively – the existentialism is right. The life is exactly how the existentialism depicts it, that's how the world looks when one lacks the naïve faith in God and in the illusion of morals. Yes, the wall, the nausea and the dirty hands[192] (dirty because of the compromises and betrayal, but also the inevitable wearing down of the days) define the horrible universe from which Christ is missing. (The apartment left by people, invaded by mice and night birds.) This description of the existentialist is not at all exaggerated; only their solution is wrong. Or, better said, they don't know a solution: the breaking through the wall to Jesus the comforter. (The comforter but also the revelator, the peace given to the Christian is also founded on knowledge, by no means inferior to that gained from Indian or Zen Buddhism.) And it is surprising: some existentialists have been in prisons: how come they didn't find the way to break through the walls?

BUGGY MAMBO RAG
…The Germans received Colonel Sturdza very correctly, but coldly. Proof that at that time still existed a feeling of military honor… And when Mackensen came in the occupied territory, in Bucharest to see Carp, the old germanophil came at the door and threw him out… What are you saying? where did you hear this? It's absolutely false… says Marcellus to Demetrios…

– André Gide: his readers and followers greatly enjoyed the words came out from the mouth of Ivan Karamazov: if there is no God, then everything is permitted.

The rationale is simple: since God does not exist, the barriers have no point, you can do – not bothered – anything. But this libertine and comforting vision (and since mamma died there is no need to go to Algeria) misses another ineluctable consequence of the formula. If there is no God it does not mean that only the man can get away with anything but the nature and the universe have no obligation toward man anymore. Who can say, if that's the order of things: it is unjust? Or: why are we wronged? Everything is permitted also against the rational being; everything is permitted also to the blind forces of nature, the ironic coincidences of the hazard, the intricate plans of the destiny. Everything is possible: it is possible the mockery, the profanation, the absurdity. (Not to mention the unpleasant consequences on a concrete plan: the murders, the assaults, the violence – they are unpleasant too when they pass from books into the streets, ask the inhabitants of the great metropolis after eight o'clock in the night.) I know someone who would be glad to be so: not to be limited, not to be forced to hurry.

The lovers of reason and justice – among those the unbelievers were usually recruited – should realize that they, most than anybody, have all the interest to exist a God. Let this contested God forbid that someone to come to wish God to exist though and not everything to be permitted.

(I wonder, Trotsky and other exiled of the communist ideal weren't they – just a little bit – happy there still are countries with different regimes where they could take refuge?)

January 1955
Fourteen hours. A call from father Mihai. I am convoked at sixteen hours. I'll see why. Did something bad happen? A sickness? – Am I a man to address (verbatim translation from French: suis-je homme á…) a lawyer in case of a sickness? I hear him smiling at the other end of the connection.

In the hall-room in the parochial house of the skete I find a lot of people, only cream and elite. I am quickly edified on the reunion theme. Father Cleopa, the spiritual of the Slatina monastery, monk of peasant origin and with reputation of saint, sits in the guest chair, and this one is on an stool at his feet, very quiet and pious, very obliging and a bit too obedient. Why this gesture of natural meekness seems traced on the words from Acts 22,3? If the one who sits at the feet of the master is Paul, then the one on the chair can be only Gamaliel.

Father Cleopa, quite young, simple, easy speaker, with gentle eyes, very dark hair, beard and moustaches, and serious gestures. They ask him all kind of questions and he answers all of them not only with great patience and just reckoning, but also with visible attention, after meditating at long. Codin Mironescu, Todiraşcu, Pillat, Alice Voinescu, Mihai Musceleanu, doctor Voiculescu, Alexandru Duţu, many youths with fiery and warm eyes listen transported and you can tell they have part of happiness. Some of them, like Pavel Sim., Virg. Cd. and others study theology in their spare time and they have examinations clandestinely. Yes, these would not leave sad from the Lord.

They stay until very late, as if sleep, rest, fatigue, businesses, schedules would not exist. And they don't even have a samovar as the Russians do.

I leave thoughtful; why do I listen from outside to all these enticing things, why am I afraid to make the decisive step?

August 1970
Meanwhile most of those who were listening to the pious Cleopa at the Mothers' skete passed through prison or at least through Security. Father Mihai is an exception. Others died.

Father Cleopa – after he lived about four years in the forest (eating mostly roots, not having the possibility to light a fire – the smoke could have been detected –, helped by some peasants, but not during snow – the foot traces would have lead the repression organs on the right path –, good neighbor with the beasts) – is now at Sihăstria, as a simple monk.

Dinu Pillat and I, leaving from Văratec, arrive at Sihăstria at noon. It is a glorious day of August: the light and the landscape belong to the incorruptible world after the general resurrection. The purity, from everywhere, strikes you, grabs you, vanquishes you.

At father Cleopa's hut on the top of the hill we arrive with difficulty. You can see that the former persecuted is hiding or is under surveillance or both. We manage, through the intercession of some monks to which we explain what do we want (and this part takes a while), to be received. The monk with the hair and the beard of a very intense black, who stood so erect, has his hair gray now and is lean. Joyful, he keeps us for more than three hours, he remained the same fluent talker. He teaches us about temptations and the distinction that must be made between the temptations from the left and those from the right. The temptation from the left we all know: is that of passions, of vice, of evil. But there is also one from the right, more surprising, coming from virtues and qualities, from the desire to do the good. (The self sufficient piety. The good imposed forcibly. God is above in heaven, all are good on earth. I have grace, what do I care, I can go and chew my bone in my corner. The exemplary, condescending literature. The sentencing morality.) We can fall by that, there is nowhere safety. Vivere pericolosamente[193]. The monk knows the Nietzschean slogan as well as Mussolini. The monastic life is as full of difficulties, potholes, ravines and despair like the darkest existentialist novel. Wherever you look, only traps. Parois[194] say the French existentialists. What a leap is required!

Out of the monastery we are welcomed again by the nature: just green and blue, calm and distinguished brilliance. What a deception! Temptation from the right too!

–   At the temptation from the right I think refers C.S. Lewis too in his book about devils. The example he gives is trivial but with huge perspectives:

The "guardian devil" of a certain Englishman prompts strongly the mortal whom he "guards" to sacrifice himself in a matter that concerns him: that specifically British of the tea. The mortal would like to drink his five o'clock cup of tea on the terrace. The wife and the mother-in-law prefer to drink it inside. Give in, prompts him the devil, be meek and kind, altruist, sacrifice yourself, humor them. The man, therefore, drinks his tea with them, and all the time he feels unhappy and wronged, the drink stays in his throat, curse in his mind both women who now see well that he made them the concession unwillingly and now they feel taken by antipathy. The devil rejoices. Three down with one blow.

What was supposed to do our mortal? Not to go to far on the way of the virtue in a secondary matter, to acknowledge his limits; to say plainly and simply that is more pleasant to take the tea on the terrace, even alone. They would have stayed inside, he outside, everybody would have been happy, the "spirit of sacrifice" lacking right reckoning (and applied where it had no place) would have been defeated and, at a greater level of modesty, not one of those three souls would have gone in the intricacies of resentment and irritation– intricacies that for the small devils are a true and preferred corso[195].

–   Dr Al. G. protests against the superiority that I allege Christianity has over the Hinduism. Love, according to him, does not lack at all in Brahmanism and Buddhism. The greatest joy for an individual is not to reach Nirvana by himself, but to help others to reach the end of the sufferance. The proof is bodhisattva Avalokittesvara whose perfection allows him anytime to access Nirvana; still, he refuses the exit from the cycles of reincarnations and, out of affection and pity for people, remains in the world under the form of Dalai Lama.

I: to guide them where? Into nothingness, nevertheless.

Under no circumstances can I understand how many European Christians felt suddenly that if their religion is not altogether bad, is, however, greatly inferior to the Asian ones.

Buddhism? But Buddhism is an easy solution. You retire – and that's it. It is a renunciation, redeployment. Christianity is something much more difficult and complex – is teandria (God+Man). Without stopping being man you also have to be God in the same time. Doesn't the head of the Christian church ask for the crucifixion of the body? But not for obtaining a state of placidity but as a mean for total devotion. Confucius? It is a very sophisticated and wise politeness (in the etymological sense). Yoga? It seems to me, ultimately, a gymnastics: psychosomatic of course, good, useful, but strictly functional, like any callisthenics. Zen is contemplation: what is its oscillating meaning?

The calling for stoicism is ever alive for many of the superior people even now. The stoicism is noble, who can deny it? But it is sour. The stoic is dignified, still his smile is tense, sour, full of resentments; of silent (controlled, without doubt) pouting.

Christianity is neither sour nor fearful in face of life. It does not propose a run away, but some other thing immensely more difficult and more efficient, the transfiguration. This is temerity and grandeur.

But one should not believe that Christianity hurts our selfishness: actually, to be good is the most selfish among the solutions, the investment that brings the highest dividend.

1940

The theory of Shalom Ash (in Der Krieg geht weiter[196]): the Jews did not acknowledge Christ as Messiah because they couldn't accept the idea that the final Good and the true Truth were shown and therefore were known.

They wanted to push them further into the future, still full of hopes, still cloaked in hiding veils.

They did not contest the grandeur of the new teaching, but to acknowledge Christ would have meant to admit that the Discovery was done, that this is it.

They preferred to further keep their undefined dreams; maybe something even greater will come...

Văratec, 1971

On the fast of Saint Mary I go to confession to father Calinic.

Among other things: a former prison mate comes to me to pluck me of money; he is reeking and sometimes he is throwing to my face rotten lies: that his kid died and he lacks the money for the funeral – to me who I know that he is not a parent. I gave him money for a while then I rejected him. I feel, though, a sort of anxiety. But what can I do with a drunkard!?

134

You should have given him the money, the confessor interrupts me. When he comes back, gave him, don't judge him! Me too – he says – I have a drunkard friend, a wretch and when he comes to me I give him a treat. Give him!

How glad I am that I became Orthodox.

Văratec, 1970

The Maestro and Margaret by Mikhail Bulgakov, insistently recommended by Pillat.

The devil Behemoth, with two colleagues, comes on Earth, in the Union, taking the image of a black cat carrying a Primus[197].

Black cat, of course, is perfect for a devil, but why the Primus?

(Zut! says the conductor lady, the cats are not allowed to travel with the bus!)

This Primus is worth all the money and is the key of the book, and is the proof of the genius of the author.

Because for such people, such devils. Behemoth is a great melancholic demon, a rebellious prince of darkness. But he knows where he happened to land and – throwing away the Byronic or Goethean cloak, the Luciferic and sumptuous cloak – he blends in, he acts according to the parochial district. The Primus is the affiliated mocking symbol (diabolo: to part, to mock) of the Soviet civilization after fifty years dedicated to forge a society preoccupied exclusively about material goods and prosperity, after fifty years of constructing the communism – triumph of the well-being.

When the devils fly over the buildings and with Asmodeic powers lift the roofs, what do they see? They see long strings of halls where, returned from work, the Soviet women cook the dinner each of them on a Primus.

This is the communism! This and not other: the comrade from the department, the lodging administration, the certificate of social origin, the mandatory denunciation, the lines, the Primus. And meanwhile a billion and a half of imbeciles, in the west, sigh, manifest, kidnap, undress, grow beards, make love in public, throw Molotov cocktails to accomplish the ideal: the Primus, the little gas stove of the poor.

The housekeepers have no choice. But the thought of that billion and half, who stays to ponder, goes crazy.

Another communism? If it was accomplished somewhere else, would have been any different? When we will build it, it will be something else.

Illusions, nonsense. You will work with the same ingredients. You will arrive in the same place. The same social racism, no more Leninist than Marxist (even if you are a nice person, although the bourgeoisie played once a progressive role, we have no choice: you are what you are, and since you cannot be otherwise, you must, therefore, be condemned.)

This is it, nothing else. Vengeful. Little. Stinking. Slum. Envious. Believer in the trinity: hate, suspicion, envy. With tongue of gossip and soul of slave. The society of the prosperity, where the kitchen is the Primus on the hall.

They know, the demons, how to incarnate, it is not by chance.

BUGGY MAMBO RAG

…In the train station of Teiuş, who do you think I met? Dragomireanu, he was going to the office of the station chief. Alecu remained in the ministerial wagon. He wanted to eat an omelet and he was asking the station chief to make arrangements with the restaurant to serve him in the wagon. I hurry to Alecu. He was in his way to Gherla, to meet Hossu, to ask him to talk to Maniu to come in October at the coronation in Alba Iulia. Maniu kept refusing. Alecu was well known in Transylvania before the war from the time he was coming under the name Ion Brad to bring donations for the Romanian schools. He had high expectations from Hossu, young bishop and a brave soul. I ate too from that omelet… Nah, dreams, he didn't come… He didn't come and the newspapers from Budapest could write Erdely[198] non coronat… God forgive him, because he died like a hero and a martyr…

Autumn 1964

Nichifor Crainic – the prisoner from Aiud who, for a kettle of barley or a cigarette, was saying that God doesn't exist – is condemned by everybody when leaving the prisons, after the reprieve.

It remains to be seen what would the judges do after fourteen years of cell regime.

On the other hand they all hurry to write in the Fatherland Voice, now, in state of liberty! Disgust. Absurdity.

Am I one of the last twenty-nine Legionnaires?

In The thirst and the hunger (third act), Eugen Ionescu solved the problem for good: after two weeks of hunger and passing of the soup vapors by their noses, the atheist in his kneels recites Our Father and the believer denies the Almighty and glorifies Darwin.

And do not lead us into temptation. Not everybody has the gift of suffering, the torture is like the bribe: all you have to do is to keep insisting, raising the offer until you match the price.

Topaze: he is incorruptible, he asks one hundred thousand francs! Orwell: there is for everybody an irresistible torture.

– God, forgiving, does not always punish our sins and mistakes. The devil, alert, does not overlook one single good deed. (On the other side of the equation the signs of the values are inverted.)

That's why it is so difficult to do the good, because you encounter at every step the strenuous opposition and the skillful obstacles of the deceitful one.

Nietzsche: "We are especially sanctioned for our virtues."

Once the man takes the decision to do the good, he assumes an immense responsibility and he put his head willingly into the noose. Truly, the good being of divine essence, the people of good will prove – here is a point where we have to concede to the devil – great audacity and even arrogance. Anyhow, before charging into the domain of the good it is necessary to know that you are going into mined terrain.

The proverbs observe the situation with cynicism: "You give, you lack", "You give with the bucket you take with the spoon", "You give with your hand and you run with your legs", "You give a finger and he takes your whole hand", "Whoever you invite for dinner, chases you from your house", and the apostle does not think differently when he writes (Rom. 7.15, 18, 19) that he does not make the good he wants, but the evil that he does not.

The evil can be done by anyone, no matter how weak he is. But the good is only for strong souls and hard tried natures. Evil: milk for children; good: meat for adults. G. Duhamel, creating poor civil servant Salavin, bent suddenly on holiness and ending up defeated, understood how things are. Holiness and kindness is not at everyone's reach. One is to play the ball on the street, another to perform fencing. It is required preparation and a tough training. For this cause the monks mortify themselves (and they strengthen themselves) in many ways before presuming to attempt good deeds.

Pity the yogi pursue departure from the world, beyond good and evil, and not the doing of good and the living of love, because they are very well trained.

The film Viridiana of Bunuel, considered by many anti-Christian and scandalous, represents too a perfect intuition of the danger of looking for holiness alone, without guidance and preparation. Viridiana is a justification of the church and the monastery and a demonstration of our little ability in learning and applying the teachings of Christ.

–   The heresy of the false meekness, somehow at the antipode of another: the angelism.

The temptation to let yourself damned to the eternal torments and to go in hell from so much love of Christ that you long to commit the sacrifice of separating from Him, this logical and demented temptation was described by Papini in one of his novels.

This temptation hovered over the Jansenists too, who were advising the monks from Port Royal to not take communion for a long time in order to suffer subtly and fiercely staying apart from Christ.

At the death of N. Iorga, Ct. N. wanted to send from Germany the following telegram to Horia Sima: "I asked to be member of the Legion in the day of the assassination of Codreanu, now I ask to be released from the Legion in the day of the assassination of Nicolae Iorga."

But he didn't do it, out of meekness.

But the temptation of the false meekness – to refrain from good deeds and legitimate joys – is the same as the sin of Judas. Judas relinquished, he humbled himself sinking in evil.

Out of meekness to give up, to consent to be the scoundrels that we are.

The explanation of the rationale by which starting from modesty and humility we arrive at demonism we can find only in the works of Chesterton who defined madness as the supreme form of logic.

Of course, the rationale of Papin's hero: I love Christ – Christ asks us to sacrifice ourselves for Him – what sacrifice can be greater than giving Him up forever? – let us commit therefore those crimes and baseness that would open for sure the gates of hell, is utmost logical. Just that is only logical, therefore demented.

As main attribute of the man, the Orthodox monks consider not the kindness, neither the intelligence, nor love, faith, patience, piety or holiness, but the right reckoning, that is a very complex virtue and difficult to express in words. (It has a formula vast like the base polymers.) In the constituency of right reckoning enters, precisely and mysteriously apportioned, common sense, and wisdom, and decency, and stillness, and will added to the above. Not one of the virtues is absolute – not even the truth -, only the skilled balancing of many can protect us from evils (this is quite easy) but also from savant blunders and sophisticated errors.

Unfortunately it is not possible to surpass the iron logic of the demented using reason but only by recognizing the truth noticed by Chesterton, that pure logic, not based and not completed by the other benefic qualities, is a dangerous disease, even nefarious.

The heresy of the false meekness also breaks the commandment to conquer the heavens. We are not required at all resignation, but the ambition, the surpassing. We are required, therefore, the concrete love that is one with desiring the presence of the groom, the will to be at His side. The side of Maria, the good side. We don't even have to pursue to be in certain place – heaven, Tabor, Golgotha, Cana – but only to be together with Christ who Himself is the truth, the way and the life.

The heresy of the false meekness opposes also the fundamental text from Apoc. 3.20 where the Savior promise to who listens His commandments that He will come to him and dine with him. Christ wants to be together with us, he demands from us the crucifixion of the body so that we can become one with Him, and not to banish us irremediably to the bottom of hell, in the frozen aseptic halls of the syllogistic dementedness.

In all this desert (or labyrinth?) only the right reckoning can help, because it is simple.

138

–   The need for sufferance – found especially at Russians and known as that of the iurodivii – represents a very special form of holiness. It is that of those who pretend to be stupid, imbecile, crazy, nuts in order to cause contempt and to provoke insults. The case of the nun Isidora, Isidora the madwoman, employed by her colleagues only for menial tasks and regarded as brainless woman until the day she is disclosed by a great eremite, to the shame of the other nuns.

Subtle mortification; it is true that it is atrocious and, hence, very worthy, but it is dangerous and equivocal as well:

a)   first because it implies putting others in the state of sin (I provoke them to be unfair, the success of your plan supposes their lack of compassion, counts on their malice);

b)   then it is a stumbling block for a lot of innocents who will mistake the faith for the nuttiness;

c)   finally, it puts the noble wisdom under the cover of madness, compromising it.

Everything happens in extremely labile regions, on quick sands; you dance on the volcano, on the knife-edge where the falls can occur anytime.

Not to mention another danger: that the pretended imbecile and nut to end up in time transforming his (her) role in reality and to become truly what he (she) pretends to be. This consideration is the most grave and brings to front the fact that the Christian life cannot be based on a pretense, a mask, a deception, a prank. In other words, a fake.

–   The church always followed the path of the equilibrium and common sense, sometimes a bit too common. On the sophisticated paths walked the heresies. Being refined, they seemed superior and they conquered the bright minds, those that cannot believe that the right reckoning is, in its simplicity, the sovereign refinement.

–   Since Christ is the one who arisen – and if Christ did not arise what for are we Christians?

–   we cannot strive toward hell, abode of the death.

I was told by Al. Pal. and Anetta that I lacked meekness and compassion toward a poor old man, that if I refused to be an accusation witness, to give statements, to be reeducated etc. – like many others, like so many people of decency and valor – was only out of pride. And maybe I would have agreed with them if I weren't edified about the heresy of false meekness.

And isn't after all this meekness – that is the same as the intention to establish the human baseness, to forbid to man to break out and to surpass it – isn't after this meekness itself a paradoxical pride, colored by the ridicule like the numbing declaration of a French bishop: in matters of Christian humility I defy any competition?

BUGGY MAMBO RAG

Sectarian B.: Then you lied at the inquiry.

General A.V.: Yes.

Sectarian B.: And you call yourself Christian? Don't you know that lie is forbidden by God?

General A.V.: I know. But I cannot apply this principle without discrimination. I am obliged to tell the truth, but not the whole truth and not to everybody.

Sectarian B.: Yes, you do. The whole truth and nothing but the truth to everybody. The lie is forbidden.

General A.V.: Even if I harm someone else? Sectarian B.: Even then.

General A.V.: Not even to save a man from unjust persecution? Sectarian B.: Not even then.

General A.V.: Then I prefer to take a sin upon myself and to atone for it. Sectarian B.: This is from the devil.

General A.V.: Let me tell you a short story. My friend, engineer Al. Ştef had a maid who has a Millenist or "Faithful" or something like that, who, anyhow, wouldn't tell a lie for nothing in the world. A very honest woman. When Mme Ştef. was home and someone was ringing the bell at the gate and she wouldn't want to receive him (she has tormented by headaches), she was asking the servant to say that she left. (I forgot to tell you that their house was in the middle of a big garden.) The believer was refusing categorically. Unpleasant situations and discussions were generated. The woman wouldn't lie. Mme Ştef. didn't want to fire her because she was honest and hard working. Finally they came to an agreement: the maid was going to the gate only after her mistress left the house and went in the back garden. Then the servant was willing to say that: "the mistress in not in the home." The undesired guest, not paying attention to the preposition, was thinking she is not home, or was thinking that the maid was not good at grammar – and the comedy ended. Well, tell me, like it or not?

Gherla, March 1962

Cold afternoon out of which it emanates, however, a far away promise of spring. Through the interstices of the planks we guess is thaw weather. I fell in a state of nostalgia and stupor. I would like to cuddle like a kid, like a cat on the oven. I am visited clearly and closely by the unending yard of the Pantelimon factory, the Armenească (Armenian) street and its unbelievable silence, the Christmas tree from the Şeteanu house, the smile of Missus Boerescu in a violet velvet dress, the forest between the river Târgul and the river Doamna at Clucereasa, the quick movements of Miss Florescu, the anti-Catholic imprecations of Lady de Branzsky, the numerous and various shouts of the ambulant traders crossing the domes of silence that were growing above the streets and alleys… And Anetta that gazes straight into my eyes, and Manole vituperating at Duqué against liberals and in favor of the Junimists…

I ask doctor Serafim Pâslaru to recite to me one of his poems, then, even more bewitched by nostalgia, I am crouching – as much as it is allowed – under the window covered with planks of the cell – between the interstices one can see a vague strip of a hill – and, as a child who retells to himself long known stories, I repeat and I systemize the theory of the nine heavens that I keep reflecting on it and that gives me comfort lately.

In the first three heavens reigns and works God The Creator, the Aldoer and Alkeeper, the Great Anonymous of Lucian Blaga, the Great Watchmaker of Voltaire, the Great Architect of the masons. From the fourth heaven up to the seventh abodes the righteous Judge, the one that frightens, the Lawmaker of the Old Testament, the God of severe justice. Starting from the seventh heaven it is unveiled – to the chosen ones – unexpected final secrets. Just that, unlike what the initiates believe, Guénonists, theosophs, anthroposophs, spiritualists or positivist people with progressive ideas, or Athènists of agnostic nuance, the divinity in the ninth heaven is not a "force" or an "energy", as impersonal and impassible as possible, a hidden coordinator or constructor, but is God with the white beard, gentle and kind, God of the farthest childhood, of the carols, cozonacs and pies, of the most beautiful Christmas nights, the one of Dickens and from Bibliothèque Rose.

Here stays Christ, the Comforter and the Giver of Rest, who promised that he will heals us of evils, filth, sins and pains, That at which think the heroes of Chekhov from Uncle Vania. (We shall rest, uncle Vania…) The uppermost, final God, from the mystery of the mysteries and the holy of holies is not at all abstract, He is not the cold Creator, not Brahma the incomprehensible and unchangeable, he is not the pensive divinity of the gnosis, unfolding the eons. And in this ninth heaven, in which Brahma does not live, certainly it doesn't reign the earthly seriousness; not a trace of the so-called seriousness of the pedants, the conscientious, the Pharisees and the accountants. We are asked to be serious in the world with the meaning of virtuous, honest, attentive to others pains; but not gloomy and not merciless executors of the regulations of the passing kingdoms and ephemeral police prefectures. The monks are joyful – only to the eyes of the people they abstain from showing it openly, but their arcane behavior is different –, the morose are the devils and the bureaucrats –, and in heaven, I bet there is only playfulness. How else could it be, since the Savior tells us clearly that only whoever is like a little child enters there? And I wonder, serious are the children or of an unquenchable gaiety?

–   Almost everybody is ready to admit the Creator, even the more compromising atheists, and the agnostics in corpore. The masons, too, acknowledge an Architect, a Supreme Being. Like Robespierre. All the sympathizers, under a form or another, of theosophy and Hinduism (and there are many of them in the world) do not fight the idea of a leading spirit. Now, even people accustomed with the scientific language of large popularity readily admit an Energy, a Force, a Motor.

A Motor was in Aristotle too. But to us, here in prison – essence of life – how ignorant they all seem, from the Stagirit to René Guénon and Edouard Schuré! It might be so, I don't deny it, up to first or second heaven. Out there, yes, it's mathematics, it's gnosis, two and two makes four, it's architectonics, there are force fields, planetary orbits, laws, justice, whatever, reckonings…

From the third heaven up, however, things change. Any trace of accounting vanishes. We are ascending toward Christ. The galaxies and the eons remain, docile, behind. The hard climbing begins. The customs are intensifying. In order to pass from the Creator to the idea of the Trinity, to the reality of a divinity not only omnipotent and giver of order, but especially good, caring for the fate of the beings; lover of men up to sacrifice, salutary and comforting. Christianity is not only a religion that bows before a Maker, but also madly believe in a Savior who gave Himself out of love to the world[199]. Losski says clearly that the Christian is not monotheist but believer in a trinitarian religion. The Christian enters in a different domain than the monotheist: moralist, right or systemized. (?)

Gradually mounting the hierarchy of the heavens, the sights are increasingly unexpected. Among constellations and swarms of galaxies, novae stars, dwarf and white, forgetting of angry preaches, volumes of theology and apologetics arguments, passing eternal sources of hydrogen – regulated by the spirit of professor Hoyle –, leaving behind judges, constructors, accountants, prophets, dignified philosophers and non-Euclidian geometers. The soul climbs always higher, cleansing herself, until the terminus stop: the place of light and green, the flowered pasture, swarming with little plump puppies and kitties with white ribbons, where it resounds the harmony of Mozart divertissements and the winged angels of Liliom endeavor to offer incessantly sweets and sherbet, where is the real God, of the children allowed – finally – to come, no matter how old or burden by evil memories, to see: the Father with white beard, in the middle, Christ, bearer of stigmas and cross at the right hand and The cleansing and comforting Spirit on the left hand.

Let us take heed, Christianity is not a simple school of honesty, purity and justice, or a noble and rational explication of life (theology, better than zoology shows us the secrets: Emil Cioran[200]); or a lofty ethics code (Confucianism, Chin Taoism); or an evasive therapeutics (Stoicism, Yoga, Zen) or a jet of questions (Taoism); or an act of obedience to the Unique (Judaism, Islam). It is more and more special: it is the teaching of Christ, of love and of the salutary power to forgive. Any other religion conceive the repairing of the sins only by the logic road of compensation (and in Brahmanism and Buddhism, through samsara it is pushed to the most absolute consequences); only the religion in which God does not accept sacrifices but He sacrifices Himself could appear the hope of the total and instantaneous erasure of the sins, through the most earthquake-like and anti-bureaucratic – therefore the most scandalous – act.

(In this metanoia, revolting for order, reason and justice, resides probably the explanation of the strange repulsion that among the other confessions, the Christianity causes to many.)

The Christian tries to respect with all his heart Buddhism, Brahmanism, Judaism, Islam... but he shouldn't forget that his religion is very different than those. It is a faith in which I believe that the final heaven is not that of mathematics or philosophers, but of the white locks and plump puppies and kitties with ribbons. (Since the Lord calls the children and compares His Kingdom with they, it wouldn't be surprising to find there what they like.) Mathematics is true, like justice, order, mechanics of spheres. But only on a certain portion. High above it is something else.

The "theologians of the death of God" fell in the other extreme: they contest God the Father and they acknowledge only the Christ. But in what way! As a symbol of man only, of the neighbor, of the human problems – that they hurry to mistakenly identify with their political preoccupations: the war in Vietnam, the civil rights of the blacks, the progress of the third world countries... Did you understand? God shut down, and Christ secularized, politicized, crypto-communized.

–   Before cybernetics maybe the scientists lacking faith in God could still find excuses. Although Bettex, in the last century, was saying that at the simple and uncultivated the unbelief is explicable but at the scholars of course not. Bacon, more than three centuries ago, he was referring to scholars too admonishing them that they cannot think the Father only because, according to the words of the Gospel, "they err not reading the Scripture and not knowing the power of God."

Cybernetics proved with certainty what the progress of sciences was unveiling little by little: the implied, absolute necessity of a Great Programmer. Biology: admits, finally, that the analyzers, (such as sight) enters in action according to a program established beforehand (innate says Monod) and they transmit only selectively – there are neurons specialized only for the sight of right lines for instance –, reality being analyzed in every situation according to preexistent criteria.

The genetic code? Fixed and invariable, programmed. The atomic structure? Only according to certain archetypal, programmed models. The language? Structured too, like the unconscious, after a program. The invariance of the species? Also the proof of some foreseen limits. The net of relatives relations? With many versions, but not infinite, therefore again patterns, programming.

These are cybernetic visions of the world, which is acknowledgment of models. Could they all be spontaneous and random? Come on, now! Cybernetics is the supreme rational scientific proof of the creation, the universal notion of programming does not allow any doubt regarding the existence of the Creator.

All these, of course, do not contain the necessity of a savior and his incarnation. These still remain under the mark of liberty, they are our most precious act, more specifically differentiating and more anti-entropy: the act of faith, as anti-destiny, as the Art for Malraux, as the anti-history of Mircea Eliade.

The hypothesis of hazard creating life seems to me, compared to divine creation, less and less probable: according as the reality unveils its amazing complexity and connectivity. Less probable in probability language is the same as zero.

(What about then the imaginary experiment with the millions of apes that type for millions of years? Will they not type in the end even Hamlet? It is a purely theoretical possibility, and the example – scholastic – it's as likely to happen as the tragic outcome that awaits the ass of professor Buridan. And even if they would type it, it would never be taken from the flux and it would not be passed in the accumulator or stocked or copied. It will still be virtual.

The fact that the example of the typist apes is inconclusive and it constitutes a pseudo- scientific allegory can be seen also from the fact that the entire rationale suffers from an elementary vice: a confusion regarding the verb to type. The apes don't type at the typewriter in the operational sense that could give birth to a combinatorial series based on which one could make probability calculations, they strike it, like kids who sit at the piano and they pretend to play. If the apes could be taught to press the keys one at a time, the example would not be good again because in this case we're not dealing with a series of random events but with intentional acts.)

–   God, specifies the Jesuit Hausherr, is not infinite but true. God is not the Infinity but the Truth. He created the Infinity, but He is a Person. (The same as He created the man a person by breathing, by the most direct and personal relation. An Idea or a Force having to solve the same problem, would have found a different way, but for sure not that indicated in Gen. 2,7: the Lord breathed into his nostrils the breath of life.)

The affirmation of Hausherr and the biblical text pull us from the "syllogism of sorrow" and "the nightmare of dialectics".

–   If I allow myself to talk of white beard, pets, sweets and flowers in the ninth sky I am not doing it out of such an extreme anthropomorphism that can't even be suspected, but because I think of spiritual states whose closest metaphorical equivalence is best conveyed by puppies and kitties etc.

–   Is that so? Aren't they by chance not only states but also their transfigured materiality?

Maybe we're not stressing enough the fact that the heavenly Jerusalem will be not another world but the same, exorcised, with other meanings and values, at

144

higher levels of purity and intensity, but not disconnected from the imagery of the beings created in the image and likeness of the divinity.

— Old Haydn was questioned why his religious music is joyous instead of ceremonious and solemn.

Answer: because every time I think of God I am filled with joy.

BUGGY MAMBO RAG

— You might be, mister, prince and descending from devil knows how many voivodes but you took a pee and you didn't wash your hands...

— Me!?

— Yes, you, don't pretend you don't know, you touched your thing and then you touched the pitcher used by us, those who do not descend from voivodes...

— But I didn't even...

— Oh, yes, you did! I'm watching you for three days, mister prince, and yesterday too, you used the barrel and you didn't wash, you want to infect us all...

— If I would have washed my hands, I would have touched the pitcher with my whole hand...

— Yes, but at least you would have been clean...

— Don't you see there is no water...

— We're not stupid. Yesterday wasn't it water? And you still didn't wash your hands. What are you thinking, to hell with these yokels...

— You put thoughts into my mind...

— Shame on you!

— Shame on you, if so, because you make trial of intentions and you are alleging gratuitous accusations...

— You should be ashamed, big shot pig...

— You stin...

— It serves you right that they put you in prison, you deserve it...

— ...king imbecile!...

Silence, silence, gentlemen, SILENCE. The cop is coming!

— From Pantelimon we moved in the Armenească street, in downtown. It's nice, but the atmosphere isn't different, just that there are more people in the streets and the buildings are closer to each other. An old peace and a sort of trust in the elements of the world reigns here too.

The street is paved, very quiet, on each side there are "boyar" houses, yards, gardens and flowers, exactly as in the suburb where we were coming from. In front of our house – a house in the corner, build out of visible burned bricks: green, red, blue, white – lives the Boerescu family. Ms Eliza Boerescu, born Florescu, is the daughter of general Ion Emanuel, former prime-minister and owner of a small castle in Calea Victoriei. In the memory of the parental residence, the house in the Armenească street has a tower too, smaller. There lives also the sister of Ms Boerescu, Miss Florescu, an "old maid", sprightly and restless, always in search for sufferance to allay. Colonel Florescu, the third brother, the black sheep of the family – degraded, now cashier at the races – is not received by his sisters.

Next door is the house of Mihai Şeteanu, counselor at the Accounts Court (?); his boys are one year older and one year younger than me respectively. The new neighbors receive us kindly. In those times the neighbors were like relatives and not even the biggest jerk would hire the maid of a friend or a neighbor. In the vis-à-vis house music is very appreciated and mother, good pianist, is often called. The piano opens for her the doors of other houses and so we come to know a lot of people from the high society.

The Şeteanu family invites me weekly and all the holidays. The hall of the house is huge and two stories high. On Christmas, without fail, a tree – as I never seen before and I won't see after. The uncle of the late Ms Şeteanu, general Zossima – with a white beard of a patriarch, wavy, one of the most famous beards of the capital – is Santa Claus.

The beautiful and roomy villa, with interior staircase, is magnificently adorned and full of guests. Innumerable presents, delicatessen, lights. Everything is gaiety, warmness and good disposition. The beard of Santa Claus seems descended from heaven to consecrate the place. Outside the street is silent. It's gentle and enchanting like in the Christmas carol of Dickens. In the morning of Christmas or of the Pascha, ladies Boerescu and Florescu are treating me with a mammoth box of candies…

Hard would be for me to believe, after many years, that all those people were beasts. As much as I knew them, superficially of course, but enough not to commit fundamental errors, I remember them rather as people of finesse, full of geniality and simplicity, people that the thought they wronged or insulted someone would obsess them, similar to the heroes of Gârleanu, Brătescu-Voineşti and from Life in the countryside.

Jilava, cell 9, 1960
Analyzing with Anatolie Hagi-Beca the Romanian phenomenon, we stop at the short story

The road becomes the traveler.

The story has a Caragialist aroma (the title; the lack of reflexive content of the characters; their scheme reduced to a phrase assiduously repeated: here at the inn, at crossroads, we need a quick lad, flash), but is a Caragialism where all the acid and venom is gone.

Now the Romanian sky is fully clear. The layers of shallow politicking disappeared; the vain ambitions, the intrigues, the restlessness – even in reduced dose – vanished. Only the archetypal background of the Romanian soul appears as it is: joyful, keen for friendship, yearning to see others happy (Niţă, if you love me, eat this fat piece of meat), unable to enjoy something alone, burning of

146

impatience to share with others any luck. (The solitaire and dark drinking, so frequently among the northern and Anglo-Saxon peoples, doesn't exist at us, at us the party implies companions and general good mood.)

In the story of Brătescu-Voineşti the mathematical series of characteristics described by Caragiale reaches its limit and integrates in a perfect sum of innocent serenity. Because the characters in The road becomes the traveler are of a visible purity, very close to the age of childhood – the individual or common one.

The conscious disappears and – although psychoanalysis is not intended – the unconscious shows itself. But what a surprise! Where psychoanalysis teaches us that behind the apparently clear and calm conscious boils the somber, muddy, self-conscious and abject unconscious, look, for the Romanian soul, things are the opposite way around.

The conscious layer caught by Caragiale still contains double crosses, ambitions, shadows… The deep layers of the Brătescu-Voineşti's story uncover the depths of a lake of great clarity, like Miorița ballad, where the same transfiguration power throbs (in the ballad, the transfiguration of the tragic situation, in the story the transfiguration through sympathy and friendship of coarse situations) and the same peace – the main heritage left to the people by the Savior.

You see, Anatolie, The road becomes the traveler is a piece of great importance for Romanian typology and immortal in our literature because it remains as a picture, or even better, as an X-ray of the character of a people. An X-ray that talks clearly and it can be easily interpreted: the deep layers of the Romanian soul are calm and serene, in the mioritical lake – modest as surface, located at the periphery of the great centers of civilization, "at the crossroads of great empires" – it reflects an utmost clear sky.

Hagi-Beca and I are more and more gladly enumerating the essences of the Romanian phenomenon for which our love – nostalgically – always is confirmed and grows.

–   Which thing created here, on this earth, managed to reach the sky? Let's think it over.

The Savior, when He shows Himself to the apostles after the resurrection, has an incorruptible body, a body of glory. To Thomas who asks Him for touchable proof, He shows the stigmas and invites him to touch them with the hand. Therefore, on the body of glory you could see the stigmas.

On the other hand, we know that the Savior ascended to heaven with this body that wore the traces of the crucifixion – bringing, therefore, forever in the heaven something from earth. This something taken from temporality: His stigmas.

Here there is the only gift made by the human world to those in the heights: the traces of torture.

Do they take place and repeat the horror signs forever and ever? Do they seem like a meteor escaped from gravitation, do they wander in spaces with their sinister load?

–   The Romanian soul so much tried by history and events. Tried but not soured. The contact with the divine peace and the joy of life was not interrupted.

–   In cell 18 not everybody knew that I was baptized. Otherwise the ex-chief of the Cross Brotherhoods wouldn't have invited me to sit next to him on the only bench and told me: now, let's talk in controversy, the Legionnaire and the Jew. Will you?

I show him that we have nothing in controversy, that where we are we all believe the same thing. Besides it would mean to give in too easily to the conspicuous policy of the administration to give rise to controversy and quarrels, putting together in the same room people with different political, social and ethnical affiliation.

By chance, after a few moments, he is taken out from the cell. I accompany him to the door and I kiss him on both cheeks. My gesture is somehow theatrical, but sincere. I feel that this is how I should proceed. Nobody scoff at my gesture. On the contrary, a solemn atmosphere fell on us. The man, leaving, is touched too. He leaves us with a smile of joy on his face saying: the traces of the Legionnaire revolver…

There is still left Mirel. Gab. who, tireless, teaches me a bunch of Gyr and Crainic's poems and the splendid piece by Sergiu Mandinescu Today same as yesterday.

Once again an atmosphere of solemnity was created in a medical office, where they brought us for dental extractions, made with pliers, by a feldsher. While waiting for our labours, the gypsy cop kills his time asking us tricky questions: how old are you? how many years were you sentenced to? what for? what have you been? did you make women at cabaret to mount naked on the table and did you sprinkle them with soda? (The issue of the naked women sprinkled with soda on the cabaret's tables is everybody's obsession, it represents for them the supreme illustration of richness and debauchery, the nec plus ultra ideal, the dream, Himalaya; is their duchess of Mortemart. Further than that no one can go, it's a kind of light speed for the relativity theory.)

He asks me if I am Romanian. I am, I answer. What, aren't you Jewish? My blood is Jewish, I say to him, but I think and I feel Romanian.

He realizes that he missed it and he gets silent. Then he attacks another one: hey, you, old man, how many estates did you have?

(My answer, paraphrasing Churchill, whose mother was from United States and who declared: I am fifty percent American and a hundred percent English, would sound: I am a hundred percent Jew and a thousand percent Romanian.)

148

–   We can find everything, we can know everything, we can learn everything.

Only the suffering no. We thing we know what is suffering, that we cannot have anymore surprises, that we reached the end.

No way! The sufferance is always new, protheic to infinity, always fresh.

–   Today same as yesterday We ring the alarm bell

But our estranged fellows don't hear us Cato is dead, Scaevola too...

–   The most extraordinary thought I've read outside the evangelical texts. It is from Kierkegaard. The opposite of sin is not the virtue, is the freedom.

–   To C.G. Jung, in Ceylon, a priest tells: "No, To Buddha you can't pray. You can't implore him. Buddha is no more. He is in Nirvana."

This is the big difference. Christ, who prayed incessantly waits incessantly for our prayers.

He watches and listens to us, always at the door.

Christ, as the Father, always works (John 5,17) and He sacrifices Himself at every liturgy.

He is not in Nirvana, to rest, to relax, on a break. He is on the site, puts the shoulder.

Only the sinners can taste Christianity in its fullness. The reason is explained by St. Simeon Metaphrastes in his prayer in preparation for the Holy Communion: "There is no sin that vanquished Thy love of men."

(The title of the book written by an elder of the Oxford Group, A.J. Russell: For sinners only. Just that it seems we are all sinners.)

BUGGY MAMBO RAG

...Therefore we start with the sonnet of Félix Anvers, the first verses: Mon âme a son secret, ma vie a son mystère... In the category of the sturgeon: huso huso, acipenser sturio, sterlet and stur sturgeon, in the salmons: sheat fish, huck and the beautiful variety of Rhine: truite saumonée which is pink... And after you mixed well the cacao with the sugar... Fanny Seculici, theosophist, died of malaria probably at Suez, when she was returning from a congress that took place in Madras... No, it is from Le lac: O temps, suspends ton vol...[201] Yes, it is Bucura Dumbravă, her brother was the captain of the Austrian vessel in which king Carol came clandestinely in sixty-six... Dear, at Sankt Moritz Titulescu[202] lived only at Suvretta House and do you know what his favorite food was? Boeuf gros sel, my dear, which is a huge peace of boiled beef, with marrow...

Aiud, May 1961

Animated discussion in the cell about the old Romanian society – old, that is before August 1944. Most of them condemn it surprisingly harshly. I even recognize accents from Shattered citadel by Horia Lovinescu. A worker even mentions the "toughness" of the capitalist society.

I had been silent, but after this remark, I intervene in the talks, showing that, in order to not be considered biased, I will refer – as always when is about communism – to proofs to be found in the texts of the adverse part only.

(Who wants, for instance, to prove the nullity of the elections, has nothing more to do than to place in parallel the number of votes obtained by every leader of the party and his hierarchical order number in the "nomenclature", which is the statute in the cadre organization, a sort of Book of precedency, of Chinese Ceremonial Register or Spanish Etiquette, to ascertain the indissoluble link between the order number in the nomenclature and the decreasing order of the number of votes. If #1 obtains 99.6% then #2 obtains 96.2, #3 95.8%; never happened and could happen that say #5 to have a superior number of votes – or equal – to #4. This very simple checking of two columns of figures – the numbers talks – is more edifying than any investigation, which would be hard to do.)

That the difference between "old" and "new" is oftentimes artificial and that the opinion that whatever is new is, somehow inevitably, better is very fragile, is proven positively by a document whose authenticity cannot be doubted because it is a creation of the "new" itself, a film realized by the regime. The document, therefore, cannot be rejected as hostile, or at least compromised by bias. Conceived and translated in images by an official director[203], with authorized actors distributed (among others the People's Artist Gr. Vasiliu-Birlic[204]), passed through numerous control steps by all the competent organs and wearing the seal of the censorship, Militia[205], and Security, the film Two tickets constitute – I said to my colleagues – an irrefutable proof of the thesis that the old society was not so tough as they believe. It is not an adversary of the new regime that says it, an agent of the reactionary forces or at least a neutral observer, it is the authors of the film made after the famous story of Caragiale – in unequivocal images and recorded words.

In the film – otherwise rather faithful to the story, well enough set and interpreted with talent

– the madman, the boss of the unlucky hero, meets the latter – who absented from work eight days in a row without calling in sick – in a tavern and drunk. And what does the madman do (the implication being that the other bosses, the non-madmen would behave even more gently)? He tells him that if he doesn't come next day to work or at least sends the keys (because he didn't have even this elementary decency), he will... request him to be fired.

This is said by the madman to a clerk who was absent for eight days, kept the keys of the file cabinets, didn't call in sick, neither announce that he can't come, nor anything else and who now is caught drunk in a tavern!

Terror: the man is threatened to be fired. And how we feel like laughing – I say to my interlocutor, the worker political prisoner subjugated by the magic of

150

the word new – when someone mentions, as yourself, the severity and the ruthlessness of the old society since we all know that after fifty years of service, for a delay of two or three minutes the poor clerk (who doesn't feel like frequenting The char with bear[206]), finding himself in the situation of not being able to get in the packed bus (thirty minutes late in its turn), would be called by the cadre, scolded like the worse fatherland traitor, interrogated like the most dangerous spy and fired on the spot or warned that he will be thrown out in the street at the first new fault.

What about the gypsy women arrested before lunch and released in the evening by the inspector because there wasn't a warrant for them? Gypsies, by the way, well treated, suspected not without reason and taken by the policeman without zeal and with gentleness.

The worker did not get upset. He might have suffered and he is a man who can be easily deceived. But regarding the intellectual D.I. Suchianu, writer and beneficiary of the old society, I will always hold a grudge against him for his chronicle devoted to the motion picture version of the play Shattered citadel. Not only that in his chronicle he demeans the very society he used to belong

– in a quite privileged position – but he also fiercely attacks the reshaping of the personality of a character – Matei – a playboy, uncaring, prone to pleasures in the play, young boyar with progressive ideas and a great heart in the film, claiming that a member of the owners class never could have had noble feelings: by definition and by virtue of the social racism he was bound to remain a family money boy, a parasite, a scoundrel.

The ridicule, here, surpasses the infamy, because Suchianu damns himself: he collaborated at "Viaţa românească" (The Romanian life), journal of the generous and leftist youth and he denies his own portrait – a portrait loaded with mysteries like that of Dorian Gray. As for the statement itself, is false, the proof being "Viaţa românească" and its redactors.

– Day after day I am more and more driven to believe that the foremost attribute of the human being is not as much the selfishness as the hate and the envy toward another.

The selfishness, after all, is not too dangerous. Hate and envy are the cause of all evils.

Along with the progress they grow and dominate the scene.

Jacques Maritain: Along with the history of the world both evil and good make progress.

BUGGY MAMBO RAG

...And Alexander Csoma from Cörösi, a Transylvanian from Trei Scaune (Three Chairs), the Cörösi village, that is Chiuruşu[207], the great specialist in Tibetan, he obtained more than Sir Charles Bell who managed only to enter in

Lhassa... the cardinal was mad with rage... using the infrared rays that penetrate deeply... with great personal sacrifices and substantial bribes he obtained in 1840 the Tibetan manuscripts, like Anquetil du Perron will obtain the Upanishad manuscripts... He died in India at Darjeling... Le ciel est si bleu, si calme...tells Marcellus to Demetrios...

– The film Two tickets remembers me another one with an extraordinary scene that all those who were investigated by the Security organs will appreciate it like a cup of old țuică, cold, like those I was savoring at Clucereasa, in the garden, during summer, in the shade, scene indeed evoking the general paradise that was not localized, as Cezar Petrescu thought, in the sweet burgh of Iassy but was spread all over that Romania that both Cezar Petrescu and the press from Sărindar bombarded aplenty, until they woke up being sorry and they said to themselves – in the cells from Jilava, Aiud, Gherla, Galați, Pitești or Botoșani, on the board of the ship Transylvania on their way to Israel with 70 kilograms and a certificate or, like Maria Banuș, trembling with repentance in front of the long forgotten spire of the Dragomirna – maybe they were wrong.

In this scene of scenes – and I remain faithful in using only pieces from the file of the opposing part – a young communist painter is arrested by the Safety[208] and brought in an inquiry office. There, after he got two slaps (where are you, major Jack Simon, to die laughing?) he is seated in a chair exactly facing the investigator and he is interrogated. The answers given by him are recorded by a typist, and the typist writes at a typewriter situated in the immediate vicinity of the accused.[209] This scene – evoked by the director of a film censored, of course, with great care

– says all and is more edifying than hundreds of volumes and thousand of articles because it recognizes that during the terror exerted by the Safety the accused was not wearing black glasses, was investigated in the presence of a third party, and his words were recorded by typing right from the tip of the tongue.

Security, together with the new, came back to the inquisitorial system; the answers are no more recorded by typing but by the redacting of the investigators, the way they proceeded in the case of Jeanne d'Arc. Her answers were spoken in French, then reformulated in Latin and stylized by the clerks of the inquisitorial court, which were changing completely the sense of the words told by Jeanne. The procedure of the inquisitorial investigation repeated.

– Have you been in the house of Gheorghe Florian?
– Yes.

And the investigator notes:

"Yes, I acknowledge that I was in the conspiratorial house on the street... at number... where I had infraction-type relations with the Legionnaire Gheorghe Florian."

When the proceedings are given for signing, the investigated exclaims:

– But I never said it was a conspiratorial house, neither that Gheorghe Florian was a Legionnaire and that I had infraction-type relations with him.

The protest is, of course, useless. And the investigator, of the same good faith as the inquisition clerks, considers it absurd. The investigator redacts in his modern Latin: in other words he transcribes in the aulic language on the institution he serves. Any establishment has its own official language and of reality knows only through the ways used by the information organs it possesses. Didn't the investigative organs agreed that in the street... at number... there is a conspiratorial house? Didn't the same State apparatuses decide that Gheorghe Florian is a notorious Legionnaire? Can you have with this kind of individual and in this kind of house any other relations but infraction-type? (Since we know that the so-called Saint Margaret, that you claim was talking to you, is in fact a she-devil, isn't it only fair and correct to note: the she-devil told me to go to Chinon?...)

Therefore is the truth that is recorded and nothing else, just that the truth perceived and recorded by the investigator and transcribed in his style, in a proper form. Because the investigator cannot approach the hierarchy in a different way than using this conventional, aulic language, there are expressed only the truths considered admissible by the institution, the house where the accused were meeting translates into the conspiratorial house where the schemers met, the tea to which we have been invited turns into the hostile séance organized through telephonic convocations (do you deny you were summoned by phone?), the voices that were talking to me become the demons were tempting me (the father inquisitor himself established that what you were hearing were actually demons).

Stylizing and highlighting.

As soon as there is no more a typewriter that clacks nicely and reproduces the words of the investigated, the bureaucratic trick works. Without tortures, without beatings...

The makers of the film couldn't conceal the historic truth. But the few spectators, probably, understood how significant was that little typewriter, so telling; it represented a whole world, a dead universe: the galaxy of objectivity.

The little machine clack-clack-clack symbolized all the real progress made through the centuries. When it was taken out from the penal investigation offices and the investigator was again authorized to record with his own hand the answers of the accused – that is to stylize them according to his conception and from his point of view and in the respective institutional tongue –, all the work of Beccaria was nullified, the historic hour was turned back five centuries and the situation in which the pure shepherd from Domrémy found herself became – but for the people from 1430 we should acknowledge the mitigating circumstance that the typing was not yet invented – that of the countless investigated people by the Security of a social order that promised too – even more consequent – that it will insure the happiness of people.

1965

The tragedy is that for centuries – and now even more than ever – even the people of good faith (especially they) see in Christianity a sort of vague and gentle cretinism, good for bigots, credulous and people in distress.

While it is fire, scandal, it is "plain craziness", more daring and more exigent than any extremist theory; it's adventure – it is the most formidable happening.

Christianity is dogma, mystics, morals, it is everything but it is especially a way of life and a solution, which is also a happiness recipe. I would say that it is super-relaxation, super-LSD. Compared to the Christian doctrine, its requirements and its results, all the intoxicants and the hallucinogens are quack tricks, minimal Hannemann dilution, Neolithic wheelbarrow.

There is no more quaking therapeutics (it requires from us the impossibility) neither more efficient medication (it gives us the freedom and the happiness without going to the heroine dealers).

Christianity gives peace, silence and rest – but not vapid and monotonous, but through the most perilous adventures, the unending fight, the most hazardous acrobatics. A trapez at great height

–   and no safety net below.

I don't understand how the wanderers for adventures and the searchers of happiness pass next to it without seeing it. I, for myself, see Christianity as a hyper lysergic acid and a "stronger" version of books like The art of being happy and How to succeed in life by Dale Carnegie.

Isichia: happiness. And not only in certain places, like the Holy Mountain. Everywhere. A universal recipe.

1971

The rock-pop opera Jesus Christ Superstar enters too, I think, in the above definition.

I consider it as something similar to the novella of Anatole France, Le Jongleur de Notre Dame, that actually is a retelling of a story from Pateric.

The jester does what he knows and he can do in front of the icon of the Lord's Mother and the Babe. He brings his tribute the only way that is open to him, that of tricks. The regular officiator, from behind a column, looks horrified at the show. But the Babe laughs and applauds and the Mother wipes with Her kerchief the sweat of the holy labor from the jester's forehead.

Bucharest, 1971 (pg 240)

The sin against the Holy Spirit: the one that cannot be forgiven.

I wander if this is not to abase the person of our fellow man – which is made in the image and after the likeness of God. Since the proof of the love of God is done by loving our neighbor (which is His being), isn't it the proof of the blasphemy hating and trampling him, reducing him to an object, treating him as if he is without spirit? Shouldn't be the Christian able to understand what Simone de Beauvoir specified so well: that the basis of any morals is the respect of the freedom of the other, the considering of him as a being who's freedom cannot be violated?

I do believe in the quasi-identity of these two words: spirit and freedom. I do believe that by robbing a man of his freedom we remove from him the mark of the spirit.

The procedures of the penal investigation based on the idea that justice is a form of the "class struggle" and the trials with "complete confessions", where the man is forced to trample himself alone till the end of the night (Judas sold Christ at night, toward whose end Céline leads us too) where he comes to hate himself to death (so that the life that he saved through treason will value nothing), where he must realize that he descended down to the last step and he cannot stand his own self – and he abjures his freedom –, where he cannot leave his self and take his cross, because he broke and burned all the bridges with the world of the spiritual powers, don't these constitute the whole and living example of the mysterious sin about which Jesus says clearly that there cannot be forgiveness?

Or about what those officers did on the American ship in Atlantic delivering to the Russians the Lithuanian sailor that managed to take refuge on their ship. They asked the Russians to come and they delivered him. Like an object. The Russians already started beating him while still on board. The sailor was screaming and he was praying them not to be given to the Russians. They gave him.

President Nixon – (Franz Ferdinand, he was more outraged when he found out that they didn't give to colonel Redl – proven traitor and spy – the chance to confess and to take communion before death) – took some vague administrative actions and there were a few resignations. But I am convinced that God did not see the things with so much casualness. (Whoever receives one little child like this in My name receives Me. But whoever causes one of these little ones who believe in Me to sin, it would be better for him if a millstone were hung around his neck, and he were drowned in the depth of the sea). Christ is gentle and humble with heart, but in the same time he was human too, completely, and once they angered even Him and he took the whip and chased the money changers from the Temple (Matthew 18,5).

This atrocious scene in the American ship, where the cruelty, the evilness and the blind imbecility (which is a sin!) are mixed in viscous equal parts, most surely stirred Christ of the Trinity, that up there still bear His stigmas and – we know it well – he knows sometimes to punish too. Woe, therefore, to the captain, the officers and the crewmen; not one protested, didn't raise his voice, didn't make a gesture, didn't set himself on fire; woe to them as all those who – quote Kierkegaard – fell into the hands of the living God.

155

(Regarding the expression "the living God" I have my own opinion: that He is not only the eternal Creator, but also the God of Abraham, of Isaac, which is the God of the living not of the dead – which is the God interested in what the living are doing –, and Christ the crucified in which bustles even in heaven the remembrance of the cruel hypocrisy, of the triumphant stupidity and the bureaucratic evilness in the world.)

– Those Americans from the ship in Atlantic could have waited at least a few more hours: they could have asked the supreme commander of the military forces, the president. The haste. The imbecile haste to apply blindly the "directives". The same haste as in the recommendation of Caiaphas – and the same hypocritical invocation of the preeminence of the general interest over the rights of the individual.

Nelson at Copenhaga, disciplined officer too: but he didn't follow the order. He didn't see it. A prince of Homburg skillful and gifted with the sense of humor. (Again my idea: it is not without fail necessary the heroism and the sacrifice, just not to be zealous, not to hurry and to be just a teensy bit – crafty. Because craftiness can be drafted in the service of the Good, the Good does not reject any help. There is a fraus pia.)

– There is another case where I think Christ will strike, the case of the only communist that underwent a process of transfiguration and reached the sanctity and the martyrdom: Imre Nagy[210]. How freely breathes the spirit and how unexpectedly he chooses his abodes: in the soul of an activist first (and for many years) full of Stalinist zeal and owner of a very beautiful pair of moustaches worthy of a proud Feldwebel. Inside this man with a typical face of gendarme or Transylvanian notary (I think in Zacchaeus, right? or in Levi, the tax collector, or in the painted Magdalena or in all those fishermen no doubt pot-bellied?) it happens within only ten days (the time is limited as in a classical play) the full transformation. Nagy is at the end of the ten days another. He didn't change his politics, he changed his soul. At the radio station it is not an honest man who speaks but an inspired man who understood.

Then the treason follows. The transfigured is sold by those who were hosting him (the Yugoslavian embassy in Budapest). The great powers don't raise a finger for the man taken to sacrifice. At the end we get involved too in this dirty business and we stain our hands with the blood of the innocent receiving him on the territory of the country (the country where more venerated than anything else is the sacred law of hospitality) and agreeing that he would be taken, moved and killed. Let his blood not be upon us and our sons!

These kind of acts nears that of Judas, on the human scale (quote Léon Blum). When the communists quarreled among themselves, they did not hesitate to use the cursed Christian nomenclature to characterize Tito[211], suddenly become the reincarnation of Judas.

–   The abasing of your fellow man is a sin against the Holy Spirit because is de- personalization. Forcing the accused to recognize, to turn in his friends, to ask for his own punishment, to sully and to compromise himself beyond remedy, to have his soul taken. This is the meaning of the Asian expression: to lose one's face. (The face, the divine image.)

The demonism makes progress, it won't just stay alone outside evolution: before, the victim was tortured and killed. Now even his soul is taken, to remain – spiritually – skinned alive. Like Peter Schlemihl without shadow. Before they were executed, those who lost their face in the trials with complete confessions, were for a while – up to the application of the sentence – truly living corpses.

1971 (pg. 305)
In United States they created homosexual churches. Against. Why?

First: Christ does not reject anyone of those who come to Him. Therefore the homosexuals too. However, as with everybody else, not to justify and confirm them in the sin, but to renounce it.

Christ did not reject the whores and the thieves, but not to bless them in their position of whores and thieves but to help them change. It would be wrong to believe that He would provide a preferential treatment for the homosexuals, receiving them without cleansing and deliverance from the slavery of their sin.

The Lord, out of pity and kindness, listens to all the prayers; the purpose of the prayer is not, however, hardening in the sin. Mauriac was saying to Gide: it doesn't matter what you renounce in particular; therefore for the homosexuals the problem can be put only in terms of self-restraint.

Second: Christianity is by its essence universal and hostile to any segregation. It is not according to the spirit of Christ's teachings to have a church for whites and another one for blacks, a church for women and another one for men, a church for rich people and another one for poor people, a church for homosexuals and another one for heterosexuals, a church for intellectuals and another one for illiterates. Similarly, it would be unchristian and ridiculous (segregation leads to ridiculous) to have special churches for hepatic, cardiac, people sick of kidney calculus…

It's bad enough that we pray to God each in our own language, that we are separated in nations and confessions, it is not necessary to create new particularities.

1945
The soviet movie The train leaves for east. Dance, songs, humor.

For who believed in the social revolution (and I'm thinking of Bellu Z., Sirena Rab., Germaine D., at Tr. in the first place), just one solution: suicide.

So many years of prison, hard labor, exile and deportation in Siberia, so much sufferance, sacrifices and hopes (princess Alexandrina Kolontay: let us go to bed early, comrades, tomorrow starts a new world) to attain what? The most abject forms of American operetta, the lowest stages of the bourgeois entertainment, the most deploring banalities of the vaudeville repertory. A lot below the level of the shows at "Marna": Titi Mihăilescu and Violetta Ionescu (these poor devils, lacking any ambition to renew the world).

The communism can socialize all the wealth, can imprison everybody, can kill whoever it wishes, but it is faced by the – firm, indestructible – durabilities: the need of fare, the cliché, the International of vulgarity, of the White Horse[212].

Pierre Gaxotte yelled too, commenting the advertising for the state loans and the state lotteries: we already knew them! This is where you're leading us? Watch out, folks!

I was expecting everything: everything but not the apotheosis of the neighborhood theaters entr'acte show. Our poor Iulian: up the skirts, down the pants.

There wasn't really, any need of G.P.U., N.K.V.D., K.G.B. or Materialism and Empiric- criticism.

Christ doesn't show idealist in his sayings. He calls the things with their real name: whore, whorish... Never He sweetens, does not use euphemisms and periphrases. The truth in its entire harshness and virulence. Like on the operation table, at the base of the scaffold. Not a veil, not an illusion, not a pampering. Because only having the crude reality in face can we tremble and leave it by transfiguring it.

Confession is an example of precise language. Penitent: I didn't quite tell the truth.

Confessor: You mean you lied?

Penitent: My behavior was not entirely correct. Confessor: You mean you stole?

–   For the Christian everything happens as if words, thoughts and facts would be recorded in a perennial film. The electric impulses express any energy and the matter is subjected to the principle of unity. The film, therefore, will be probably unique. By playing it everything that was covered, hidden, concealed will be known, it will come into the light, it will be discovered and exposed; the film that would make Satan to roar with laughter if the compassion of Lord would not have kept for the devil the surprise to play a film on which the repentance and forgiveness erased everything.

If that's so, it would be strange not to be completely engaged by every act, that every example, no matter how insignificant – in the depth of the cell, in the basement of a police station and under the blinding light of the inquiry room – not to have an absolute value.

BUGGY MAMBO RAG

158

Preda, Radu and Stroe[213]... Clothos, Athropos and Lachesis... I was sent by Vaida[214] in Portugal to study the Constitution of Salazar... It's called mizzenmast... It's called cardanic axis... It's called dendrite... It is translated by the past conditional...

– That the art, contrary to what believes including Nego, is not a devilish thing, it's proved by the remark that it is based, like the faith, on liberty and doesn't have value if it's not a product of the artistic liberty and doesn't propose to the listener or the reader a case of liberty. The theater, especially, cannot live except fueled by liberty; built in deterministic perspective, on the objective epic (Brecht) or on physiological fatum, is dead. The physiological fatum (frigidity, sterility, impotence, inversion) – exactly like the chronic diseases – causes compassion but not the artistic interest. A game that is over because one of the players got sick is not interesting; a session of a totalitarian parliament, where everybody knows in advance the result of the vote (unanimity), might be a ceremony, but it will never have dramatic nature. The secret of every drama is the absolute liberty of the person. The most captivating suspense proceeds from the discretionary liberty of the individual – its paramount form being of course the play that we play with our own soul.

– Woe to us if there would not be in the Gospel the parable of the unfair judge. It makes available to us the – hard, clumsy, desperate – solution of insisting.

And the fact that we are not dealing with an unfair judge, even a righteous one but a generous boyar is shown by another parable, of the workers hired at the vineyard. Pay attention, however: we are tempted to prefer to renounce the pay rather than see the one hired in the eleventh hour receiving the same pay.

–We are revolted, as the elder son in the parable of the prodigal son, by the unfairness of God toward the righteous. For the good son he never killed the fat calf; to his friends he never gave a feast and he didn't give them the occasion to drink and dance. All the good things only for the prodigal son.

The righteous, protesting, proves a sloppy lecture of the text. It is true that for them there was no calf, neither feast, nor dancing or ring in the finger... There was and there is something else, something mentioned in verse 31 of chapter 15 in Luke: all that I have is yours.

Therefore, the righteous has something, and he can't complain is little: all of the Father's.

– Father Paulin Lecca (from the Cozia monastery) divides the world in four categories:

That of the prodigal son that never returns to the Father. There are of this kind, lost among pods and pigs.

That of the prodigal son who returns and enter at the royal feast.

That – very numerous, maybe the most numerous – of the righteous son, who is good, but he's lukewarm and proud and although he is righteous, he doesn't enter at the feast!

That – alas, rare – of the righteous son who is not only good but also has a warm heart and participate at the royal feast. Examples: St. Virgin, St. John the Evangelist. They represent the ideal.

(According to the Nemo-Balotă theory about Doktor Faustus.)

–"The song of man"

In the Old Testament the man manifests his supremacy over the rest of creation and his

ability to elevate himself, answering – together with Moses, the patriarchs, the righteous and the prophets – when he is called by God with the words: "Here I am, Lord!"

Present, aye Sir, ready for orders, anytime available and ready, unfaltering, prompt. He is fulfilled, spiritualized and filled with Godliness when he follows the will of the Creator.

In the New Testament the highest stage that can be reached by the creature is that indicated by the Lord in what He said to Thomas the Unbeliever: Happy are those who have seen and believed but happier are those who have not seen and yet have believed.

To believe without concrete proofs and contracts. Papers and certificates. The less mercantile thing that can be. The most noble. To trust. To not doubt. To receive the truth – as the artistic emotion of N. Schöffer – without going through the devious way of the reason of the cerebral cortex. To take at His word Lord Christ, who Himself is the Word.

[1] Nicolae Steinhardt signed the political testament with a false name and also used pseudonyms for the characters in his book as a precaution in case the manuscript would be confiscated by the police, which eventually happened.

[2] After the fact (French).

[3] Talking hostile means talking against the regime, in the communist jargon.

[4] An inferior form of politeness for aged men without education and social status.

[5] This name and the following are rustic, folkloric names.

[6] The Romanian political police (Securitate).

[7] Romanian for John, here with the meaning of the average man.

[8] Greek governors of Moldavia and Muntenia in the XVIII century, working for the Turks, originally from the Greek district Fanar in Istanbul. The Fanariots were infamous because of their corruption and greediness.

[9] Literally Suck-Juice, the type of the picturesque retard.

[10] Dracula, whose nickname was Țepeș, the Impaler.

[11] Ancient Slavic name for ruler of the land, king.

[12] Master, today used mostly in a derogatory sense.

[13] Romanian philosopher, famous in the thirties. He was the mentor of an entire generation of Romanian intellectuals and the spiritual leader of the Romanian fascist movement.

[14] Bloody battle during World War I where the Romanian army obtained a great victory against the German army.

[15] You will not look for me. (French)

[16] From bon Dieu, good God (French).

[17] In Romanian, in original, șmecher (approximately trickster), which means a type of human with a cynical philosophy of life, who looks for the easiest way, who assumes the others to be as dishonest as he is, thus justifying generalized dishonesty as a way of life. This philosophy is widely spread among Romanians and is considered by many one of the main faults of the nation's character. Apparently it is an heritage from the time of the Turkish occupation.

[18] A great Romanian poet (1850-1889)

[19] Diminutive from Nicolae.

[20] The Romanian fascists were called Legionnaires due to the original name of their party, The Legion of Saint Archangel Michael.

[21] In English in original.

[22] Expression coined by the philosopher Lucian Blaga to designate the Romanian culture, inspired by the folkloric ballad Miorița, considered one of the most representative folkloric cultural creations of Romanians.

[23] Allusion to the Ballad of master Manole, where the builder Manole embedded his very wife in the walls of a monastery so that the building could withstand.

[24]   Inutile canal ordered by the communist authorities connecting the Danube river with the Black sea. Actually the canal was just a pretext for sending political prisoners to forced labor.

[25]   Hint to the homonym novel written by Petru Dumitriu, in which the building of the canal is presented as a heroic deed of the working class.

[26]   Penal punishments given without trial, by simple administrative decision.

[27]   Cațavencu and Farfuridi are comic characters in a play by Caragiale, representing politicking demagogues.

[28]   Alludes to the chronicle of Miron Costin, written in the XVII century.

[29]   In English in original.

[30]   The author probably refers to the moral intransigence that was part of the Legionnaire ideology.

[31]   The statements taken by the Security were handwritten.

[32]   Carol II, king of Romania in the thirties, the father of king Michael I.

[33]   King of Romania (1859-1867)

[34]   In English in original.

[35]   It refers to Marx and Engels, and the fact that some Western communists were thinking that the communist doctrine as conceived by the two philosophers was good while Stalin and the other communist leaders just betrayed the ideal.

[36]   It must be a misunderstanding. This idea attributed to the philosopher Ştefan Lupaşcu is not consistent with the ensemble of his works.

[37]   Originally from Bessarabia (Basarabia), a province in the north-east of Romania; today this is an independent state named Moldavia (Moldova).

[38]   City in Transylvania.

[39]   Picturesque city in Moldavia.

[40]   Famous poems written by Mihai Eminescu.

[41]   Child-like pronunciation of the previous French verses.

[42]   My father Parsifal bore a crown/ I am his son, the knight Lohengrin (Richard Wagner, The flying Dutch).

[43]   Trip on Rhine (German).

[44]   English tea (French).

[45]   Iancu Jianu, a famous outlaw in the first half of the XIX century, similar to Robin Hood.

[46]   The wanderer passes still inside/ A threshold turned to stone by pain/ There in the room shines/ Suddenly on the table bread and wine. (German)

[47]   In Romanian context, "Legionnaire Jew" sounds paradoxical and comical, like "Nazi Jew".

[48]   I am the thief Orbazan (German). Allusion to the homonym character from the Caravan of Hauff. (V.Ciomoş' note.)

[49]   One is required the impossibility (French).

162

[50]   No one is required the impossibility (French).
[51]   In English in original.
[52]   A handsome old man (French).
[53]   Traditional Romanian sweet bread made on Christmas.
[54]   In English in original.
[55]   Even if I am sentenced to fifteen years (French).
[56]   In English in original.
[57]   Idem.
[58]   Death and life (Latin).
[59]   The town of Pantelimon was swallowed by Bucharest in its development and became a peripheral district of the capital city.
[60]   The southern Romanians from the Balkans or Aromanians, are often called Macedonians.
[61]   Strong alcoholic beverage, very popular in Romania, made from prunes.
[62]   Black age (Sanskrit).
[63]   Word (German).
[64]   Speak (German).
[65]   Much-too-human (German), term consecrated by Friedrich Nietzsche.
[66]   Romanian historian, politician and journalist at the beginning of the XX century, but also a spiritual leader with a tremendous impact on the public conscience. He died in 1941 assassinated by the Legionnaires.
[67]   As if (German).
[68]   Town in Moldavia famous for its wines.
[69]   Humuleşti is the native town of Ion Creangă, writer of folkloric inspiration.
[70]   Ionel Teodoreanu, brother of Alexandru O. Teodoreanu (Păstorel), wrote the novel of pastoral inspiration At Medeleni.
[71]   Mihai Sadoveanu, president of the Writers Union.
[72]   Romanian writer and critic in the late half of the XIX century.
[73]   Author of literary reportages.
[74]   The author from Paris is Mircea Eliade, who wrote the fantastic novels The secret of Dr Honigberger and The night of Sânziene (The equinox night). Sânziene are fabulous female creatures in the Romanian mythology.
[75]   A series of Romanian sayings and proverbs.
[76]   Constantin Noica, Romanian philosopher in the second part of the XX century, spiritual leader of the Păltiniş school which today has a large influence in Romanian culture and politics, was the "chief" of the batch of arrested. Caught by the police in the possession of a forbidden book, he tried to minimize the importance of the fact by stating that a large number of people already have read the book, thinking that the police cannot arrest everybody. His miscalculation lead to the arrest of

the twenty-five people here accused in the courtroom.

[77]   Upon my word, darling (French).

[78]   Before the people (Latin).

[79]   At a later time the Legion change its name to Iron Guard.

[80]   Corneliu Zelea-Codreanu, the leader of the Legion, was called the Captain.

[81]   Politician and arts Mecena in the last half of the XIX century.

[82]   The "kingdom" means Muntenia and western Moldavia, which from 1859 until 1918, when Transylvania joined them, formed together the kingdom of Romania.

[83]   Avram Iancu was the leader of the Transylvanian revolution in 1848. He fought the Hungarian revolutionaries that were pursuing the forcible integration of Transylvania in Hungary and declared himself loyal to the Austrian emperor.

[84]   From Eugen Ionescu, French writer of Romanian origin, founder of the absurd theater.

[85]   Allusion to the revolutionary movement in the Romanian countries in 1848.

[86]   French philosopher of Romanian origin.

[87]   The forbidden book because of which Noica and the others were arrested.

[88]   In medieval Romania the executioners were recruited only among gypsies.

[89]   Allusion to the anthroposophic movement initiated by Rudolf Steiner. (Note of Virgil Ciomoş)

[90]   In English in original.

[91]   Idem.

[92]   Ibidem.

[93]   Ibidem.

[94]   The Pope is the offices (French).

[95]   In English in original.

[96]   In English, in original.

[97]   In English in original.

[98]   Mental hospital near Bucharest.

[99]   Vassals and generals of the legendary voivode of Muntenia Michael the Brave (1593-1601)

[100]   Originally from Oltenia, a province in the south-west of Romania.

[101]   Leader of the social-democracy movement in Romania

[102]   In English, in original.

[103]   Special units of the Legion.

[104]   The order given by the general Ion Antonescu (later marshal), the supreme commander of the Romanian army, in 1941, meaning the liberation of eastern Moldavia (Bessarabia), on the left side of the river Prut, occupied by Soviet troops in 1940.

[105]   Mihai Antonescu, the closest collaborator of general Antonescu.
[106]   Capital city of Transylvania.
[107]   Leu (lion), the Romanian currency.
[108]   Allusion to Geo Bogza's literary reportage with the same title.

[109]   Ion Luca Caragiale, a satirical writer, whose main works were outlined from the end of XIX century to the beginning of the XX century.
[110]   Being and Time, the philosophical treaty by Martin Heidegger.
[111]   Romanian poet.
[112]   Romanian playwriter.
[113]   French people, one more effort if you want to be republicans (French).
[114]   Eugen Ţurcanu, former Legionnaire, converted to communism in prison, while still an inmate was given permission by the authorities to apply a brainwashing program to the political prisoners by unlimited use of torture. Educated young men of good family were turned into sadistic torturers.
[115]   Important Romanian political leader between the wars.
[116]   A barren plain in the south-east of Romania, that was colonized in the fifties with political prisoners.
[117]   See St. Simeon the New Theologian, Moral Teachings, in Filocalia. (Virgil Ciomoş note)
[118]   The nouns antler, horn and cornel have the same singular form in Romanian.
[119]   The nests were administrative units in the Legion.
[120]   Badger in French.
[121]   The people of good faith (French).
[122]   In Romanian "semănătorist", pertaining to a literary and political movement that exalts the traditional, folkloric, Romanian values, the peasants, and cultivates a sentimental, pastoral mood. The "sowerists" were the target of many ironies and criticism.
[123]   The communist regime renamed many streets after communist leaders like Ştefan Furtună.
[124]   Here I stand; I can't do otherwise. Lord help me. Amen. (German)
[125]   Bastards (French). Allusion to the philosophical term coined by Jean-Paul Sartre in his novel The nausea, by which he designated the people that out of hypocrisy and material interest pretend that existence has meaning and sense, at the expense of others.
[126]   In English in original.
[127]   Allusion to the Romanian proverb: "The stupid is not stupid enough if he is not vain too."
[128]   King of Romania at the beginning of the XX century.

[129]   The interlocutor was apparently a former important member of the Conservative party, the opposition party for the most part of the reign of Ferdinand.

[130]   Horologe, sinister, frightening, impassible god... (French).

[131]   In English in original.

[132]   Idem.

[133]   Queen of Romania, wife of Ferdinand.

[134]   The hostage (French).

[135]   Romania, after the union with Transylvania in 1918, was occasionally called Grand Romania. It refers to the totality of territories where Romanians make a majority or on which Romania has a legitimate claim.

[136]   Leaders of the Conservative Party.

[137]   The Liberal Party, the government party for most of the reign of Ferdinand.

[138]   Birch tree (French).

[139]   Romanian sayings.

[140]   God created man in His image and he did it well (French).

[141]   Romanian historian between the wars. One of his most famous theory was that the Dacians, the ancestors of Romanians were already monotheists when Christianity arrived in Dacia, which he thought explained the quick conversion of the Dacians to Christianity. This theory was proven wrong in the fifties by archeological discoveries showing that the Dacians were politheists. However, to this day, Pârvan theory still has adepts.

[142]   In English in original.

[143]   Russians living in the Danube Delta; originally they were religious refugees from Russia.

[144]   Romanian writer of Jewish descent who lived in the first half of the XX century.

[145]   Market in Bucharest.

[146]   Members of Junimea (Youth) a cultural and political organization in Romania in the second half of the XIX century that was the most influential group in the Conservative Party.

[147]   The quay of Dâmbovița, the river that crosses Bucharest.

[148]   From where flames were bursting (Yiddish). The problem was the word "flacărăs" (flames), formed by adding the Yiddish ending "s" for plural to the Romanian word "flacără", which sounds very weird. The correct Romanian plural form of "flacără" is "flăcări".

[149]   The northern German belief (German).

[150]   The great zero (German).

[151]   Character in the novel with the same name, the type of the mean, absurd and stupid drill sergeant.

[152]   Reason for war (Latin).
[153]   But, to have faith, add this too, that the sins are given to you for this.
[154]   Prime minister of Romania between the wars.
[155]   Ezra 4,3
[156]   To perceive (French).
[157]   Hermann Oberth, German scientist from Transylvania, the first who rigorously defined the concept of space flight.
[158]   Some Romanian verbs have past tenses that are only slightly different and may be easily confused; I tried here to find a similar example in English but the analogy is far from perfect. (translator's note)
[159]   Romanian voivodes in the XV century.
[160]   Quote from the poem The Latin nation by the Romanian poet Vasile Alecsandri.
[161]   Picturesque county in Transylvania.
[162]   The court of miracles (French), the name of the interlope world quarters in The hunchback of Notre Dame by Victor Hugo.
[163]   Prime minister of Romania.
[164]   A fascist government that lasted a few months in 1938.
[165]   The supreme deity of the Dacians, the most important Tracian tribe, the ancestors of Romanians.

[166]   The dance the poet is talking about is "hora", a Romanian folkloric ring dance which in the past was taking place every Sunday evening in the civic center of the village and was an important part of the social life of the village. Oftentimes future couples were getting acquainted during the dance.
[167]   Constantin Brâncoveanu, voivode of Muntenia around the year 1700.
[168]   August 23rd 1944, the day when the Romanian army turned weapons against Germany and general Antonescu was arrested by the order of king Michael I.
[169]   Mongol invaders.
[170]   Szlachta, the Polish noblemen.
[171]   Carol-Robert d'Anjou, king of Hungary in the XIII century.
[172]   Caragea, voivode of Muntenia in the first half of the XIX century, during whose reign a devastating outbreak occurred.
[173]   Silistra, Turkish garrison on the Danube from where the Turks were watching the Romanian voivodes.
[174]   Russia.
[175]   Disease that affects the grape-vine.
[176]   Janissaries were children taken forcibly from their parents, converted to Islam and raised as soldiers loyal to the sultan.
[177]   Turkish sultans and generals in the Middle Age.
[178]   Iuliu Maniu, the president of the Peasant's Party.

[179]   O, gladsome light of the heavenly glory.
[180]   I made here a literal translation of the Romanian version, because it seemed to me more expressive than the English version. (Translator's note)
[181]   From Ioan Ianolide I found out that it was Valeriu Gafencu himself, one of the "saints of the prisons". (Author's note)
[182]   Literal translation of the Romanian version. (Translator's note)
[183]   The prototype of the spoiled kid from the homonym sketch of Caragiale.
[184]   The good old times (French).
[185]   Romanian proverb about hypocrisy: He neither ate garlic, nor his mouth smells.
[186]   The usual life. (French)
[187]   In this paragraph there are repeated allusions to a poem by Ion Barbu, The dogmatic egg.
[188]   Oftentimes the communist regimes wanted to appear as peace loving and they were forcing people to sign petitions to international forums and to demonstrate on the streets for peace. These manifestations lacked moral value because they were not the expression of the free will of the people but only of the political ambitions of the communist leaders.
[189]   The virgin, the lively and the beautiful today. (French)
[190]   Fish tail (French). It means a conflict without winners, undecided.
[191]   In English in original.
[192]   Allusion to literary works of the existentialist philosopher Jean Paul Sartre.
[193]   Live dangerously (Italian).

[194]   Walls (French).
[195]   Avenue (Italian).
[196]   The war goes on (German).
[197]   Soviet made gas appliance with no oven, just burners.
[198]   Transylvania (Hungarian), literally, "beyond the forests", the same as Transylvania in Latin.
[199]   "Not nails but love kept Christ on the cross" (Saint Clarisse) (Author's note)
[200]   Romanian philosopher in the XX century.
[201]   The lake: Oh, time, suspend your flight... (French).
[202]   Nicolae Titulescu, prominent diplomat of Romania between the world wars, president of U.N.
[203]   The quality of "official" film director of the regime attributed to Jean Georgescu by Steinhardt is unfair. The director Jean Georgescu had a well-established domestic and international career long before the onset of the communist regime in Romania. The film discussed here and other films of Jean Georgescu are today considered masterpieces of the Romanian cinematography.

Although Jean Georgescu never directly opposed the regime eventually he was considered subversive and was forbidden to direct.

[204]   Grigore Vasiliu-Birlic, popular comedian in the fifties.

[205]   The Romanian police during the communist regime.

[206]   The tavern mentioned earlier.

[207]   The Hungarian and the Romanian versions of the village name.

[208]   Siguranță, the analogous institution of Security before communism.

[209]   Actually, the reason why the Safety is presented in a mild light in the communist films is because of the horror of reality of the authorities. Everything had to be adjusted, nothing was supposed to be too strong, too explicit, everything was supposed to be presented in a conventional, euphemistic way. This idea is further developed below by Steinhardt.

[210]   The leader of the democratic Hungarian revolution in 1956, crashed by troops of the Warsaw treaty.

[211]   Communist leader of Yugoslavia, who struggled for independence from Soviet Union, defying Stalin.

[212]   Imaginary cabaret.

[213]   Names of generals of Mihai Viteazu.

[214]   A prime minister of Romania between the world wars.